VERDI

The Man in his Letters

GIUSEPPE VERDI

VERDI

THE MAN IN HIS LETTERS

As Edited and Selected

by Franz Werfel and Paul Stefan

Translated by Edward Downes

BOOKS FOR LIBRARIES PRESS
FREEPORT, NEW YORK

INTERNATIONAL STANDARD BOOK NUMBER:

0-8369-5538-2

LIBRARY OF CONGRESS CATALOG CARD NUMBER:

71-130565

PRINTED IN THE UNITED STATES OF AMERICA

TABLE OF CONTENTS

LIST OF ILLUSTRATIONS

A PORTRAIT OF GIUSEPPE VERDI

by Franz Werfel

I

GIUSEPPE VERDI'S life was eighty-eight years long. Almost sixty of those years were lit up by a swiftly growing and ever-blooming fame. His was the great, steady, world renown that can only be captured step by step as a real victory, the fame that smiles upon the rarest and most illustrious artists alone. But particularly at the start of his career another and more dazzling aura surrounded his name. It was bestowed by an agitated nation, at the moment of its self-appraisal and self-shaping, upon the man above all others who gave artistic expression to its distress and its yearning.

Between 1820 and 1870 the Italian nation went through its period of revolt, of rebirth, of union. This was the great cultural and political rebellion against tyranny and oppression at the hands of foreign rulers and foreign methods that has gone down in history under the name of *Il Risorgimento*. The *Risorgimento* was a national revolution, not by any means a nationalist revolution in the modern sense. This was assured by the very names of its spiritual begetters. Gioberti

[9]

was a Christian universalist, Mazzini a democratic and social universalist. This was the period when the rude choruses, the wild *cabalette* and *strette* of Verdi's operas first took the air. These were the tongues of flame to set inflammable temperaments ablaze. As early as the forties Giuseppe Verdi was a sort of incarnation of the Italian popular soul—he, who would never work, as an artist, for an ulterior purpose; he, who never heeded aught but his heart as he wrote.

Adolphe Adam, the composer, tells of the frantic cult carried on under the master's name in Rome, Milan, and Naples. The frenzy—it cannot be called anything else—that such youthful works as *I Lombardi, Attila, La Battaglia di Legnano* then excited, made on the stranger an impression almost of embittered fury.

For years an inscription could be read, hastily chalked on the house-fronts of Milan and Venice, Rome and Naples. For the police to rub it out was useless; within an hour it would be back again in every nook and corner of all the cities: "Viva Verdi." Obliquely it signified more than simply *Long live Verdi, the composer.* For the five letters of his name formed an acrostic of a far more dangerous cry, which horrified the Hapsburg, Papal, and Bourbon police not a little: "*V*iva *V*ittorio *E*mmanuele *R*e *d*' *I*talia!" This was the name of the national king from whom the Italians then expected all the blessings of the future.

With such things Giuseppe Verdi himself had nothing to do. He was a good patriot, and had a cool, objective eye for the realities of social life. But in his letters he writes again and again: "I know nothing of politics, and hope politics will let me be!" He honestly withstood the great statesman Cavour, who finally broke him down and forced him to accept a deputy's seat in the first parliament of united Italy. Cavour well knew what the name of Verdi meant to the prestige of a national assembly. But the master confessed frankly: "There are supposed to be 450 deputies in Italy. This is not true. There are only 449, for Verdi is no deputy."

At the first performance of his opera *La Battaglia di Legnano,* an incident occurred that brilliantly illuminates the inflammatory effect of Verdi's music on the Italian people in 1848. One of the most powerful scenes shows the hero imprisoned by his own brother in revenge for supposed adultery, so that he may not enjoy the honor of going out to do battle among the Italian knights against Emperor Barbarossa's German oppressors and barbarians. The scene is a barred room in a castle whose foot is washed by the broad Po. In the wildest colors the music depicts the marching songs of the Italians going out to battle, and by contrast the desperation of the captive patriot condemned to the ignominy of absence from this struggle against arrogance and baseness. The contrast, in which the steady roar of the stream is also marvelously interwoven, makes one of the most stirring pieces of music that Verdi ever wrote. The scene ends with the hero, who has no other road of escape, plunging with a magnificent cry of triumph from the window into the river, saving his honor by this perilous leap to freedom.

At this very point a sergeant of dragoons in the gallery of the Teatro Costanzi did the same thing the tenor was doing on the stage. Deprived of his reason by the irresistibly tempestuous rhythm of the music, he tore off his tunic, and leaped from the parapet of the gallery into the orchestra, where, surprisingly enough, he neither broke his back nor seriously injured anyone else. I think I may safely say that in the whole history of music there is no similar example of "incendiary effect."

How strange! One would suppose that the life of a man who was master of such passions, whom his works could raise to the summit of symbolic existence, one would suppose that such a life would not only lie open before us, but more than that, be our common property, preserved, explained, and explored to the last detail. But such is not the case. Of monuments, tablets, streets, and squares bearing his name there are plenty, and not in Italy alone. But in the year 1910, when I began, being enthusiastic and indignant at the prevailing injustice to Giuseppe Verdi, to take an interest in the figure of this man and master, there were only a very few trivial biographies, all just alike, and one analysis of the works by a certain Basevi, written (believe it or not) in 1857.

Compare this with the great example of the opposition. Even during the lifetime of Richard Wagner, who died in 1883, whole libraries were written about him. The number of books dealing with him by now far exceeds a round thousand. And never a year passes in which this number is not augmented by several fat tomes. Not a champagne or millinery bill made out to him but is published with the most conscientious philological *apparatus criticus*. A whole Alexandrian scholarship has lived and continues to live on the analysis of his motifs, his chromatic harmony, his theories, and philosophical problems.

Why should matters be so entirely different in the case of Giuseppe Verdi, who never yielded an inch to his adversary in the world of opera, and continues to dominate the repertory with the same if not greater permanence? Why is this so?

"How can you," I hear someone say, "compare the operatic composer Giuseppe Verdi with Richard Wagner, who was not an operatic composer but the creator of the musical drama out of nothing, the great reformer of composition, a poet of high rank, a theorist of lasting influence? Remember the celebrated phrase of Hegel the philosopher, who called Napoleon 'the spirit of the universe on horseback.' Hegel would have called Richard Wagner 'the spirit of the universe in sound.' Giuseppe Verdi, on the contrary, is no more than an excellent master of music, who has sung his way into the heart of humanity with a few sweet melodies, and that is all. As a man and an artist he is in the old tradition. His figure cannot tempt us to explore it. Presumably it is not very interesting and not particularly fruitful."

No one would more quickly agree with this view than Giuseppe Verdi himself. But the question remains: Can an "uninteresting person" create a work of genius that has already survived the crisis of mortality, that has passed into its second "classical" flowering without ever withering at all—something that can be said of only a very few works of art? "Elemental vigor" and "animal full-bloodedness" are the sort of phrases quickly to hand in one's embarrassment to explain how something imperishable could come from an uninteresting human being. What is stirring in a melody? Its beauty? That is a matter of period. Tunes from the sixteenth century are scarcely beautiful to us unless we are moved by the man who sang them. Only the utterance, the revelation of the heart that it contains, makes a melody moving. There is no work of art that is not a confession.

Here this mystery of Verdi is connected with our question:

[13]

a soul-stirrer, yet the biographies show only a respectable, humdrum life? A king of passion, yet not a love-letter has been published?

I will whisper the answer.

It is Verdi's own fault. He always tried to remove the traces of his private life. Verdi never knew the pose of having no pose. Certainly he wrote letters to women, which he certainly did not demand back so that he might destroy them. Why should he? But, you see, those letters are not there. Neither is anything definitely there that might betray his innermost humanity, the heart of his heart, which never wept openly except in melody. This veiling of himself was not intentional, it was an organic characteristic; not a virtue, but an instinct of the first order. Giuseppe Verdi was that very rare thing among artists, a dissembler, a person who made small ado about himself and his sufferings. This is remarkable indeed, since after all making much ado about oneself and one's sufferings is an important prerequisite of artistic output.

This is why Giuseppe Verdi the human being, of whom a good many facts are recorded, is so little known. We look into his life as we would look through a window into a neatly arranged room. Everything is in its proper place. The stroller passes on: "What can anyone see there?" he thinks. But another, stepping away from the window, ponders uneasily: "I saw something, and still I didn't see anything." The magic of a life hidden not in darkness and mystery but in sober daylight keeps luring him back.

This is the magic of Giuseppe Verdi's letters. They do not surrender to the first glance, for they are a very peculiar document of shame and pride.

II

Giuseppe Verdi was born in 1813, the same year that brought into the world his great rival, the enemy and dragon-slayer of Italian opera, Richard Wagner. The little house where Verdi was born stands in a small village in the former Duchy of Parma, bearing the name of Roncole. Not far away the Po sends its muddy torrent across the vast plain that stretches down from the curve of the Alps to the Adriatic. This plain was Verdi's homeland, which he loved and served throughout a long life.

Above the narrow front door of the crumbling little house in Roncole, which is preserved by the State as a national shrine, was a sign: *"Sale e Tabacchi,"* and perhaps also, *"Vini nostrani."* Carlo Verdi, the tavern-keeper and grocer of the hamlet, sold to the starved peasants of the Napoleonic and post-Napoleonic era the few poor luxuries they enjoyed. His son Giuseppe grew up in the most abject poverty. A smoke-blackened tap-room, an open fireplace, a shop-counter, and two tiny bedrooms adjoining, were enough for the family. On Sunday a few peasants brooded over their wine in the tiny tap-room.

The mythology of Verdi's childhood is very scanty. One pretty story tells of the terrified tumult that filled the towns and villages of Parma when the marauding troops of Eugène Beauharnais left the country, and the soldiers of the Holy Alliance occupied it instead. Among the latter, the Cossacks in particular enjoyed a reputation as bad as it was undeserved for butchering or at least abducting children. And the women of Roncole, the story says, roamed the neighborhood,

seeking a safe hiding-place for their littlest ones. Young
Luisa Verdi (her maiden name was Utini) took her baby,
Beppino, wrapped him in her apron, and, with the new-born
infant, climbed to the top of the *campanile,* the belfry of the
village church. There she knew she was safe from the bear-
skin-capped kidnappers, although the icy December winds
blew with Cossack fierceness about her and the baby. This
legend is not a bad symbol of a man who was to tower above
the country all his life, as lonely, high, and resounding as a
campanile.

Of all human capacities, music is the earliest to be in evidence. Most great musicians were probably child prodigies.
Whether they were so in the eyes of the world depended on
the surroundings they grew up in. Not all six-year-old
geniuses have had for fathers a Leopold Mozart, that excellent music-master, model pedagogue, and tireless impresario
all in one. Still it must be accounted greatly to the credit of
the poor tavern-keeper, Carlo Verdi, that one day he took his
rude staff in hand, and tramped the dusty highway to the
county seat, Busseto, to ask the advice of an important personage about his little son.

It is not known who first drew his attention to Beppino's
musical nature. Carlo Verdi and his wife were completely un-
tutored souls who knew nothing of music. (Yet the parents
were very early at considerable expense to put a rickety spinet
under Beppino's tiny hands.) It may have been Bagasset to
whom Giuseppe Verdi owed his discovery. Bagasset stands
with one foot in mythology, the other in biographical reality.
Bagasset was a wandering musician who strolled about the
neighboring villages, playing at church festivals, weddings,
and other gala occasions. Judging by the sound of his name,

Bagasset should have tooted the bassoon or the clarinet. Actually, however, he sawed out the popular tunes of the day on a whining fiddle. It is said that little Verdi dogged his footsteps, and sat beside him by the hour when he was performing somewhere. Bagasset was warmly remembered by the Maestro, who was not a sentimental man. Visitors at the country seat of Sant' Agata are said to have met the old strolling musician there as late as the end of the fifties.

If Bagasset was not the discoverer of Verdi, probably the pastor of Roncole was. There had been difficulties with the pastor during Mass on Sunday. Beppino usually assisted at the altar. But this particular Sunday the organ was playing. The organ very seldom played in the church at Roncole—almost never except when an organist from the neighborhood came to the village on a visit. Beppino, absorbed in the swelling tones, completely forgot his surroundings, and failed in his duties during the Holy Office. He did not make the responses. He did not kneel. He forgot to swing the censer. The pastor had already growled softly at him twice. When this proved unavailing, he gave him a nudge, whereupon the little lad fell in a faint on the altar steps. This scene indicates an extremely delicate nervous system. Village lads do not usually fall in a faint when awakened from musical dreams by a gentle poke in the ribs. At the same time the scene shows the close connection between native genius and the capacity for intense concentration.

But no matter who was the first to think there was a musician in Beppino, only one man far and wide could help—Antonio Barezzi. The village innkeeper of Roncole had modest business relations with him. Prosperous Antonio Barezzi was the largest merchant in the city of Busseto. Today we would say he was the owner of the most splendid department store in town or county, where every kind of wares could be had, from foodstuffs to farm tools, from textiles to saddlery and hunting guns. Barezzi's house, on the main marketplace, was one of the most stately in all Busseto. Above the vaulted storerooms of the ground floor were the living quarters of the family, including a large hall where the members of the Società Filarmonica met for rehearsals two or three times a week. For Signor Barezzi—to whom Carlo Verdi presented his request touching on Giuseppe—was not only a good man of business, but far more, a rabid music-lover, for which his memory will bloom eternal. Antonio Barezzi called himself President of the above-mentioned Società Filarmonica—a pompous title that must not, incidentally, be taken to indicate a philharmonic orchestra in the modern sense, but a primitive brass band, a "Banda Municipale," such as is fortunately maintained to this day in the tiniest villages of Italy. The president was also a member of the orchestra. He doughtily tooted the clarinet. On Sunday after High Mass there was usually a concert in the town square. Otherwise they participated in solemn church functions, and carried deserving fellow-citizens to the grave with a solemn, querulous accompaniment.

Whether in those days an opera season occasionally strayed to Busseto, and the Società Filarmonica was privileged to function as a theater orchestra, scholarship can no longer determine. But from the bottom of our hearts we hope so. For in the first place an Italian town is almost unthinkable without a traveling opera troupe, and in the second place President Barezzi's musical ambition was high. Not contenting himself with arranging Rossini overtures and popular opera potpourris for his venturesome philharmonists, he independently commissioned local composers to write marches, church music, and even cantatas. Signor Antonio was also constantly on the lookout for new talent. To this local pride and ambition of his we owe the fact that he did not simply eject Verdi the tavern-keeper, but sent for Beppino, then ten years old, to come to the house and be looked over.

Honest Signor Antonio proved that he had a keen eye. After the first visit of the shy, awkward, taciturn village lad he decided to pay out of his own pocket for Giuseppe Verdi's musical education and regular schooling. From that moment Antonio Barezzi was the guardian angel of Verdi's youth, a portly, easy-going, perpetually curious, rather commonplace guardian angel with a heart as warm as a child's.

Beppino was now sent to board with a maker of wooden shoes named Pugnatta. Life here was perhaps even more poverty-stricken than at home. But what did that count for now that the great dream seemed to be reaching fulfilment?

The musical luminary of Busseto at the time was a certain Maestro Provesi. In the early nineteenth century even the smallest Italian town had a local musical figure. In many cases these men were priests. Priests had played an honorable part in the musical history of Italy, especially as teachers. The celebrated Padre Martini of Bologna was still universally remembered—a wizard of counterpoint who survived from the classical age into the new century. Rossini, and for a while young Donizetti, too, had studied under him. True enough, honest Provesi was no Padre Martini. His skill was modest. He taught his pupils the first elements of harmony and musical composition. No less important, however, was the humanistic training that the boy owed to the priest who taught him at the secondary school, Don Seletti—a good command of Latin, a profound knowledge of the Bible, and a highly polished feeling for language, versification, and meter, which was to be astonishingly revealed in his many letters to librettists.

But even in the first few years of his training the boy had to perform practical services of every sort. He was sent as an organist to villages all over the province. In winter this was no small matter. He had to go out in the black of night, and trudge by the hour along the frost-bitten highway to be in time at the church in some remote village. One Sunday morning in January there was almost a mishap. The climate of the region is very harsh; that morning there was a blustering storm; the boy went astray in the darkness, and fell exhausted in the snow somewhere off the road. Finally a peasant came along in a cart, and heard his cries for help.

Another share of his musical services fell to the Società Filarmonica. Signor Antonio very soon began to trust his protégé. Only a few years had passed before Giuseppe was the factotum of the orchestra. He learned quickly how a piece of music is arranged and orchestrated for that kind of musical organization. Along with these arrangements he began to write various marches, serenades, and overtures for the Società himself. The most important thing, however, was that he gained an exact knowledge and command of the special nature of the instruments, particularly the winds. Decades later, when he used the bass clarinet and double bassoon, instruments of modern romantic orchestral coloration not very common at that time, thus embarrassing the smaller theaters, he said with a laugh, "Even as a young lad between

1820 and 1830 I composed solos for bass clarinet and double bassoon."

But once again it was Antonio Barezzi who realized that his Busseto Società Filarmonica and honest Maestro Provesi were not the school for a composer with a great future. And that such a future awaited Giuseppe, Signor Antonio no longer questioned. He had grown very fond of the lean village boy with the fine, clear brow and the strangely deep-seated blue eyes. He received him into his own family, where he grew up among the Barezzi children. Giuseppe had now finished the Latin school. He ought to go to Milan, thought the merchant of Busseto. There, at the celebrated Conservatory, he should receive his musical ordination. Those who had gone through the Conservatory classes had a head start in their careers. Besides, Milan was at that time the musical capital of Italy, as Naples had been a generation or two earlier. It was the great mart for singers, maestros, and impresarios, and, above all, the mart for all opera scores. In Milan was the world famous Teatro della Scala, with its tremendous stage and auditorium. The Scala was the dream of all musicians. To an Italian, of course, music and opera are one and the same. It would cost a pretty penny, Signor Antonio reflected . . .

Before the examination commission of the Imperiale e Reale Conservatorio di Milano the eighteen-year-old Giuseppe Verdi suffered one of the severest defeats of his life. Here, under the presidency of the redoubtable Basily, were assembled the musical pedants and pigtails of the Lombard capital. Only one of the professors, old Rolla, a friend of Abbé Provesi's who had received a letter of recommendation from him, was not quite so icy to the ill-dressed and unim-

pressive village youth. Verdi submitted some of his compositions, presumably written for the "Banda" of Busseto. The
eyes of the examination commission rested unkindly upon
them. Then he was instructed to play something on the piano.
The bashful Verdi, although an accomplished pianist, was
never fond of showing off, least of all before commissions.
To please the bewigged pedants and prove his own good taste
he should have chosen some sonata by Galuppi, Scarlatti, or
something by Mozart. Instead he played a dry-as-dust vir-
tuoso piece by Kalkbrenner.

A few days later old Rolla informed him that he must put
the Conservatory out of his mind. Let him look around for a
teacher in the city.

A better business man and worse music-lover than Antonio
Barezzi would probably have said after this that that fellow
Verdi had turned out to be a fraud.

Signor Antonio said nothing of the sort, but told Giuseppe
to stay on in Milan at his expense, and pick out a teacher.
Giuseppe found one. His name was Lavigna, and he was the
conductor at the Scala. Judging by his success, Maestro
Lavigna was not a bad master. His hobby, Verdi himself tells
us, was the analysis of the score of Mozart's *Don Giovanni*.
Every morning he used to say: "Well, Giuseppe, today we'll
have another look at the introduction and the grand finale."
This choice of subjects seems to point to Lavigna as the
man who awakened in his pupil the fondness for dramatic
contrapuntal contrasts that astonishes the student even in
Verdi's early operas, and reaches its highest perfection in
Rigoletto.

The young man from Roncole stayed in the capital for
several years. He tried every way of earning his living as a

musician. He failed. Disappointment followed upon disappointment. On the advice of a well-wisher he began to compose an opera to an old libretto of the celebrated Felice Romani. (Afterward he wrote out with his own hand the whole material of the opera, solos, choruses, and orchestral parts.) But who had any use for the tragic opera of a young man from Roncole?

It was no use. Time passed. The disaster grew more and more acute. One could not dawdle about the great city forever, making constant demands upon Papa Barezzi to keep from starving. One day Verdi had a letter from Busseto. It reported that the position of organist there had fallen vacant, and been thrown open to competition. Why should he not compete for it?

Hard as it must have been for Giuseppe Verdi to come home defeated, having drawn a blank, home he went. He sought and secured the organist's position, though even this modest good fortune was spoiled for him by all sorts of intrigues and rivalries. Antonio Barezzi received him with open arms. The failure at Milan had not shaken his firm belief in Verdi.

During the three years that he served as organist at Busseto, the young maestro finished his opera, *Oberto, Conte di San Bonifacio*. In later times Verdi needed three or four months at most to have a work finished and on paper. By disposition he believed in rapid, nay, frenzied work. Only in his eighties, finishing his last and next-to-last operas, did he take as long as he had for his first product.

We possess an album of romanzas that may date from the days of *Oberto*. They are of great biographical interest because they show a sadness of soul, a melancholy that has none of the rhythmic elasticity of the later Verdi. These romanzas sing in resigned tones of death and exile. Memorably enough, Gretchen's two songs from Goethe's *Faust* are in the album.

The sadness of this first creative period is surprising because it was during those very three years that Verdi laid the foundations for his life's happiness, or at least believed he was doing so. Margherita Barezzi, one of Signor Antonio's daughters, fell in love with him, and he with her. Margherita was a pretty creature, and highly musical. The pair had met over the piano. The girl was a true daughter of her father. She shared his faith in and admiration for Verdi; she was fired with ambition for him and his career.

It was a simple love story, quite without complications, the kindliest that could be imagined—two fine, healthy young people, well suited to each other, who had known each other from childhood. There was not even an angry rich-merchant papa to rage at his daughter's taking a poor devil instead of a rich suitor. On the contrary, he was delighted with his daughter's choice, for after all he was getting for a son-in-law a genius whose intellectual father he himself was. The wedding soon took place. Encouraging reports came from Milan, making it seem not impossible that a theater manager might put on *Oberto*. Verdi would try his luck in the capital once again. Now he was not alone. He had a wife who loved him; and there was a child on the way. This time he would, he must, succeed!

With warm blessings and a monthly allowance from kindly old Signor Antonio, the young couple took the mail coach to Milan. It would be a very modest, limited life that lay before them, but the proud Margherita knew what it meant to be the wife of a young artist who, though he might be struggling now for recognition, was assured beyond doubt of great fame. In a damp inhospitable house in one of the inhospitable alleyways near the Porta Ticinese they found very small, cheap quarters. But gray-shrouded Destiny waited, immobile in the corner of that dark dwelling, upon the new tenant, Verdi—an implacable tragedy such as few men and artists have had to endure.

Giuseppe Verdi tells of this tragedy in his own words elsewhere in the present volume. Simple and utterly unadorned, this one literary document that we possess from his hand has an incomparable purity and dignity. It is very characteristic, too, that the real tragedy, the death of his two children and his young wife, which came blow upon blow, is reported here in a few lines. He speaks at greater length of the agonies caused by unpaid rent. Again and again it is the same bashfulness, the same pride. Verdi is muffling his heart.

The autobiographical sketch ends with a description of the opening night of the biblical opera *Nabuccodonosor,* or *Nabucco,* as it was popularly abbreviated.

Nabucco was Verdi's third opera and first success after the crushing reverses of his youth. This work, which celebrates its hundredth birthday in 1942, abounds in beautiful music, true Verdi music. It is full of long melodies, sustained, syncopated, rhythmic, but full above all of sweeping choral passages depicting the yearning, the sadness and wildness of the biblical exiles. In the most splendid of these choruses, *Va pensiero sull' ali dorate,* Verdi reached the highest summit that any musician can attain. That tune made him, then and for all time, the singer of his people's liberty. The very day after *Nabucco* opened, people were singing the song in the streets. It became the anthem of revolt against foreign rule and oppression. For the past hundred years every Italian child has known and sung it. Who can tell?—we may hear it again as a hymn of Thanksgiving when the present oppression and foreign rule in Italy are overthrown.

The psalm from *Nabucco* runs through Verdi's life like a sort of reminiscence. One of his biographers tells the following moving story: When Signor Antonio, very old, was on his deathbed, Giuseppe Verdi hurried to his bedside from Turin, or perhaps it was from Paris. He sat quietly beside the dying man, who was breathing heavily. Barezzi could barely speak. Or possibly he lacked the courage to confess his wish. His eyes uneasily indicated the open door to the next room. Verdi understood his benefactor. Slowly getting up, he went softly in to the piano, and played the chords of yearning from *Nabucco*: "*Va pensiero*—Fly, thought, on golden wings."

This story was published during the master's lifetime, and we can accept it; for, great disavower of all untruths and exaggerations that he was, he made no denial. The last word of the good merchant of Busseto was very rightly: "Verdi . . ."

With the triumph of *Nabucco* the story of Giuseppe Verdi's youth comes to an end; indeed we might almost say his biography ended then, in so far as action, grave misfortune, and outward struggle are concerned. What follows is one great upward climb, interrupted of course by reverses and bypaths, but all moving unmistakably in one direction. The outward struggles become inner struggles, hidden from the world, but none the less intense for that. From here on the biography of Verdi is the biography of his operas. It becomes a biography of nineteenth-century Italian opera and its life-and-death struggle.

But what, then, do we mean by opera?

III

At the heart of the cities stand the great opera houses. This is true not only of Milan and Naples, but equally, and more significantly, of Paris and Vienna. The Metropolitan Opera is not exactly the geographical center of Manhattan; still, every New York child knows the social glamor that has always surrounded it. The historical fact that places of public musical entertainment where Thespians, the dagger already in their hearts, sing glorious melodies for minutes on end before dying a stage death, can occupy the places of honor along with cathedrals, parliaments, and royal palaces in the great cities (instead of being banished like the circus or vaudeville to the amusement quarter) is one that we have long since learned to take for granted. Yet it deserved to be anything but taken for granted. What was it, we ask, that gave to the admittedly dubious form of art called opera the robust vigor to capture and hold for centuries such a place in the life of civilized mankind?

About the end of the sixteenth century a few highly intellectual, fine-drawn aristocrats formed a literary and musical circle in Florence. These esthetic gentlemen, still wholly under the spell of humanism, speculated and argued at great length about Greek tragedy. In their discussions they reached the conclusion that the Greeks had not declaimed the dramas of Aeschylus, Sophocles, and Euripides, but sung them. Anyone who wanted, therefore, to accomplish the exalted object of reawakening Greek tragedy—this not altogether modest goal was what the gentlemen had fixed on—must set dramatic action, monologues, dialogues, and choruses to music. The academic discussions of these high-born Florentine dilettantes were the origin of opera. It was the very opposite of the process in the title of Nietzsche's celebrated pamphlet—*not* "The Birth of Tragedy from the Spirit of Music," but the birth of a new music from the spirit of tragedy.

In the very first years of its existence this reborn classical tragedy had the inestimable good fortune to attract a true musical genius: the composer Claudio Monteverdi. His works show in an oddly abbreviated way the whole antithesis in the new art form, the inner contradictions that were to determine its history for all time. At first Monteverdi was entirely in the spirit of the learned Florentines. "Orfeo" and "Ariane" sing endless and shapeless recitatives, strange arcs of sound, noble in expression, that remind us of the principle of "endless melody." This monotonous exaltation is but seldom varied by a sustained phrase or a refrain of the accompaniment. But in his last work, *L'Incoronazione di Poppea,* Monteverdi abandoned the high style of a tragedy only apparently reborn, and made unhesitating sacrifices to the really new-born, true, highly seductive Muse of Opera.

In *Poppea* the nobly expressive recitative is secondary. Ariettas, arias, duets, and choruses succeed one another in abundant variety, and even the ballet makes its appearance.

But the great, smashing victory awaited Claudio Monteverdi's successors, the Cavallis, Cestis, and the rest. Of this victory there is one striking proof. By about 1650 the city of Venice, then the opera town par excellence, had no less than eleven opera houses. Today there are scarcely as many cinemas.

What was it, then, that brought this heady success to the new kind of art? Certainly not the erudite theory that had cradled it.

It was *the human voice,* especially the Italian voice, finding expression in a powerful form hitherto unknown: tense, dramatic song. Here at a blow was a new type of singing, a hundred times more effective than the old, cool, objective style of the canzonette that the common people had trilled, or the polyphonic madrigals of the musical world. Four basic types of human voice became differentiated. The soprano broke down into a high, light type and a heavier but warmer one. The mezzo-soprano with its range formed a bridge to the mellow contralto. The flexible tenorino, able to vie with the roulades of the coloratura soprano, also developed. But in this key the greatest popularity was enjoyed by the tragic hero, the true tenor, whose high As, Bs, and Cs gave the audience well-remunerated shivers of delight.

Finally, in the deepest voice range, the grave bass, the more youthful baritone branched off with its torrential manly resonance. Opera thus immensely developed and enriched that most important of all musical instruments, the human being. (It is perhaps more than chance that Italy in the same period made another outstanding contribution to music—the violins of the Cremona masters. Amati and Guarneri humanized, deepened, and dramatized the voice of the violin much as the opera did with the human voice.)

The maestros soon realized that the new, dramatic way of singing, the "Bel Canto," needed a fresh kind of music. Neither the customary *canzonette* nor the polyphonous phrases of the common madrigal would do for opera; still less would the exalted, psalm-like recitatives of Monteverdi's monodies. What the new theatrical form needed was broad melodies that would fit the peculiarities of the human voice; soulful or explosive tunes shaped into periods that the listener's ear could recognize and retain, just as it must catch every sentence of spoken drama to understand the action. So far as the drama that is the basis of every opera was concerned, however, the maestros soon discovered that music and song melted it like wax. Thus within a few decades after the Florentine days the reborn tragedy more or less went to the literary dogs. It became a libretto.

Nobody goes to the theater to learn the plot of a play whose comprehension is hindered in the extreme by the gratuitous singing of one or more voices that swallow all the words beyond hope of recognition. This is the very reason why the opera has so often been called a paradox, even if a glorious paradox. And it is also the reason why rationalistic people and races like the northern Europeans and Anglo-Saxons have always cried down the opera, fought it, and kept trying to parody or even reform it, as the Germans have done. Is it not truly preposterous for a dying man to assert in a melting G-flat that death cannot part him from his beloved, whereupon the beloved, in the same tone and tune, despairingly maintains the contrary, until at length both repeat their contradictory statements and identical tunes, finally starving (as the old theatrical joke has it) on the sustained B-flat? It is preposterous; yet in this very preposterousness lies the secret of the triumph opera has gained. Very few people today know the depth of this secret, which is connected with the most delicate ecstasies man is capable of, the sense of the unreality of all things and the featherweight joy of irony. . . .

But preposterous or not, the opera built up its form step by step. Arias and duets were augmented by more complicated arrangements, trios, quartets, quintets, and finally the great ensembles in which all the voices join. The rhythms of the orchestral accompaniment grew livelier. Great Monteverdi himself had used the excited tremolo of the violin as a dramatic effect. His successors considerably enriched the orchestra, which has remained as our symphony orchestra down to the present day. The recitative likewise grew brisker, particularly in the comic operas. Interrupted by the dry chords of the harpsichord (*recitativo secco*), it gave the singer an opportunity to distinguish himself as an actor also.

As early as the generation after Monteverdi the opera began its triumphal march through Europe, which can perhaps be compared only with the conquest of the world by the films; and it must be remarked that the films are not or not yet an art form. All the princely courts, large and small, vied in keeping an opera house and a group of singers of their own. And since Italy and Germany alone had well over a hundred such courts or sovereign cities, we can easily judge the importance attaching to the opera in the baroque age.

Along with the intoxication of song there was now a new element to confound the senses: costuming and décor. Particularly in operas written specially for gala occasions, *e.g.*, coronations, enormous sums were lavished on the scenery. Great painters and architects were summoned to intensify the spell of the stage. Gods appeared and floated away by ingenious machinery in the flies. Traps opened with a hellish red glare to swallow up Stygian spirits. Costumes, processions, dances, grew more and more splendid. The "total work of art," the "work of art of the future," came into being long before Richard Wagner coined those ugly terms.

The dangers are obvious. The first derived from the singers; they never had their fill of showy vocal acrobatics, and their vanity and greed for applause endangered the effect of the music. The second danger came from the empty ostentation that drowned all higher spiritual emotions. For the third danger the audiences of the time were responsible, consisting as they did entirely of noble personages who gossiped, flirted, intrigued, and talked politics in their boxes, now and then turning toward the stage for a minute or so to hear some favorite tune. But still geniuses kept arising whose masterpieces combined the highest musical and dramatic values with the indispensable concessions.

Opera stems from the Italian nature, the Italian voice, the Italian soul. Its platonic idea, its essence lies in excited singing, *canto concitato*. When it is untrue to this essence, even in the hands of the greatest musician, it goes astray, finally ending up in one or several blind alleys, as the musical history of the last few decades shows. Up to the French Revolution there was no opera at all except Italian opera. Gluck and Mozart, though their musical diction was foreign, wrote Italian operas. *The Magic Flute,* written to a German text, is not a sufficient rebuttal. It is not an opera, but an operetta. The Paris "Opéra Comique" too is operetta, not opera. So far as the French "grand opera" goes, its founder was Lulli, an Italian maestro.

In the last two decades before the French Revolution this state of affairs began to change. The serene, clever society of the eighteenth century was gradually displaced by duller

plebeian masses. It was a tremendous movement full of magnificent forces and bitter animosities. The nationalism of the
European peoples arose under the impact of that movement
—particularly German nationalism, even though at first it
still wore a mask of universal idealism.

Italian opera, like every true branch of art, is supra-na-
tional on a national foundation. It rules the world, although
it preserves its own language.

But here comes national animosity, saying: "Why Italian
opera? Why this empty tonal trifling by vain, ridiculous, vocal
virtuosi? Why these flat little tunes, bawled out to the sopo-
rific accompaniment of a mandolin-like orchestra? Must we
let our earnest and exalted musical taste be prostituted by
these strangers who pocket our money? Can we not create
a national opera of our own?"

While such words as these were heard ever oftener and
ever more imperiously, the new, the nineteenth century
dawned. In a short span of time, from Haydn to Beethoven,
German instrumental music had captured the peak. Again a
new language had been established. Again the genius of a
nation had conjured up a fresh form of art almost out of
nothing. The language here was darker, the form more
learned and involved. For another race was expressing itself,
a race that no longer took its life with such fearless ease as
the high-born past had done. The human voice was pushed
into the background, the tense singing and sweet melodies
that enchanted so effortlessly. The Germans and northern
Europeans were no singers. Now the instruments spoke. They
could not pour out their confessions with the glowing authority of the human voice. They were not so aristocratic.
They were committed to a sort of collective democratic ex-

change of opinions, like the parliaments that were the political wish-dream of the time. The expert calls this musical discussion among the instrumental voices "thematic." Thus the modern orchestra owes its rise to a German assault on the Bastille of the Italian voice and *bel canto*. The symphony replaced the human voice by introducing a new force into music: Nature, its life and fabric. Again it is highly instructive to see by a glance at the history of civilization that through some deep-seated connection the natural sciences grew up at the very same time as the symphony orchestra.

But even so, Italian opera was anything but beaten. On the contrary, in the first half of the nineteenth century it took a new rise; for in spite of all the symphonies, people's pleasure in tunes and singing remained inexhaustible. National operas did split off, but the result was pitiful. In Germany between Mozart and Wagner there were, all told, two musical dramas of universal stature: Beethoven's *Fidelio,* an incomprehensible and uncomprehended exception, and Weber's *Freischuetz,* a most original opera, which however never reached world popularity.

In Italy, on the other hand, during the same period, between Cimarosa and Verdi, there flourished three masters who dominated the world beyond all contradiction. The greatest of them was Rossini, a true original genius, the inventor of a new type of comedy set to music. Magnificent as many of his serious tunes were, e.g. in the *Stabat Mater,* he was the only creator of truly comic music who ever lived. The grand crescendo in all his overtures, the breakneck pace of his recitatives, the frantic chatter of his ensembles were a musical achievement such as no one before or after him equalled. But the two younger maestros, Bellini and Donizetti, are very rightly alive even today. Wagner and Verdi alike ascribe to Bellini, who died almost as a youth, the invention of the long, modern vocal melody. The finale of *Norma* has its echoes as late as *Tristan*. And Donizetti on his part, quite aside from his merry masterpieces (*Don Pasquale, Figlia del Reggimento, Elisir d'Amore*), had a special ear for romantic love songs, to which Verdi is frequently indebted.

This was roughly the situation of Italian opera when the young man from Roncole began his career with the tremendous success of *Nabucco*. We would naturally suppose that after such fierce blows of Fate Verdi would have been happily contented at seeing his success lift him, in the turn of a hand, to the ranks of the great, along with Rossini, Donizetti, and Bellini. But on closer scrutiny we find that even in the days of his first triumphs Giuseppe Verdi had not a moment of quiet and contented happiness. While he wrote opera after opera, a deep unrest clutched his heart, a nervous uneasiness betrayed in many letters. He could feel the coming crisis that was later to set the whole tone of his correspondence, either implicitly or openly. He could feel the crisis of Italian opera, whose destiny lay in his hands.

IV

To do justice to Verdi's accomplishment between 1842 and 1851, between *Nabucco* and *Rigoletto*, we must cast a glance at the musical theater of the leading countries at the time. A French or German composer worked under quite different conditions from what an Italian did. France was Paris, and therefore there was in France only one opera stage, the Grand

Opera—"La Grande Boutique," as it was derisively called. The road to this pretentious palace was as good as barred to a young musician. The doors of the great opera opened not to talent but to connections, guile, intrigues, and universally recognized mediocrity. This was the experience of young Richard Wagner, who had to starve in Paris. And the young French musicians shared his experience. The art of the nineteenth century in France had to make its way against the "Salon" in every field.

In small-town Germany with its decorous "Court and City Theaters" there was not even the impulse of protest and desperate ambition that the metropolis gives to all those who are striving. The enemy Wagner had to defeat at home was none other than the provincial likeness of everything that was applauded as success in the great world. In untouched solitude he built up his sound-swept cloud theater out of nothing.

How different was Italy! That country was still inexhaustible soil for the most intoxicating of all the arts. As wine was the Italian sun turned fluid, so opera put it into sound. The opera troupes were still traveling from town to town. There were an imposing number of magnificent singers, who had in their throats not only the national gift of voice and the certain something of *bel canto,* but overwhelming expressiveness and the tradition bred by two hundred years of an opera civilization. And the strand was not severed. As one vanished, another appeared. After a Malibran, a Rubini, and a Lablache came a Coletti and a Tadolini; after these shining stars the sun of Adelina Patti rose, and then came a Tamagno, a Maurel, and finally in our own century Caruso and Battistini.

In Italy opera is life, and by no means an unimportant

part of it. Basevi gives statistics to show that within the first decade of the Verdi era in Italy more than five hundred new operas were written and performed. (To appreciate the full weight of this figure, we must keep in mind that nowadays there are frequent years when no new work is performed at all in the largest opera houses.) Whereas everywhere else the supply of dramatic music far exceeded the demand, in Italy the reverse was true. Furthermore, until late in the second half of the nineteenth century the opera houses of the world lived almost entirely on the Italian output. The maestros were swept helplessly into the swift torrent of activity, and were no longer free to take refuge on the shore. Thus the magnificent talents of Bellini and Donizetti came to an early end. The latter went mad at forty-five, and it is still uncertain how much of his malady was due to the exhaustion of a brain and a nervous system that sometimes produced as many as six operas a year. The opera is a dangerous goddess. It is intoxication and release. Like ancient tragedy, it is truly descended from Dionysus. Often indeed it strikes its priests dead with the fatal thyrsus, the ivy-twined staff.

Even Rossini, a true genius, suddenly fell silent at thirty-seven after *Guglielmo Tell,* and although he lived to be seventy he never wrote another opera. If this was what happened to the great, what must have been the lot of the comet swarm of lesser lights, the Mercadantes and Pacinis, every one of whom after all had it in him to sing a true melody? Only Giuseppe Verdi alone, the strongest of them all, remained victorious, with, against, and above the current.

We must remember: in the time during which young Wagner could concentrate his efforts on four works, from *Rienzi* to *Lohengrin,* young Verdi was compelled to write *seventeen* operas. Compelled? Yes, compelled. It may be true that the spirit of a young man who had struggled through a hard childhood, hunger, failure, a dreadful blow of fate, would succumb more easily than others would to the temptations of money and success. But this was not what forced upon Verdi the killing output of his first working decade. It was the audience, the people themselves. It was the active, overpowering *need* for his music all over the country. His employers, the impresarios and publishers, merely exploited this national need.

In *Nabucco* the twenty-eight-year-old maestro spoke the decisive words: *"Va pensiero."* The majestic new anthem sounded. The tingling agility of Rossini, the divinely gentle melancholy of Bellini, the sensually ecstatic melodiousness of Donizetti gradually faded into the shadows of the past. Quite beyond the purely musical values, suddenly something new struck a surprising chord: energy and angry passion. Roughness, "Ruvidezza," the Italians call it. Hidden under this *ruvidezza* is a pounding, a grinding, an underground rumbling, which produced the amazing effect known to Italy under the apt name of *furore*. (For instance the dragoon in the Teatro Costanzi.)

The Scala at Milan performed a few of the young composer's scores. Soon Naples, Rome, Venice, Florence, Genoa, Trieste, had their turn. Each city wanted a new opera for its Carnival. What a heady potion it must have been for the peasant lad from Roncole to find the world thirsting for his music, which but yesterday no one would touch! He made contracts. But they weighed him down grievously once the first intoxication was over. For instance, a contract said: "The composer shall receive the libretto four months before the first orchestra rehearsal." The maestro had, in other words, only a few weeks to familiarize himself with the libretto, make changes, sketch out the music, elaborate it, and finally finish the score. Thus *Rigoletto* was set to music and orchestrated within forty days—a stupendous accomplishment even mechanically, and artistically quite beyond belief. Giuseppe Verdi never put down musical ideas in notebooks for later use. All his music sprang to life straight out of the libretto. Thus we have to admire not only the imagination but the capacity for work that could get the immortal profusion of tunes in *Rigoletto* down on paper in a single month. The Maestro wrote: "In my younger days I often sat at my desk without interruption from early morning until late at night, with nothing inside me but a cup of black coffee." Again he sighs: "I must go back to my music, though it is real agony."

While most of the maestros around him composed in order to supply the demand, our young artist, who might have taken an easier road, made life difficult for himself and others. He did something quite unheard-of in refusing to allow the singers supplementary arias and rondos; he would not tolerate the slightest alteration in his music, and people had to grit their teeth and hold the final rehearsal in costume and mask. So, when his artistic conscience was in question, he tyrannized over the tyrants. And the ones over whom he tyrannized most implacably were the fiercest tyrants of all, the theater managers and publishers. We have no need to tell such stories to any reader of this correspondence. But it would be a mistake to read any kind of greed or avarice into his letters to middlemen. Verdi was not concerned with money. The deepest sense of justice alone fixed his relationship to the men of business. At the very time when other young composers were wearing out shoe-leather trying to procure a performance somewhere, Giuseppe Verdi was fiercely ready to withdraw any of his operas, no matter how great the financial loss, if a single one of his artistic stipulations was not met. Even in his early days he began including in his contracts a clause by which any change or omission in a score, even the mere transposition of a part, carried a penalty of a thousand francs. The publisher was made liable for it. Money was mere empty air to Verdi the moment art was put in question. Never for a single instant of his life was his thinking commercial. When he was thirty-three he forbade Ricordi, the publisher, to let the Scala at Milan perform his new opera. Imagine: the Scala was the great shrine of the Italian melo-drama, and Verdi scarcely more than a beginner. A success at the Scala would bring in a fortune. But never mind! At this shrine they had treated his music lightly. Therefore he put a ban on the Scala, which was never really revoked until the creative period of his old age.

It would be a grave mistake to take the expression "tyrant" too literally, and suppose Verdi a dictatorial character who could not forget a bitter childhood, and was retaliating, once he had attained some small power, on all those who were subject to it. The Maestro never demanded anything for himself personally except that he should be left out of account. Whatever he required had to do with the objective cause represented by a work of art that is to be offered to the public.

He would repeat a hundred times over: "I wrote the opera this way and no other way; probably someone else would have done it much better. But as I couldn't make it any better myself, the opera has got to be played as I planned it, or else everyone will suffer a fiasco—the impresario, the singer, and I."

Seventeen works came into being in this fashion, among them such beautiful and daring ones as *Macbeth, Luisa Miller, La Battaglia di Legnano*. The greatness of Verdi by comparison with his predecessors and competitors can best be judged by the fact that under these back-breaking conditions his work was never irresponsible or superficial, understandable as that would have been. His purity of artistic purpose challenged the Italian show business, and imposed his own laws upon it, so far as his operas were concerned. The impresario, the singer, the conductor, the orchestra, and not least the librettist had found a terrible new taskmaster. Particularly in the matter of librettists, the letters show us that Verdi was always his own playwright, planning the scenario for himself, shaping the characters, writing the dialogue, and leaving the literary men with nothing to do but turn his swift prose into meters that he had carefully worked out beforehand. The librettist served him solely as a verse-maker. Even today there are critics who maintain that Giuseppe Verdi draped his music on lifeless librettos, like a dress on a window-dummy. This, they say, is the failing that distinguishes Italian opera from high musical drama.

Actually, however, the Maestro not only illuminated every character and every situation to its depths with the incorruptible sensitivity of a great dramatist before starting to work on the composition, but did the same for each word down its very syllables. His letters to his librettists are the living proof that never a word was too unimportant for him to weigh its suggestive effect. The analysis of the librettos of *Un Ballo in Maschera* and *Aida* contained in the present letters ought to be part of the curriculum in every dramatic and musical school.

It was another important trait of his character that the Maestro, despite his superiority, never insisted on the poet's removing or adding anything; with all modesty he would simply clothe his wish in the form of a suggestion.

Nothing could better characterize the relationship of Verdi to the theater than the following excerpt from the yellowed memoirs of Nini Barbieri the singer, describing the rehearsals and performance of the opera *Macbeth*. This took place in 1847, in the days of the most extreme Italian melodrama, which was usually whipped to the footlights after two or three orchestra rehearsals. By way of comparison: the German musical drama was hardly born. Richard Wagner had just finished *Tannhäuser*. Of the three Shakespeare operas that Verdi composed—it is still uncertain whether part of the music was ever written for the fourth, *King Lear* —*Macbeth* is the earliest and in a sense the most interesting. Considering the age and society to which it was presented, the theme was impossibly daring. Scotch mist, witches, ghosts, murders, darkness, and not a trace of a love story to bring in a lilting tune. And the composer of this dreadful "thriller" was a child of the Italian sun! Today we know that the solution Verdi found for the subject was as bold as the subject itself. *Macbeth* is not a bit less new and revolutionary in the history of opera than *Tannhäuser*. Verdi at thirty-three, hand in hand with Shakespeare, took the leap from the old melo-drama to the modern musical drama without being untrue for a single beat to his own style or convictions. But Italy was not yet ripe to understand him. Although the première of *Macbeth* was a success, still it was a

[42]

success of misunderstanding. Verdi could feel that no one would follow him into the new country he had conquered.

The singer who played Lady Macbeth describes very vividly the struggle that the Maestro carried on against the conventional theater on behalf of his *Macbeth*.

"More than a hundred piano and orchestral rehearsals of *Macbeth* were held, for Verdi never seemed satisfied, and kept demanding that the singers give a more and more concentrated rendering of their parts. With his excessive requirements and reserved, taciturn character they had very little liking for him. In the morning and evening, when the Maestro came to rehearsal, all eyes on the stage and in the rehearsal rooms would search his face to see whether he had some new torture for us. If he came in with a pleasant smile, it was as good as certain that he would demand endless hours of overtime rehearsal. As I remember it, the opera had two climaxes—the sleepwalking scene and my duet with Macbeth after the murder. No one will believe it, but it is a fact that the sleepwalking scene alone required more than three months of rehearsals. For three months I tried, morning and evening, to play the part of a person talking in his sleep, uttering words, as the Maestro insisted, without moving the lips. Eyes closed, the whole face as rigid as a mask—often it was enough to drive one crazy . . .

"Incredible though it sounds, the duet with the baritone, *Fatal, mia donna, un mormore,* was rehearsed a hundred and fifty times. Verdi was determined that in our mouths the music should seem rather spoken than sung. Well, even that was got through with. On the evening of the final rehearsal, Verdi absolutely insisted on everyone's singing in costume, something previously unheard-of. And there was no such thing as defying his will. At last we were all dressed, and the orchestra was waiting with instruments ready tuned, when Verdi suddenly beckoned Varese, the baritone, and me to him in the wings, and asked us to do him the favor of running through that accursed duet once more with him in the rehearsal room.

"He was a tyrant who had to be implicitly obeyed. I can still remember the black look Varese shot at Verdi as he came into the rehearsal room, his hand clutching the pommel of his sword as if to transfix the Maestro like King Duncan. But he too submitted, and the hundred-and-fiftieth trial took place with the impatient audience already making an uproar in the theater. But anyone who merely said that the duet was enthusiastically received would be saying nothing at all. For it was something unheard-of, something quite new, something unimagined. Wherever I sang Macbeth, every night of the Teatro Pergola season (where it was first performed), we had to repeat the duet two, three, four times, once even five times!

"Nor shall I forget how Verdi, silent and uneasy, kept circling about me before the sleepwalking scene on the opening night. It was evident that for him the success of the opera, great as it already seemed to be, could only be decided by that scene. I will let the newspapers of the time be my judge whether I captured the musical and dramatic intent of the great master. All I know is this: the storm of applause had not yet died down, and I was standing in my dressing-room, trembling in every limb, unable to utter a word, when the door flew open—I was already half undressed—, and Verdi stood before me. He gesticulated, and his lips moved

[44]

as if he were trying to make a speech, but not a word came out. I could not speak either, only laugh and cry. But I saw that Verdi's eyes were red too. He squeezed my hand, and rushed out. It was a magnificent reward for those months of work and strain."

The cool objectivity of the thirty-year-old was admirable. He was no touchy author, skulking shyly around the theater, upsetting the cast by remarks now abject, now presumptuous. Young Verdi walked into the auditorium, and by virtue of an inflexible will and an inborn authority the master who would take absolute command was there. It was not important that a man by the name of Giuseppe Verdi had written the work to be performed. His work was now separate from himself. It no longer belonged to him. He had only to make sure that everything he had felt and thought through should be transposed into reality with the greatest possible perfection. The vainest of all human institutions, the theater, encountered the incredible phenomenon of an artist without vanity.

We have, then, seen how Giuseppe Verdi was guided by the requirements of the Italian opera, and how he soon began to determine those requirements for himself. With all his love of the new and daring, he could not, like Richard Wagner, shatter the sacred canons of the opera form, established through centuries and handed down by his predecessors. More than that, he actually hoped, by wise development and tireless innovation, to preserve, keep, and hand on to an unknown future the hallowed form of *bel canto*. This after all was the meaning of his mission and his struggle from the very beginning.

V

At thirty-four years of age Giuseppe Verdi first reached the outside world. He wrote *I Masnadieri* (Schiller's *The Robbers*) for Her Majesty's Theatre in London, and *Gerusalemme* for the Grand Opera in Paris. This was the first long journey he ever took, to rehearse the two works on the spot. England and English ways made a great impression on Verdi, the realist. Through all the fog and coal smoke of London industry he recognized the vigor of the Anglo-Saxon race. "Who can resist this nation?" he exclaimed. But he confessed also that the fog and smoke made him ill, that he was yearning for the sun of home, counting the days.

Verdi had far less admiration for Paris than for London. "I have no great longing to go to Paris . . . The city is without special attractions for me, but I shall like it very well, because I can lead the kind of life I want to lead there. . . ." How prophetic was this "I shall like it very well"! He was to like Paris very well indeed. "It is a great pleasure to be able to do as one pleases here." A constant urge for independence was one of Verdi's strongest characteristics. From now on he spent several weeks, often even months, of every year in Paris, enjoying his stay most when it was not disturbed by performances of his operas. When he did work in Paris, he worked more leisurely than in the old days. He generally settled in the faubourgs. He would stroll for hours on the boulevards, through the gardens and along the quays on the Seine.

But alas, Paris was not only the city of the boulevards, of Montmartre, of gardens and quays where one could take the fresh air, strolling free and unobserved through the silver-gray of early spring as if one had no duty to the jealous goddess, Opera. Paris was also the capital of the intellectual world, the center of the politics, literature, painting, and music of the whole age. Here the great artists of all countries first received the cachet that gave them world rank. And in Paris likewise the moths gathered around the flame. These were the literati, the journalists, the theatrical people, the critics, the dilettantes, the frequenters of cafés, the snobs. They cooked up public opinion on books, plays, operas, pictures. This was a realm of presumption united in the esprit de corps of negation. After all, anyone who is a cipher almost becomes a unit if he calls a unit a cipher.

The man from Roncole made his first acquaintance with this realm of presumption, headed by the higher criticism, when he came to Paris. It is indicative, and we are almost inclined to take it for a trait of character, that the first operas Verdi wrote for the "Grande Boutique"—*Gerusalemme* and *I Vespri Siciliani*—were almost more Italian than those he had written for Italy. And this at a time and in a city whose nerves were already beginning to be frayed by Italian music. Rossini, Donizetti, Bellini had been accepted and domesticated as typifying the gracious light-heartedness of a fading era. But enough of that, thought the literati and critics. Here was this man from Roncole daring to put his vulgar male choruses in polka time on the grand-opera stage!

At all the rehearsals there was a whispering behind Verdi's back: "Pas de bon goût." Again and again the awful words "bad taste"—and then the dagger thrusts: "Banality," "triviality." True, the audience applauded these banalities, they captured the people, and the hand-organs played them in the courtyards of Paris. But to offset this, Verdi could read in the newspapers of Paris and all the other great cities what a pitiful street musician he was, and how his popular operatic music was worlds beneath that which could be taken seriously as true art.

Probably no master in history has ever been treated so ill by the "higher criticism" as Verdi. A good example is the reviews of the celebrated Viennese critic Hanslick. When this brilliant stylist attacked Wagner (to which attack he owed his fame), he did so with obvious misgivings of conscience, with reservations, respectfully, as it were in self-defense. Quite otherwise with Verdi. Here Hanslick rolled up his sleeves at leisure, for he had nothing to fear. With witty relish he exposed the ludicrousness of his victim. And the other luminaries of musical criticism in France, England, America, and Germany followed the same course.

Then when *Aida*, the *Requiem*, *Otello*, and *Falstaff* made their appearance, these gentry were not in the least abashed. They pointed out with the benevolence to which, after all, old age has a right that the bad boy had improved; they even ventured the melancholy remark that there had been considerably more "red blood" in the naughty pranks of youth than in these masterpieces of maturity.

The way Giuseppe Verdi managed to deal with this ill usage at the hands of critics and intellectual snobs was a marvelous proof of spiritual fortitude. He was not exasperated; but neither was he self-satisfied with his popular success. He did not swerve an inch from his path; neither was he rigidly unyielding. He looked the forces of negation squarely in the eye. He tried to find the truth even in scorn

[48]

and dispraise, and to see his own back, as it were, with the coldest objectivity.

He never for an instant questioned the laws of the Italian operatic form, forged in a hundred fires. Dramatic singing was and would remain king, divided between recitatives and arias. In the recitatives the action advanced, producing the necessary calm for the arias. A sustained melody required to be relieved by a quicker, electrifying rhythm. This is not only an operatic law, but a prime law of music in general, which a composer offends against to his own cost. And so, at a time when all the electrifying accelerations, known as *cabalette,* had long since been extirpated root and branch, Verdi asked the librettist of *Aida* to furnish the necessary verses for such a *cabaletta,* expressly adding: *"Cabalette* are perfectly acceptable to me." The opposing tendency could not shake his conviction.

In Paris Verdi heard a great deal of music, and certainly not that of Auber and Meyerbeer alone. Presumably he met with an occasional piece by Berlioz in the concert-halls. An alien world, an antagonistic world. He recognized progress; he meant to progress himself. But the musical progress that found expression in broken color tones and romantic torment of the nerves was not his kind. Giuseppe Verdi had other talents to contribute to the battle going on for a new art: an uncompromising sense of proportion, polished acuteness, inexhaustible feeling and invention, justness to the point of mania, and an enlightened realism that was scarcely understood until recently, but has come to mean eternal youth for his music.

The realist reached out for new subjects, subjects inconceivable in the lyric theater as it had previously existed. He put a hunchbacked cripple on the stage (*Rigoletto*) and a tubercular cocotte (*La Traviata*). For perhaps the first time the traditional opera stage was trodden not by costumed singers, but by suffering human beings. Now that three generations have been familiar with these most popular of all operas, we can no longer realize the revolutionary courage required to approach such provocative themes in defiance of censorship and the reigning esthetic code. And the Maestro —as he says himself—would not have been afraid to turn the most treacherous of all situations into a true Verdi love duet: the seducer and the seduced in the bedroom. "That would be a duet, a magnificent duet . . . but we should be whipped out of town."

So that we may have a proper understanding of his life and works, let us sum up once again: an Italian of vigorous peasant stock, whose apprentice years came during the time when Rossini, Bellini, and Donizetti dominated the opera houses of the world with a yearly triumph, and it was the dream of all dramatic composers to emulate these three bright stars. An Italian from a wretched village, from the deepest poverty, who was not accepted for the Conservatory at Milan, and had to learn his trade from a theater conductor who went through a few opera scores with him for no reward in order to teach his pupil the skills essential for success. An Italian who presumably heard very few classical or pre-classical pieces of music in his youth. An Italian who soon became the father of a family under harassing circumstances, who had to struggle desperately, and for whom art could not be a dream, but had to mean bread. An Italian who, through a dreadful occurrence, lost everything, wife and children; whose opera was hissed off the stage during those days of horror; but who pulled himself together on the threshold of nothingness, and within a few years turned out three times six melodic dramas, some to become immortal, while his music as a whole blossomed into the marching song of national rebirth.

One may well ask whether after such a career this Italian would not have had every right to be weary. Might he not have been satisfied with what he had attained? What was the world to him; what were Paris, the critics, the snobs; what was German music? "After *La Traviata*," Verdi once wrote, "I could have taken things easy, and written an opera every year on the tried-and-true model. . ."

He did not take things easy. He did not sidestep the crisis that threatened Italian opera. He met the challenge of that crisis. His clear mind remained free. Abuse of the opera, as old as opera itself, began to pile up from all sides, not least in Italy. Verdi turned an attentive ear. He did not fly into a rage when he saw the enemy conquering position after position in his own country. In later times he merely shook his head when invited to join a "chamber music society" or the "committee of a symphony orchestra." Why, could not these fools see that they were serving a strange god ill-disposed toward singing—that they were giving aid and comfort to the enemy? The enemy of pure song, the enemy of Italian opera, was the symphonic tendency, or in other words German music, along with its priests, worshipers, and imitators the world over.

Giuseppe Verdi knew his own goal. He recognized that at this turning-point any artist who stood still and dwelt in the past was lost. With cool, keen eyes he watched the enemy. He was always ready to accept even from the foe anything that squared with his own natural conviction. And so Giuseppe Verdi moved forward bravely and circumspectly, like a good soldier.

The road from *Nabucco, Ernani, Macbeth,* to *Rigoletto, Il Trovatore, Un Ballo in Maschera,* and then to *La Forza del Destino* and *Don Carlos,* is a straight climb. But the advance is the smaller marvel, as against the man's fidelity to himself during this progress. There is no essential difference between the scores of *Nabucco* and *Otello.* It is not the form that changes significantly, but the spiritual expression, which is ennobled beyond all imagining.

At one particular time, it is true, the hazards around Giuseppe Verdi multiplied. This was between 1865 and 1870, when the Maestro wrote *Don Carlos* for Paris, a work that betrays an almost frantic straining of every nerve, even a certain overloading. Acute ears immediately caught the danger. It was no less a figure than the composer of *Carmen* who expressed his anxiety for Verdi in a letter written after *Don Carlos.* What, was even this old, strong Italian to succumb to the new god? The danger that Bizet saw threatening Verdi had a name: Richard Wagner.

This is not the place to draw comparisons in musical history. And anyway, comparison of great opposites is a simple and therefore very precarious matter. These two men often lived near each other in space, and they never met. That is symbol enough.

The question whether Giuseppe Verdi matched the greatness of Richard Wagner or not is unimportant. All that matters is the fact that he was the only one to hold out against that greatness. Wagner was more than a brilliant playwright and dramatic composer, he was the creator of a new musical language. No matter whether one loves or hates that language, all his contemporaries succumbed to it, and so have all his successors down to the present day. All composers after 1870 spoke and still speak the language of Wagner, with variants that will be blurred a hundred years hence. Even the cacophonies and rhythmic spasms of ultra-modern music spring from an effort to burn Wagner's language out of the blood-stream by an artificial fever.

The vigor of Verdi's personality saved him from two evils —being seduced by Wagner, and becoming antiquated through Wagner. He once said to the Marchese Monaldi: *"Vi pare, che sotto questo sole e questo cielo io avrei potuto scrivere il Tristano o la Tetralogia? Siamo Italiani, per Dio! In tutto! Anche nella musica!"* But it was not sun and sky alone that saved him from losing himself; the opera of Italy, for which he had had to work so hard in his younger days, saved him to become its saviour. Not for a moment did he waver in his principles. The drama is man. Therefore the opera too is man—that is, the human voice; that is, singing. The melodies of the instrument called man obey different laws from the themes of the orchestral instruments. Anyone who does not realize this mistakes the meaning of opera and the conditions necessary for its existence. If the human being and his melodies are pushed into the background in favor of any orchestral fabric, no matter how compelling, the idea of opera is destroyed. Verdi once called it "the invasion of the baroque." And he was right when he said that this invasion of the baroque was by no means new in the history of opera, but had occurred once or twice already in the course of the centuries. To him wrong did not become right simply because a great man did it with every resource of his genius. Verdi shrugged his shoulders. How uncomfortable the Germans made him, with their perpetual rebellion against the fundamental facts of humanity, their fanatical craving to conquer and devour everything that might oppose them! . . .

The Wagner peril may often have shaken Verdi's self-assurance, but never his artistic conscience. He looked around him. All the composers, Italian and non-Italian, were wavering, more or less submitting to the new principle. The Italian opera was like a beleaguered fortress; and within this beleaguered fortress the traitors of the "Fifth Column," as we would call it today, were at work. A friend of Verdi's, the conductor Angelo Mariani, one of the most influential musicians in Italy, had gone over to the Wagnerians, and he put on *Lohengrin* at Bologna, with tremendous thumping of the publicity tub. Once again Giuseppe Verdi muffled his heart. He even sat with a copy of the piano score at the dress rehearsal, and looked his adversary in the eye.

About this time Verdi, still under sixty, summoned all his forces, and made a triumphant sortie from the beleaguered fortress. This sortie bears the name of *Aida*. Although it was written to order for the gala opening of the Suez Canal, this strange occasional piece has historical significance of a high order. *Aida* stands for the self-defense, salvation and renewal of Italian opera as against the assault of the symphonic drama. It is the final relieving of the beleaguered fortress. In this music Verdi struggled to give to excited song, *canto concitato,* a fanatic force of expression previously unknown even in his own works. One dramatic melody rushed headlong upon the heels of the next, and each one depicted with the sharpest perfection the passion of the characters involved. The instrumental accompaniment was accompaniment still, even with all the sunset gold that had come into the colors, and the quivering variation of the rhythms. Today we have discovered at last that *Aida* is not merely a popular opera written for an occasion, but a victorious battle in a long war.

The European critics of the time, faced with these new facts, hastily improved the opportunity to distinguish themselves in regard to their old friend by misunderstanding his epoch-making work from beginning to end. Whereas to them Verdi had once been the tasteless theater composer with a few pretty tunes, after *Aida* he quickly advanced to the post of imitator and puny offshoot of Wagner. This horrid stigma he was never again to escape.

Let it be said again and again, with every emphasis: Giuseppe Verdi adopted *nothing* from Richard Wagner. Though jealous Wagnerians may lay claim here to an unusual harmony, an orchestral coloration, there to a series of tones, a reminiscence, it is all empty labor; such things are in the air of the times, in the common development. They mean nothing at all. It would be equally futile to maintain that Wagner had been influenced by Verdi because, for instance, the "Pact Motif" in the *Ring of the Nibelungs* resembled the descending series of notes characterizing the agreement between *Rigoletto* and the bandit Sparafucile at the end of the scene. From *Nabucco* to *Falstaff* the language of Verdi is always the same, a curt, hard, aphoristic language, and nothing is more alien to it than the long-drawn expression of Wagner, meant to persuade and overwhelm the listener. The last two works, *Otello* and *Falstaff,* still criticized by the obtuse as being like Wagner, are precisely the best proof of this statement. Not a single symphonic measure is to be found in them that would subordinate the song to the thematic fabric; but we do find the entire older opera brilliantly abbreviated with new inspiration. What had been an aria was now compressed into the small space of a "phrase," drenched in melody and harmony; man singing was triumphant as always, and the orchestra never took the lead, but obediently lived and trembled with man and his fate. In *Otello* and *Falstaff* the esthetic contradictions that have always been inherent in the "reborn tragedy" are almost resolved.

It is plain that Verdi suffered through and from Wagner. This suffering was a secret motif of his letters and utterances from the time of *Don Carlos*. It broke through whenever he wrote about "music of the future" or "high art," about the founding of symphony orchestras in Italy, about the decline in singing, and similar subjects. Once he complained with unaccustomed frankness: "A pretty fate, to wind up after more than thirty-five years' work as an imitator of Wagner!" And again: "If only I had never written *Aida,* or at least never published it!", and he went on: "Not a word did I hear that was worthy of art!"

He was right. Despite the world success of *Aida* no one understood the battle that was fought out in that work.

It is hardly too fantastic a supposition to connect the long hiatus in production between Verdi's sixtieth and seventy-third year with the depressions here hinted at. "Why should I write?" he keeps asking.

Yet still Giuseppe Verdi never hated Richard Wagner, although there must have been tale-bearers in abundance. The great Italian probably knew that the great German despised him, for that is the kind of contempt one can feel, and it is the severest test of a man's sense of justice. (Wagner was in the habit of citing the aria of Germont the father in *La Traviata* on the piano as proof of the decline of Italian

[56]

opera.) Yet Verdi never made the slightest remark pointing to any hatred of Wagner. All hatred is plebeian, for it presumes that a spirit can be degraded. Verdi's spirit could not be degraded.

The Verdis—several years after the death of Margherita Barezzi the Maestro had married Giuseppina Strepponi, the diva of his *Nabucco,* and a popular idol—the Verdis usually spent the winter months in the mild climate of Genoa, in a big apartment on the second floor of the Palazzo Doria. It was in one of the high-windowed rooms of that palace, on the evening of February 13, 1883, that seventy-three-year-old Giuseppe Verdi opened his newspaper, and read the dispatch announcing to the world that Richard Wagner had died suddenly a few hours before in the Palazzo Vendramin at Venice. What was in the Maestro's heart as he slowly put the paper containing this report back on his desk? The most conscientious biographer, scrupulously refraining from all fictional adornment, could hardly keep from dreaming in retrospect of that great moment . . .

Wagner was dead. The fire whose smoke and flames had choked Italian opera and its master for decades was extinct. Wagner was dead. But Verdi was alive, and the living man is always right. The living man is victorious over the dead, invariably. And the victor was not only alive at seventy, but sound, healthier than in his youth, and he could feel the strength for new deeds, whereas the dead man must now remain mutely idle forever. Would it not have been only human if the black lightning of unutterable triumph had quivered through Verdi's heart at that moment?

Fortunately we have a document to show. It is a letter to

Giulio Ricordi, the son of the publisher, his young friend and confidant.

Here is the letter, faithfully reproduced:

"Sad sad sad!

"Wagner is dead!

"When I read this news yesterday, I may truthfully say that I was completely crushed.

"Let us say no more! It is a great personality that has disappeared. A name which leaves a mighty imprint upon the history of art. . . . ."

It is impossible to study the facsimile of this letter long enough. First, the "Triste triste triste," with no commas, the words breathed on paper in almost tremulous script. It is unquestionably a magnanimous expression of true regret, behind which no secret satisfaction can hide. The word Wagner is written with V instead of W. It seems as if in his emotion Verdi were unable for a moment to recall his rival's painfully familiar name. And then, most striking of all, Verdi has crossed out the adjective "mighty" (potente), replacing it with the superlative "most mighty" (potentissima). The justice of the Maestro, no lover of superlatives, would not permit the weaker term he had first chosen.

Thus a warrior dips his sword to the fallen foe. With a pure heart.

V I

At the same time of life when Giuseppe Verdi first came in contact with foreign countries, with the great world, with Paris, he bought a house, home, and fields on his native soil, not far from Roncole. This considerable country estate is named after the hamlet of Sant' Agata. Like the giant in the

Greek myth, the Maestro now could touch the earth from which he sprang, renewing his strength from it. Though art and his own work might require long stays in Milan, Genoa, Rome, Naples, Paris, yes, even Saint Petersburg and Madrid, though he had to violate his principles by making a European tour as conductor of his *Requiem* in 1875, he was everywhere an impatient guest; at Sant' Agata alone he was at home and under his own roof.

When Giuseppe Verdi bought the estate of Sant' Agata, it was a run-down establishment off the main road, a flat, dreary piece of land with a tumbledown house, in the middle of the most desolate neighborhood imaginable. The Maestro had spent many long weeks in Florence, Naples, Rome; had not those landscapes and their beauty lured him to settle under the cypresses, laurels and mimosas? Had he so little "artistic" feeling that he must needs choose the most monotonous and melancholy spot in Italy for his permanent abode? The peasant lad of Roncole was not tempted by the hills of Tuscany and the magic gardens of Sorrento, but by the prosaic yet fertile soil of his fathers. There he built his house.

He built a manor house. It is a bright, fairly extensive building, a ground floor and second storey, completely unadorned. Around this house, as grave and clear as its master, stretches a great park. Close at hand are trimmed hedges, flowerbeds and circles. But the further the park reaches from the house, the more it is left to itself. Verdi's pride was the beautiful trees. Oh, it was not easy to bring the shoots here, to plant and raise them.

Years passed. The crowns grew thicker and closer, and then long, dark avenues ran through the park, which had once been a stretch of desert. The Maestro had a happy touch with growing things. Nevertheless the old dissembler wrote in late 1865 about the "wonders of Sant' Agata":

"Four walls protect me against the sun and against the inclemency of the weather; a few dozen trees, largely planted by my own hand, and a puddle that I would dignify with the name of 'lake' if I had water to fill it. . . ."

The interior of those four walls, which did far more than protect him from sun and weather, gives the same impression as Verdi the man. The study was large, not remarkably light. One might call it sunny darkness. A massive desk stood in the room, a second, smaller desk to the left of it. Next to that a heavy bookcase. Among Verdi's books were not only several editions of Shakespeare, but the theoretical writings of Richard Wagner. The latter in turn were a proof of the long, concerted struggle that the Maestro carried on for the existence or non-existence of Italian opera. Pushed over against the side wall stood a big piano, a gift from the firm of Erard. Over it hung a portrait of none other than good Signor Antonio, the excellent merchant of Busseto.

All this was very simple, with but little of the overcrowding characterizing the period between 1870 and 1900, which could never get enough of heavy curtains and furniture like fortresses or mountains that scarcely left room to force one's way among them.

Now let us hear a visitor describing Sant' Agata. It is Antonio Ghislanzoni, the librettist of *Aida:*

"Nature has bestowed no charms on this landscape. The plain rolls monotonously on. Rich for the countryman, poor for the poet. In the middle of a long avenue of poplars the eye, surprised and touched with melancholy, rests upon two weeping willows that flank a garden gate. The two giant trees, which would scarcely attract attention elsewhere, tease the mind here like some strange and unfamiliar spectacle. He who planted those trees at this spot can be no ordinary man . . . He may even be a misanthrope, for a drawbridge furnishes the only communication between his property and the world."

As Ghislanzoni goes on with his description, although he praises the beauty of the park, he cannot escape a certain melancholy. He comes to the conclusion:

"If a genius inhabits this house, it must be a genius of pain and passion."

Having cast a glance at the strange lake in the middle of the park, the visitor ends his observations.

"The broad lands of the master spread out beyond the lake. Their cultivation bears testimony to the scientific principles that he has introduced here from less naturally fortunate foreign countries. Verdi's gift of keen observation has turned every advance in English and French agriculture to the profit of his own country. While the weeping willows, the dark thickets of trees, the melancholy lake, all reflect the dreamy passion of the artist, the fields outside reveal the orderly energy and acute understanding of the man."

The last sentence raises a great contradiction. Dreamy passion and a sense of reality! Can this conflict be resolved within a single soul? The nineteenth-century conception of artists denied the possibility. To that age the romantic was the archetype of the artist. The romantic blithely ignored reality. He did not feel himself bound by "bourgeois" morality. He was proud of not understanding about money, business, the requirements of the human life that went on far below at his feet. If he had to go hungry, he regarded it as sacrilege against genius on the part of bourgeois society. Since religion was fading away, and people no longer believed in God, the romantic artist in his overweening pride set himself up as a sort of substitute. Do not the features of Richard Wagner shine through this hasty sketch?

In the outer conduct of his life, too, Giuseppe Verdi remained the great contrast to his rival. The author of almost thirty opera scores, the composer of the *Messa di Requiem* and *Quatro Pezzi Sacri,* was anything but the mere proprietor of a splendid estate and a handsome country retreat. He was a conscientious farmer, a large-scale agriculturist through and through, and this not in the ordinary but in the creative sense. He had his fair share of all the work, plans, schemes, alarms, troubles, cares, joys and pains of the real, serious land-owner. The model estate of Sant' Agata brought about reforms in the agriculture of the whole district. Constant new innovations and improvements surprised the conservative, skeptical peasants of the province. Verdi dug canals, introduced the threshing machine and the steam plow, started dairy farms round about, built roads.

He kept increasing his holdings. The soil of Sant' Agata swallowed a considerable part of the sums his operas earned. Music made Verdi a rich man. He was proud of the fortune that he owed to his pen. No wonder that envy circulated every imaginable slander upon his person. Verdi, they said, was greedy and miserly. But this greedy miser never worshipped money for a single hour of his life. He never put his money to work on the stock exchanges, in the world of shares and complicated interest. What he did not spend on living and farming, he invested in the more patriotic than profitable Italian funds. Verdi was never avaricious; he was the very opposite—he was thrifty. And he could think and act selflessly, like a patriarch, in a thrifty and constructive fashion, as the following episode shows.

About 1880 Italy went through a grave economic depression. Unemployment waxed from month to month. People in town and country, and particularly in the country, could no longer earn their bread. Emigration to America assumed alarming proportions. While the romantic artists of the time simply took no notice of such things, the Italian operatic composer Verdi immediately turned to in his own locality with a vigorous hand. In the middle of winter he left the comfortable Palazzo Doria, and went to Sant' Agata. There he not only started a long-planned remodeling of the house, but had three large dairy-farms and agricultural establishments set up on his own land, so that he could give work and bread to two hundred unemployed peasants and their numerous families. Soon he could exclaim with satisfaction: "Nobody is emigrating from my village now!"

Giuseppe Verdi, whose prophetic eye foresaw the world wars of our day during the Franco-Prussian conflict of 1870, predicted no less prophetically: "For you must know, you city-dwellers, that the misery among the poor is great, very great, immensely great . . . And if nothing is done to meet it, whether from below or from above, we shall live to see a great catastrophe. . . ."

Verdi was no friend of the socialists, as indeed he was no friend of any one political party. But his was a resolutely responsible social spirit like that of no other musician in his day. And he saw not the slightest contradiction between speech and action.

He showed the same integrity and purity of character in

all questions of public welfare. He hated it when it was only the alms to ease the consciences of the well-to-do. He refused to participate in anything that smelled of "benevolence," of "charity." He would take any burden upon himself, even that of doing good. For instance he not only built the hospital in the neighboring town of Villanova out of his own pocket, but supervised the administration of the place, looked after the wine, milk, and meat, and made sure that the patients were not stinted in any way. But if the papers printed a story that Giuseppe Verdi had made a donation for the renovation of the little church in his native village, or that Busseto was to have a theater, he would fly into a rage; and this newspaper scribbling was not too trifling for him to correct it with brusque denials.

His servants and employees, too, the master of Sant' Agata treated like a patriarch. They feared him, for he was a real master, caring for his property even when he was away in Paris or Genoa. "Is the coachman exercising the horses every day?" (Verdi loved his horses as Leo Tolstoy did.) Who had dared to turn over the key of the machine shed to unauthorized persons against his orders? What? The cholera was raging in northern Italy, and the overseer did not even think it worth while to write him a line as to whether all was well at home? But it was not his property alone that the master cared for with all his heart, it was his people even more. There is testimony to this in his will, where even the least and youngest of his servants was not forgotten, and in a multitude of other cases. For instance to save some poor wretch, the son of a coachman, from military service he moved heaven and earth, wrote begging letters (what an agony!) to influential acquaintances, and was finally forced to realize that even the great Verdi was a little man in the eyes of bureaucracy.

The Maestro suffered a great deal of annoyance in his days at Sant' Agata from the affair of the theater at Busseto. This went far back, into the lifetime of Barezzi. Old Signor Antonio, a celebrity himself through the glory of the man he had discovered and helped—oh, fame is a drink that does not quench the thirst it feeds—had probably originated the idea that the city of Busseto should build a Teatro Verdi in honor of its great son. A few Bussetans approached the Maestro with the idea, and immediately sustained a sharp rebuff. The years hurried on. Meanwhile the plan of a Festspielhaus at Bayreuth came into being, dedicated to the works of one man. "Bayreuth" became a regular headline in the European press. Who knows, perhaps the Bayreuth festivals made the honest Bussetans even more eager for their Teatro Verdi. They went after Signor Carrara, the Maestro's attorney. The refusal was even sharper than before: "I tell you, I have never seen the use of a theater in Busseto."

Several times more the game was repeated, always with the same result. Verdi did not want a Teatro Verdi.

Often as he had thrown himself body and soul into giving his music a perfect performance, he never thought for a moment of establishing a fixed tradition, let alone of making Busseto into a Bayreuth. His labor of love in his old age was not to be devoted to his own operas, but to the human beings who had been the voice of those operas, the veterans of song and orchestra pit. On the Piazzale Michelangelo in Milan the Maestro bought a piece of ground. On this plot—on the outskirts of the city, from which one saw the blue range of the Alps on the horizon—he put up an imposing new building.

It was a home for aged musicians, bearing the more tactful name of *Casa di Reposo*. In this house of rest a group of old musicians, a hundred at a time, were and still are housed and fed for the remainder of their lives. Along with the endowment given by the Maestro, the royalties on Verdi's operas form the permanent income of the home. As long as those operas live and bring returns, a hundred retired artists will have food and shelter, generation after generation.

Here is the every-day routine of Sant' Agata. Giuseppe Verdi rises early. Like most Italians, he takes nothing but a cup of unsweetened black coffee. Then he goes out on horseback—in later years he has the carriage hitched up—to inspect the work in fields, barnyards, and at the dairy farms, or to call on some of his tenants. He is the squire, not the maestro. Between nine and ten he comes home. Meanwhile the mail has arrived. The mail is of course the great daily event at any country house. Signora Giuseppina has sorted the letters, separating the nuisances attendant on a celebrity from the important correspondence. Some time is spent every day in dealing with this. If guests come, they generally arrive about noon. Verdi's equipage usually fetches them from the nearest railway station, Firenzuola-Arda. His circle of friends is small, and grows no larger despite the vast number of connections formed in the course of a long, brilliant life. Only seldom does an outsider come in, like Monsieur du Locle, the Director of the Paris Grand Opera, who asks Verdi in vain for a new work for his institution. After 1870 the group of friends consists chiefly of the singer Teresina Stolz, a Czech with a superb voice who created *Aida* at the Scala, Giulio Ricordi and Arrigo Boito, the poet-composer of *Mephis-*

tofele, a vigorous talent and more vigorous intellect who writes the masterly librettos of *Otello* and *Falstaff* for Verdi.

The main meal comes at about six in the evening. Verdi has the reputation of a lover and connoisseur of good cooking; though he does not compare with Rossini in that respect, he sets a splendid table. He loves the light wine of Italy and heavy Havana cigars, nor does he disdain a game of cards after the evening meal.

Music seems to cut no great figure in the house. Verdi is not fond of musical discussions. He warns some of his visitors that they will find no scores at his house, and a piano with broken strings.

Yet sometimes, later in the evening or at night, after the guests are all gone, Signora Giuseppina will be sitting alone in her room. Perhaps she is thinking how it all came about. Once, long ago, she was the young, radiant diva, and the Maestro a modest, rather somber man to whom her patronage helped bring victory and great glory. And now? Muffled tones come from Verdi's room. Peppina drops her sewing, and lifts her head. What is this? Why, that's new! What the woman does now requires some courage. But she cannot help herself. Slowly, on tiptoe she creeps nearer, listens at the door, and finally opens it. One of those melodies has just been born that seem as old as the world the very first time they are heard: "Addio di bei giorni" from *La Traviata.* "Ai nostri monti ritorneremo" from *Il Trovatore.* "Rivedrai le foreste inbalsamate" from *Aida.* Giuseppe Verdi's face is hot, his eyes are moist; the tremendous emotional power of his soul, which he hides so manfully from the world, is revealed now to his wife, his old companion in music . . .

VII

The signature Giuseppe Verdi put at the end of his letters changed somewhat as decades passed. One need not be a graphologist to understand the spiritual meaning of the twined circle that the Maestro drew more and more closely about his name. The signed name itself represents the ego, exposed to the shameless presumptions of a perpetually exigent world. No matter how strongly this ego believes itself armored with hardness and equanimity, it is and remains a touch-me-not, achingly excitable, mortally wounded by every unkind breath. To protect this ego, which is embodied in the name, the writing hand puts a sort of hedge around it, a sheltering fence or wall, at once cautious and vigorous. This is the meaning of the loop that encircles the name, leaving a smaller and smaller opening for the admittance of the world as time goes on:

Excitability and sensitivity of the ego are the natural and necessary concomitants of every artist personality. In most cases they lead to a morbid access of self-conceit, to an egocentric intoxication that would deny the autonomy of the outer world, and subjugate that world to the desires and purposes of the perpetually suffering ego. Quite otherwise with Verdi. Through all his letters from young manhood on runs the pedagogical determination to push the ego into the background. Fie upon this ego writ large, with its vain self-mirroring! We meet with a chained and sifted ego that has been many times subdued, and seldom permits itself an unchecked outburst. On the other hand all the cool, critical forces hostile to self-conceit come to the fore.

If a playwright or actor has a failure he will generally put the blame, once he recovers from the first stupefaction, not on himself but on his associates, on an unhappy combination of circumstances, or even on the audience. The vain egocentric is quite incapable of thinking himself wrong. Verdi, on the contrary, records failures suffered by himself with a coolness bordering on a kind of strange malicious satisfaction.

He is still young, and has the success of *Nabucco* just behind him; a new opera, *I Lombardi,* is performed at Venice. So much depends on his not suffering a reverse now! Fifteen minutes after the curtain falls upon the last act, the thirty-year-old writes to a woman friend:

"*I Lombardi* have fizzled completely. It was one of the truly classical fizzles. Everything was disliked or just barely tolerated. . . This is the simple but true history, and I tell it without pleasure, but without pain either. . .

Some ten years later *La Traviata* suffered a failure of such proportions, on its first performance (also in Venice), that the final curtain went down to the pitiless laughter of the audience. Imagine this happening to *La Traviata* on the first evening of what was to be its perennial stage life! And Verdi wrote one of his rare autograph letters that have become famous:

"*La Traviata* was a fiasco yesterday. Was it my fault, or the singers'? Time will tell."

This letter of three sentences is like a crystal. A gem of human veracity.

The man who cultivated this chaste truthfulness was an operatic composer, and lived in the world of the theater, a world of constant overweening pretension and self-adoration. No wonder that his aversion to what he called "advertising" started early, and sprouted later into the most acute disgust! Other artists are delighted to see their names often in print, even if only in connection with gossip or vapid anecdotes. Even as a young man Verdi was made violently uncomfortable by such occurrences. And in his old age he suffered from a strange onomatophobia: "I am horrified," he said, "when I read my own name; it smells dusty. . ."

At the time of *Aida* the name of Giuseppe Verdi became one of the show-pieces of world publicity. The Khedive of Egypt commissioned an opera for the opening of the Suez Canal. The choice, according to the rapturous tales of publicity, wavered between Richard Wagner and Giuseppe Verdi. And the publicity went rapturously on: the Khedive was paying two hundred thousand louis d'or upon delivery of the score. (Actually it was a hundred and fifty thousand francs.) The material for the opera came from the great Egyptologist, Mariette Bey. Emperors and kings announced their attendance. The entire press of the world was sending special correspondents to Cairo. Day after day the chant of publicity went on, compounded of truth and exaggeration. Would not any author have rubbed his hands? The name of the work was echoing in everyone's ears long before it was written.

But the Maestro's stomach was turned by the constant tub-thumping. When Filippo Filippi, the critic (incidentally one of the deserters to Wagner), proudly informed him that he too was going to Cairo for his newspaper, Verdi burst out into a song of fury, a veritable diatribe against advertising:

"I have a feeling that if this sort of thing goes on, art will no longer be art, but an empty trade, a pleasure journey, a hunt, a mere something that people run after, to which they would like to give, if not success, at least publicity at any price. What it makes me feel is disgust and humiliation! I always think with pleasure of my early days, when I came before the public with my works almost without a friend, without a soul to talk about me, without preparation, without the well-known influence; I was ready to take any bullets that came, and more than happy if I succeeded in creating a musical impression. And now, what machinery for one opera! Journalists, soloists, chorus men, directors, professors, etc. Each one must contribute his mite to the structure of advertising . . ."

Disgust and humiliation. How infinitely more disgusted and humiliated Giuseppe Verdi would be today! Presumably he would have a radio somewhere in the house, and from it, between two battle reports, two arias, two symphonic movements, a repellent, humanly indifferent voice would come out to sing the praises of an automobile, a soap, or a laxative! And what would he say of an art that no longer even pretends to be ashamed of advertising, but surrenders to it nakedly and openly?

Even the sedate, easy-going publicity of that day was

enough to send the blood to his head. What did all these people mean by their "German bustle," stewing a work of art for months in the "witches' cauldron of public opinion"? When he quoted this, Verdi was thinking of Meyerbeer and the Wagner of the Paris *Tannhäuser*. Can any cause in this world be sustained by persuasion? What have connections, dinners, diplomats, ministers, patronage, bribery, newspaper stories to do with a work of art? Is a work of art any the better because a mandarin of criticism nods at it, or a clique of half-baked minds is artificially worked up about it? There is an incorruptible relationship between tune and listener: either the tune sticks to the listener's consciousness, or it evaporates forever. Any attempt at prompting or mediating is contrary to nature, nay, impossible. Not only his innate repugnance but his clear thinking made it impossible for Verdi to understand how creative human beings could so completely mistake the laws of life. Thus even theoretic work on behalf of his own cause was unknown to him. This was where he differed most sharply from Wagner. He was not a Messiah, but *simply* a master of Italian operatic music. And how could a master over-rate or under-rate himself and his work? How could a master venture to thrust upon the world anything that it did not take of its own accord? Mastery is sure repose within the natural organization of things.

And so it was an actual fact that during his long stays in Paris throughout forty years Giuseppe Verdi never gave any interviews, was scarcely ever visible at great receptions, avoided the salons as sedulously as he did the coteries of the artists, and jealously preserved his untouchable solitude. He knew neither Meyerbeer nor Berlioz nor Gounod personally, and in fact he seems never to have met Rossini, of whom he thought very highly.

This same Rossini once discovered that his countryman from Roncole—he called him "The musician with the helmet on his head"—who after all was hoping for success as an operatic composer in Paris, could not even be persuaded to pay the necessary and usual calls.

The hedging line around Giuseppe Verdi's signature drew closer and closer. Then came the years of silence, the years of the strange hiatus in his output. His successful operas dominated the repertory of the world without diminution. But there was quiet around him now. He no longer had to curse publicity. Divine honors were paid to the name of Richard Wagner. Verdi was merely considered a popular operatic composer. No progressive music-lover of the time would have dared to give him the same rank as his rival.

The connoisseurs nodded mournfully: *Aida* was the swansong of Italian opera, which had been annihilated once and for all by the musical drama of Wagner. The world was convinced that the old Maestro himself had spoken his last word with *Aida,* and would write no more. Verdi was seventy. The papers began to bestow on him, free of charge, the honorary title of "The venerable ancient of Sant' Agata." He was seventy-two; seventy-three.

And then one evening at the Scala in Milan the tremendous, dissonant opening chord of *Otello* came crashing out, that blow of a giant's fist, smashing the stone of the tomb. "I am here still!" Italian opera cried, and this in an orchestral medium that no one would have thought it capable of.

And the venerable ancient of Sant' Agata was eighty when the Scala echoed with the first chord of *Falstaff,* a fierce new proof of strength, this time on the weak beat of common time. Tempestuously bidding defiance to the accustomed measures, *Falstaff* burst upon an astonished world. By these two works Verdi hurled the Italian opera, which without him would have succumbed to the crisis, like a golden discus into a remote future. The dream of the learned gentlemen of Florence was fulfilled, if in an unexpected way. Here were none of the good old vices that had become attached to opera in the course of the ages. But neither was there the bloated excess, the garrulous monotony and superabundance of the symphonic drama. And everything, everything was song. *Otello* is the suffering mortal who is musically revealed down to the faintest tremor of his nervous system. Never before had music succeeded in reproducing so sharply the physiological process of spiritual anguish.

And *Falstaff* is the comedy of overcoming the world, just as *Parsifal* is the mystery play of overcoming the world. But what a contrast! In *Falstaff* the innate irony of Italian opera takes wings again; there is a sort of underlying terpsichorean feeling that the things of this world are not quite real, but the sport of the gods. The work ends with a tremendous choral fugue, expressing in this most earnest of all musical forms the conviction that everything on earth is a jest:

"Tutto nel mondo è burla."

Yes, everything on earth is a jest. And within this jest man is *"Il nato burlone,"* the born fool, the unconscious jester of fate. Pleasure passes away, even pain, more real than pleasure, passes away. All that remains is the strange fame, the jest in the cosmic form of a fugue. But in *Falstaff* too everything, everything is pure song. There is even a loving couple that sing the sweetest melodies. It is a true that these tunes breathe a touching coolness which by no means belongs to the love-songs of *La Traviata* and *Aida*. It cannot be denied that a man of eighty wrote those songs. They are like the enchanting frost flowers on a window, through which the deep blue eyes of old age smile out upon a sunny winter landscape.

But now the time to cease work was irrevocably at hand. Verdi had covered a long, long road, a road of labor, a road of the soul. He had fought his battle through to the end. His uncompromising nature, a "thou must" as hard as diamond, had never allowed him to weary, never to temporize, and had kept him young, a man of the future, up to the very arctic zone of life. Fame had been no temptation to him, and even true inspiration no excuse. His constant intellectual labor produced not nervous exhaustion but another kind of hard work, farming. Progressively, year after year, there developed within this man of the theater a divine striving for anonymity, or, to put it more clearly, a striving for an existence without outward seeming.

There he went, the old man, through the streets of Milan, Genoa, Rome; everyone turned to look, but it no longer troubled him. The hedge of anonymity had grown together around him. It was seldom that now he had an outburst of anger or disgust. Like a bluish shadow the chivalrous humor of *Falstaff* lay upon its old creator, rendering him gentle.

Sometimes still a cloud would gather over Verdi's head. The King of Italy and his ministers were planning to make the Maestro "Marchese of Busseto." Unpleasantly surprised, he humbly requested to be spared this elevation to the nobility: he would feel ridiculous. This was neither pride nor democratic principles, but a delicate sense of dignity.

During those years Verdi often stayed at the spa of Monte-

[75]

catini. Montecatini was alive with organ-grinders. The Maestro had to run the gauntlet of his own tunes, for the hand-organs relentlessly ground out the *Miserere* from *Il Trovatore* and the quartet from *Rigoletto*. One day Verdi assembled these honest men of music, and paid them a stiff ransom to desist from further propagation of his songs. He may have succeeded in the little watering-place of Montecatini, but he did not succeed anywhere else in the world.

But another time, in Rome, Verdi happened by chance to hear a distant orchestra playing the introduction to the last act of *La Traviata*. Unable to control himself, he began to weep, melting over his own coals, as Goethe has it.

"Old as I am, there's still a little heart left in me," he once confessed, "and I can still weep. . ."

After Giuseppina died, the peaceful companion of half a century's life and music, he could no longer endure the loneliness of Sant' Agata. He moved to the Grand Hôtel Milan in Milan. There anyone might see him, in the lobby, in the writing-room, in the lift, even in the restaurant. He put no outer barrier between himself and the crowd, as if he no longer bore the burden of his own name. He did not turn away callers. He received not only his friends Ricordi and Boito, but such young musicians as Mascagni and Giordano. He watched the world and the new century that had dawned. But already he seemed to be on the far shore.

The end came suddenly. A stroke. The cause was a shirt stud. A niece who was taking care of the Maestro had gone out of the room for a moment. He was just dressing. The stud slipped from his fingers, and rolled under the bed. But old Verdi was the old Verdi still. He did not believe he needed help or attendance any more than he ever had. He knelt down quickly, and stuck his head under the bed to look for the little button. And then death came to him.

But death had no easy time with him. For seven days the struggle went on between death and Giuseppe Verdi. That iron body, that magnificent generator of all earthly harmonies and rhythms, defended itself valiantly. Outside, in front of the Grand Hôtel Milan, a dark, silent crowd stood gathered for seven days. The traffic was diverted from the Via Manzoni. Nobody in the city seemed to speak above a whisper.

D'Annunzio, the poet, wrote a great ode about the death of Verdi. He saw the figures of Dante, Michelangelo, and Leonardo in the Milan hotel room, bending over the unconscious form. The finest stanza of the poem tells with ecstatic rapture what Verdi meant to the people of Italy and to the world:

> *He nurtured us, as Nature's hand,*
> *The free, circumambient universe*
> *Of air, sustains mankind.*
> *His life of beauty and manly strength,*
> >*Alone,*
> *Swept high above us like the singing seas of heaven.*
> >*He found his song*
> *In the very breath of the suffering throng.*
> >*Let mourning and hope echo forth:*
> >*He loved and wept for all men.*

On January 27, 1901, the heartbeat of Italy stopped for an instant. Italy knew that the music of Verdi was like the air, without which there could be no life. But now he was gone, he who had found his song in the very breath of the suffering throng, who lived for all and wept for all in his melodies. Italy would give her great son such a funeral as had never been seen before.

With accustomed foresight, none other than the Maestro in person upset the plans. When the will was read, people were dismayed to find the following provision:

"I wish my funeral to be very simple, and to take place at daybreak or at the time of the angelus in the evening, without singing or music."

This was what had to be done, and done it was. But fortunately there was another clause in the will. Verdi wished to be buried in the chapel of his Casa di Reposo. This required some time and preparation, and made a second funeral necessary, about which the will was silent.

"The second interment, a few months later—the coffin was taken from the Milan Monumental Cemetery to the Casa di Reposo—, was a great national ceremony. Hundreds of thousands swarmed around the cortège. The royal family took part, the government, the army on parade. And then came one of the great and rare moments when people and music become one. Without any preconcerted plan, by some inexplicable inspiration, there suddenly rose out of the monstrous soul of the multitude the chorus from *Nabucco* with which Giuseppe Verdi had become the voice of consolation and hope for his people, sixty years before.

"Va pensiero sull' ali dorate!" The song of the enslaved by the waters of Babylon, after the words of the Psalm. . .

Opinion about Verdi's music fluctuates with the times, yet it is hard to imagine that human hearts and ears will ever be closed to the slender beam of his dramatic melody. His life is a parable, an example pointing toward the future. In this time of change and upheaval we have buried so many gods! The grease-paint has never melted off faster than it does today on the frightened cheeks of the mountebanks who have been playing the hero. The feeling for genuineness has grown implacable, and with it has grown our supply of disappointments. Modern art as it developed during the first three decades of this century is one of the culprits responsible for the chaos of values. No one believes in it any more. The great masters have no posterity. Fanaticism has entered into the birthright of culture. Vulgar disbelief in all higher levels of existence is rising in a torrent.

At such a moment as this, a life full of truth and without illusions, like that of the poet and farmer Giuseppe Verdi, seems a very star in the murk. Especially the young artist, the musician, writer, singer, actor, who is at the beginning of his career can find in Verdi's letters, if he knows how to read them aright, mysterious sources of strength like those of a radium bath.

(TRANSLATED BY BARROWS MUSSEY)

AN AUTOBIOGRAPHICAL SKETCH

St. Agata, 1879

*At his Sant' Agata home in the year 1879 Giuseppe Verdi
dictated the following description of the darkest days of his
life to his friend, Giulio Ricordi. This sketch appears to be
the only literary document we have from Verdi's pen. Pougin,
who published it for the first time, rightly praises the touching simplicity of its style. Not only for purely human reasons
but for historical reasons as well, it belongs at the head of
this collection of letters, since it tells us about the youth of
the master, which is hardly touched upon in his correspondence.*

IN 1833 or 1834 there was in Milan a Philharmonic Society
which was made up of good musicians. It was directed
by a maestro Masini who, while he was not distinguished by
any higher knowledge of music, at least had patience and per-
severance, the qualities necessary for an amateur society. At
that time they were preparing Haydn's "Creation" for a performance in the Teatro Filodrammatico. My teacher, Lavigna, asked whether I would like to attend the rehearsals,
for the sake of what I might learn from them. With the greatest joy I accepted.

Nobody noticed the young man who sat quietly in a dark corner of the hall. The rehearsals were conducted by three maestri: Ferelli, Bonoldi, and Almasio. One fine day, through some strange coincidence, all three failed to appear. The performers had already begun to get nervous when Masini, who lacked the courage to sit down to the piano and play from the score, turned and asked me to serve as accompanist. With the scant confidence which he may have felt in the ability of an unknown young artist, he said: "It will be enough if you simply accompany from the bass."

But at that time I was fresh from my studies and was not to be intimidated by an orchestral score. I accepted and sat down at the piano to begin. I remember very well the ironical smiles that passed among those dilettantes. My youthful face, my scrawny figure, and my poor clothes commanded but little respect.

However, the rehearsal began, and little by little I began to warm to it. Then as my excitement grew, I stopped merely accompanying, and began to conduct with my right hand while I played with my left. After the rehearsal was over I received compliments and congratulations on every side, particularly from Count Pompeo Belgiojoso and Count Renato Borromeo.

Following this incident, whether the three maestri mentioned were too busy to continue with the burden of the work, or were prevented for other reasons, the direction of the concert was completely given over to me. The public performance achieved such success that we repeated it in the great hall of the Casino de'Nobili in the presence of Archduke Rainer and all the Milanese society of the day. A little later Count Borromeo asked me to compose a cantata for voice and orchestra, on the occasion, if I remember rightly, of a wedding in his family. I ought to say here that I reaped no pecuniary profit from all this, and that I gave my services without any payment at all.

Masini, who, it seems, had gained confidence in the young artist, now proposed that I write an opera for the Teatro Filodrammatico, which was under his direction. He sent me a libretto which, after being revised by Solera, became "Oberto, Conte di San Bonifacio."

I accepted the offer with delight and returned to Busseto, where I had meanwhile received a position as organist. There I remained for about three years. When I had completed the opera, I made the trip back to Milan, taking my finished score with me in perfect order. As a precaution, I had made separate copies of all the singing parts myself.

But now the difficulties began. Masini was no longer director of the Teatro Filodrammatico. Hence he could not put on my opera. But whether he had real confidence in me, or only wanted somehow to show his gratitude (after the "Creation" I had helped him again and again, rehearsing and conducting various other works, including "La Cenerentola," and always without remuneration), he refused to recognize any obstacle, and promised to do everything in his power to have my opera produced at La Scala as the gala annual performance for the Pio Istituto. Count Borromeo and Attorny Pasetti promised Masini to support his plan, but to tell the truth, their support consisted of a few banal words of recommendation. Masini, on the contrary, went to great pains, and he found a powerful ally in the cellist, Merighi, whom I had known at the Teatro Filodrammatico and who had faith in my talent.

[82]

At last we succeeded in arranging everything for the spring of 1839. And in such a way that I had the double good fortune of having my opera produced at La Scala, and of obtaining four such really extraordinary interpreters as Strepponi; the tenor, Moriani; the baritone, Ronconi; and the bass, Marini.

The roles were distributed and rehearsals had hardly begun, when Marini fell seriously ill. Everything came to a standstill, and no one could even dream now of producing my opera any more. Terribly disappointed, I was preparing to leave for Busseto, when early one morning I saw an employee from La Scala enter my room.

"Are you the maestro from Parma, whose opera was accepted for the *Pio Istituto?*" he asked gruffly. "Come to the theatre. The impresario is expecting you."

"Is it possible?" I cried.

"Yes, Signor. I have instructions to bring the maestro from Parma, who was supposed to have an opera produced. If you are the one, then come."

I went.

At that time the impresario of La Scala was Bartolomeo Merelli. One evening in the wings he had overheard a conversation between Signorina Strepponi and Giorgio Ronconi, in the course of which Strepponi expressed a very favorable opinion of "Oberto, Conte di San Bonifacio," and Ronconi had agreed with her completely.

I presented myself to Merelli, who informed me without any preliminaries, that in view of these friendly judgments, he would be disposed to produce my opera next season. However, if I accepted, I would have to make certain alterations in my score, since other singers than those originally decided upon would take the roles. To a person in my circumstances, this was a brilliant offer. Young, completely unknown, I had found an impresario who had the courage to stage a new work of mine without asking a financial guarantee, which, incidentally, I could not possibly have given. Taking all the expenses upon himself, Merelli proposed only to divide with me whatever sum I might receive from the sale of my score in case the opera should be a success. No one should suppose this was a poor bargain for me, for this was a beginner's work.

As it turned out, the opera was successful enough so that Giovanni Ricordi, the publisher, consented to buy the rights to it for 2000 Austrian lire.

If "Oberto, Conte di San Bonifacio" did not exactly create a sensation, at least it was sufficiently popular to be given a fair number of performances which Merelli decided to augment with a few that were non-subscription. It was sung by Marini (mezzo-soprano), Salvi (tenor), and Marini (bass). As I mentioned, I had to rearrange my music somewhat to adapt it to the voices of my new singers. I also wrote a new quartet, the dramatic setting for which was suggested by Merelli himself, while I had Solera do the verses. This quartet proved one of the most fortunate pages of my score.

Merelli now made a proposition which was extraordinary for those days. He offered me a contract to compose, at intervals of eight months, three operas, which should be performed either at La Scala or at the Imperial Opera House of Vienna, which was also under his direction. He, for his part, undertook to pay me 4000 Austrian lire for each opera, and the price of the sale of the scores was to be divided equally between us.

I immediately accepted and shortly after, Merelli, who was leaving for Vienna, commissioned the poet, Rossi, to write a libretto. This was "Il Proscritto." I was not really satisfied with this libretto and had not yet begun the music when Merelli, returning to Milan in the early months of 1839, told me that he absolutely had to have a comic opera for the fall season, that his repertoire demanded it. He would look for a libretto for me at once, he said, and I could work on "Il Proscritto" later. I couldn't say no, and Merelli gave me several libretti by Romani to read; which had been forgotten either because they had been unsuccessful or for goodness knows what other reasons. But no matter how conscientiously I read them, not a single one appealed to me. The situation became more and more pressing, so finally I chose the libretto that seemed the least bad of the lot. Its title, "Il Finto Stanislao," was later changed to "Un Giorno di Regno."

At that time I was living in a modest apartment in the neighborhood of the Porta Ticinese with my little family: my young wife, Margherita Barezzi, and our two little children. Hardly had I begun to work when I came down with a bad case of angina which kept me in bed for a long time. I had just begun to recover when I remembered that the rent, for which I needed fifty *scudi* was going to fall due in three days. Though that was no small sum for me in those days, still it was not serious. But sickness and pain had prevented me from making any advance provisions, and the communications with Busseto (the mail went only twice a week) made it impossible to write my excellent father-in-law in time for him to help me. I wanted to pay my rent the day it was due, at any price. So reluctant as I was to resort to third persons, I decided to ask the engineer Pasetti to beg Merelli for the fifty talers, either as an advance payment or as a loan for eight to ten days, long enough to write to Busseto and receive the sum mentioned.

There is no use of my going into the reasons here why Merelli did not advance me the fifty écus. It was not his fault. But I was deeply distressed. I could not resign myself to overstep, even by a few days, the date on which my rent fell due. Thereupon, my wife, who saw my agitation, took her few jewels and, I know not how or by what means, got the sum together and brought it to me. I was deeply moved by this proof of her devotion and swore to myself to return everything to her, which happily I was soon able to do, thanks to my contract.

But now there began the most terrible series of misfortunes for me. At the beginning of April my little boy fell ill. The doctors were unable to find the cause of his suffering, and the poor little fellow wasted slowly away in the arms of his mother who went nearly mad with grief. But this was not enough. A few days later my little daughter sickened in her turn, and this child too was taken from us! And even this was not all. During the first days of June my young helpmate herself was seized with an acute encephalitis, and on the nineteenth of June, 1840, the third coffin was carried out of my house.

I was alone! . . alone! . . In a little over two months I had lost three loved ones. My whole family was gone! . . And in this terrible anguish of soul, to avoid breaking the engagement I had contracted, I was compelled to write an entire comic opera!

"Un Giorno di Regno" was not successful. Part of its failure was certainly due to the music; but the performance, too, must take part of the blame. My soul rent by the misfortunes that had overwhelmed me, my spirit embittered by the failure of my opera, I persuaded myself that I could find no more consolation in art and resolved never to compose again. I even wrote Pasetti (who hadn't shown a sign of life after the fiasco of "Un Giorno di Regno") asking him to obtain from Merelli a release for me from my contract.

Merelli called me in and treated me like a capricious child. He refused to believe that art could have been poisoned for me by a single poor success, etc., etc. But I stood firm until he finally gave back my contract, saying: "Listen, Verdi, I can't force you to compose. But my faith in you is as strong as ever. Who knows, one fine day you may decide to take the pen up again. In that case, all you have to do is to let me know two months before the opening of the season, and I promise that the opera you bring will be performed!"

I thanked him. But even these words were powerless to make me change my decision, and I left.

I settled in Milan near the Corsia de' Servi. I was discouraged and no longer gave a thought to music. Then one evening, just as I was leaving Christofori's Gallery, I found myself face to face with Merelli, who was on his way to the theatre. Heavy snowflakes were falling from the sky and Merelli, shoving his arm under mine, persuaded me to accompany him as far as his office at La Scala. On the way we chatted of this and that, and he told me he was in difficulties because of the new opera he had to give. He had commissioned Nicolai to write the opera, but Nicolai was dissatisfied with the libretto.

"Just imagine," cried Merelli, "a libretto by Solera, superb!! . . magnificent! . . absolutely extraordinary!! . . Tense, grandiose, dramatic situations, beautiful verses! . . But this pig-headed Nicolai can't see reason and declares the text is impossible! . . I am in a terrible quandary and don't know where on earth to turn to get another quickly."

"I can help you," I comforted him. "Didn't you have 'Il Proscritto' written for me? I haven't composed a single note of it. The text is at your disposal."

"Bravo! . . . That's what I call luck!"

In the course of our conversation we had arrived at the theatre. Merelli summoned Bassi, who was poet, stage manager, *régisseur,* librarian and various other things rolled into one, and bade him find out immediately whether there was not a manuscript of "Il Proscritto" in the archives. It was found. But at the same time Merelli picked up another manuscript and showed it to me, exclaiming: "There! That is Solera's libretto! Think of turning down such marvelous material! Take it, and read it!"

"What should I do with it? No, no, I am not in the mood for reading librettos."

"Eh! It won't bite you, will it? Read it and then you can give it back to me." And he forced the manuscript into my hands. It was a thick brochure written in a large hand, as was the style then. I rolled it up, took leave of Merelli and started back to my lodgings.

As I was walking back, I was seized with a sort of vague

anxiety, a profound sadness, an anguish that gripped my heart! . . . Back home, I threw the manuscript on the table with an almost violent gesture, and remained standing before it. In falling, it had opened of itself; without my realizing it, my eyes clung to the open page and to one special line:

"Va, pensiero, sull' ali dorate." *

I skimmed through the following verses and was deeply moved by them, the more so since they were almost a paraphrase of the *Bible,* which I have always loved to read.

I read one fragment, I read another. Then firm in my resolution never to write again, I closed the brochure and went to bed. . . . But bah! "Nabucco" kept running in my head! . . . Sleep would not come. I got up and read the poem not once, but twice, three times, so many times that by morning I can say I knew Solera's libretto by heart from beginning to end.

But in spite of all this I was by no means disposed to change my resolution. During the day I went back to the theatre to return the manuscript to Merelli.

"Eh," he said, "it's beautiful!"

"Very beautiful!"

"Well then, set it to music!"

"Positively no! I don't want to have anything to do with it."

"Set it to music, I tell you, set it to music!"

With these words, he stuffed the pamphlet into my overcoat pocket, seized me by the shoulders, and not only threw

* "Fly, oh thought, on golden wings." The words to the melody of the great nostalgic chorus of the Jews in "Nabucco," which laid the foundation of Verdi's fame, and which was struck up spontaneously by the crowd at Verdi's funeral.

me out of his office, but slammed the door in my face and locked himself in.

Now what?

I went back home with "Nabucco" in my pocket. This verse today, tomorrow that, here a note, there a whole phrase, and little by little the opera was written.

It was autumn, 1841. I remembered Merelli's promise, went to see him and told him that "Nabucco" was finished and could be performed during the coming season of Carnival and Lent.

Merelli declared he was ready to keep his promise, but at the same time he pointed out to me that it would be impossible to perform my work the coming season, because he had already accepted three new operas by famous composers. To give a fourth new opera, by a man who was almost a newcomer, would be dangerous for all parties concerned, and especially for me. Therefore, according to him, it was more sensible to wait till spring when he had no other obligations, and he promised to engage good singers for me. But I refused. Either during Carnival or not at all! . . . And I had good reason for firmness too, for it would have been impossible to find two artists better suited to my opera than Strepponi and Ronconi, both of whom I knew had been engaged for Carnival, and on whom I set the greatest hopes.

Merelli, who wanted to oblige me, was in a very difficult position himself, as impresario. Four new operas in one season was a real risk. But I too had good artistic arguments in my favor. To make a long story short, what with "Yes" and "No," objections, perplexities, and half promises, time slipped past, the billboard with the repertoire appeared, and "Nabucco" was not on it.

I was young and my blood was hot. I wrote a foolish letter to Merelli, in which I gave free rein to my fury. But I must confess, hardly had I sent it off before I was seized with remorse. I was afraid I had spoiled everything.

Merelli sent for me. When he saw me he said, brusquely: "Is this the way to write a friend? But bah! You're right. We shall give this 'Nabucco.' Only one thing you have got to realize. The other three new operas are going to involve me in tremendous expenses. Therefore, I can afford no new costumes or scenery for 'Nabucco.' You will have to be content with the best arrangement of whatever we can find in the warehouse."

I agreed to everything, so anxious was I that my opera be given. And I saw another billboard appear on which at last I could read "NABUCCO."

This reminds me of a comical scene which had taken place a little earlier between Solera and myself. For the third act he had written a little love duet between Fenena and Ismael. I didn't like this duet. It cooled the heat of the action and seemed to me to detract from the biblical grandeur which characterized the whole subject. One morning when Solera was at my home, I pointed this out to him. But he wouldn't agree because that would have obliged him to re-do a finished piece of work. We argued back and forth. I remained firm and so did he. At last he asked me what I wanted in place of the duet, and I suggested the prophecy of Zecharias. That didn't seem a bad idea at all to him, though he was full of "ifs" and "buts" and "becauses" up to the moment when he finally said he would think the scene through and then write. That was not what I wanted, for I knew the good fellow, and I knew that day after day would pass without

Solera's making up his mind to write a single verse. So I locked the door, put the key in my pocket and said, half joking, half seriously: "Now, you don't get out of here until you have written the prophecy. Here, take the *Bible.* The words are there. All you have to do is to put them into verse."

Solera, who was quick to anger, didn't take the joke well at first. There was an angry gleam in his eyes and I passed an uncomfortable minute, for he was a perfect colossus and could have made quick work of my frail person. But all of a sudden he sat down quite quietly at the table and in a quarter of an hour the prophecy was written.

In short, toward the end of February, 1842, the rehearsals for "Nabucco" began, and on the ninth of March, twelve days after the first piano rehearsal, the première took place. As my interpreters, I had Strepponi, Bellinzaghi, Ronconi, Miraglia, and Derivis.

This is the opera with which my artistic career really begins. And though I had many difficulties to fight against, it is certain that "Nabucco" was born under a lucky star. For everything which might have hurt it turned out to its advantage. I wrote a furious letter to Merelli, after which one might have expected the impresario to send the young musician to the devil. And just the opposite happened. Crudely mended and cleverly rearranged, the old costumes appeared magnificent. The old scenery, brushed up a little by the painter, Perrani, produced an amazing effect. The first scene in the temple, particularly, aroused such enthusiasm that the public applauded for at least ten minutes. At the dress rehearsal nobody yet knew when or where the military band was to come on the stage. The conductor, Tutsch, was in the greatest embarrassment. I simply pointed one measure out to him, and at the première the stage music entered on the crescendo with such precision that the audience burst into applause. . . .

However! We should not always depend on benevolent stars. And experience taught me later how right our proverb is: "Fidarsi e bene, ma non fidarsi e meglio." (Faith is good, but scepticism is better.)

THE LETTERS

To Opprandino Arrivabene   October 18, 1880 (A)

*Francesco Florimo, librarian of the Conservatory of Naples,
had urged the publication of Bellini's letters. Vincenzo Bellini (1801–1835) was one of the most popular opera composers of his day. His greatest masterpiece, "Norma," which
was admired by both Verdi and Wagner, is still performed
today.*

Dear Arrivabene: Thank you for the article on Bellini. All
in all, I think Florimo has done his deceased friend a poor
service. At the same time, he has provoked a letter from
Romani's wife, which makes Bellini look very, very small
before the public, and who knows what may yet come of
all this? But why should anyone go and drag out a musician's letters? Letters which are always written hastily, carelessly, without his attaching any importance to them, because
the musician knows that he has no reputation to sustain as
a writer. Isn't it enough that he should be booed for his
music? No, sir! The letters too! Oh, what a plague fame is!
The poor little great celebrated men pay dearly for popu-

larity. Never an hour of peace for them, either in life or in death.

I leave you and go out into the fields. That is my present occupation. The weather is beautiful and I walk from morning till night. It is a very prosaic life, but it makes you feel very well.

(from Bragagnolo-Bertazzi: "Vita di Verdi") (J)

But alas! I was born poor, in an impoverished little village, and had no means to give myself any sort of training. They put a ridiculous little spinet into my hands and soon after, I sat down to write. Note after note and nothing but notes. That's all! But it is sad at my age to be forced to doubt so gravely the worth of all those notes. What remorse and despair that means! Fortunately at my age I haven't much time left to despair.

Roncole, October 24, 1829 (A)
To the Vestry of the Church of St. Giacomo at Soragna

Illustrious Sir: It having come to the knowledge of Giuseppe Verdi, resident of the commune of Roncole, that through the voluntary resignation of Signor Frondoni, the post of organist in the parish church of Soragna is about to fall vacant, he offers himself as replacement for the present incumbent, contingent of course upon the requisite public as well as private investigation of the applicant's capacity to discharge the sacred functions. Consequently, he begs your Lordship to admit him among the competitors for the above-mentioned position of organist, assuring him of the most conscientious and tireless service, and every effort to deserve the general approbation. Confidently and with the expression

OIL PAINTING BY FORMIS *Courtesy Musical Courier*

THE COMPOSER'S BIRTHPLACE
AT LE RONCOLE

of his deepest respect, he declares himself Your Lordship's grateful servant, Giuseppe Verdi.

To Caponi-Folchetto   *October 13, 1880* (I)

My dear Caponi: It was not in 1833, but in 1832, in the month of June (I had not yet completed my nineteenth year) that I entered a written application to be admitted as a paying student at the Milan Conservatory. Furthermore, I underwent a sort of examination at the Conservatory, submitting several of my compositions and playing a piano piece before Basily, Piantanida, Angeleri, and others, and old Rolla too, to whom I had been recommended by my teacher in Busseto, Ferdinando Provesi. About a week later I called on Rolla, who said, "Forget the Conservatory. Choose a teacher in the city. I advise Lavigna or Negri."

I heard nothing more from the Conservatory. No one answered my application. Nobody, either before or after the examination, spoke to me about the ruling. And I know nothing about the verdict of Basily, which Fétis reports.

That's all.

I write you hastily and briefly, for you are busy, but I have told you all I know.

My wife sends her thanks and greetings and I shake your hand warmly.

To Pietro Masini   *Milan, 1837* (J)

Dear Friend: Yesterday at last the impresario came and I presented myself immediately in the name of the commission, without waiting for an introduction. But he answered that he couldn't take the risk of producing a new opera, which might or might not be successful. At first I thought all this was just a lot of talk, to get people to pay court to him. But no matter what I said, I couldn't persuade him to discuss the matter and his replies were always the same. If I hadn't been the first one to talk to him I would certainly have thought some enemy had prejudiced him against me. But that was impossible. Depressed and enraged, I had to return without a spark of hope.

Poor young people! What's the use of working and studying if there is never to be any encouragement? Tell me, couldn't you talk to Merelli and find out whether a performance might be arranged at some theatre in Milan? Tell him I want to have the score examined by ranking artists, and if they reject it, then the opera should not be given. You would be doing me a great service. You might perhaps be able to pull me up from nothing, and I would be eternally grateful. Get in touch with Piazza too and tell him about it. I shall await your answer in Borgo San Donnino near Busseto.

I embrace you heartily, and remain your faithful friend.

Verdi refers here to a contract for the performance in Venice of "I Lombardi."

Dear Count: I have received the contract. I think I see some points in it which might be objectionable, and since neither you nor I would like to get ourselves into litigation, I have made some modifications which of course you can accept or refuse.

I cannot bind myself to Article 2 of the contract, because the Director might refuse both the first and the second libretto and so we might never see the end of it. The Director may be quite sure that I shall endeavor to have a libretto written that I can feel, so as to compose it as well as possible. Hence, if the Director does not have confidence in me, let him have the libretto written himself and charge it to me, always provided that the cost is not more than I can pay.

I cannot bind myself to Article 3, because (as I wrote in my last letter from Udine), I always do the instrumentation during the piano rehearsals, and the score is never completely finished before the rehearsal preceding the dress rehearsal.

In Article 7, the phrase "after confirmation of the third performance" must be deleted, because the third performance could never be confirmed for many reasons and I ought not to be bound by it.

A tenth article must be added, as noted below.

2. The libretto in question will be published at the expense of the Maestro.

3. Maestro Verdi pledges himself to be ready to put on the new opera about a month after the production of "I Lombardi," providing, however, that as many rehearsals as are necessary for a good production are held.

7. He is to be paid 12,000 (twelve thousand) Austrian lire, in three equal installments, the first on arrival in the city, the second at the first orchestral rehearsal, the third after the dress rehearsal is held.

10. The artists who are to take part in the new opera of Maestro Verdi shall be chosen by the Maestro himself from the roster of the company.

I am not sending back the contract because it would be too voluminous. But I shall return it or destroy it, as you direct. If you reply to this letter by return mail you may address your letter to Parma, otherwise to Milan.

With the highest esteem, I remain yours devotedly.

To Count Mocenigo　　　　　*Milan, June 29, 1843* (H)

Dear Count: I am sending you the sketch of "Catherine Howard." I should like to propose two other plots, which would be far superior to this one, but I don't know whether they would be practicable. One is "Cola di Rienzi," a splendid plot, but however carefully it might be treated, the police might not sanction it. The other is "La Caduta dei

Longobardi," which would also be excellent, but I should need a baritone to sing Charlemagne and a real bass to sing the last King of the Longobards, Desiderius.

To Ignazio Marini   *Milan, June 11, 1843* (A)

I hear with the greatest pleasure that you are coming back to us. The Milanese will greet their favorite bass with transports of joy. I have recently written two operas, "Nabucco" and "I Lombardi," that have parts for you in which you may one day shine. In "Nabucco" the part of the Prophet and in "I Lombardi" the part of Pagano seem as if they had been written for you. And I must tell you that I should like enormously to hear you do them. I am going to write for the Carnival season in Venice, for I didn't want to risk writing another opera in Milan just now, and I was obliged to refuse all the kind offers Merelli made me.

To Giuseppe Cavalieri   *Venice, December 12, 1843* (A)

Venice is beautiful, it is a poem, it is divine, but . . . I wouldn't stay here of my own accord. My "Ernani" is getting along and the librettist is doing everything I want him to. I rehearse "I Lombardi" twice a day; and all are doing their very best, above all la Loewe.

The first time we met was at the first rehearsal of "I Lombardi." We exchanged a few complimentary words and that was the end of it. I haven't been to pay her a single visit yet, nor do I intend to unless it should be necessary. In all, I can only speak well of her, for she does her duty very conscientiously, without the slightest shadow of caprice. Laugh if you like, but I shall be in Milan as soon as "Ernani" is put on.

[101]

To Giuseppina Appiani   *Venice, March 10, 1844* (A)

"Ernani" which was produced yesterday had quite a success. If I had had singers who were, I won't say sublime, but at least able to sing in key, "Ernani" would have been just as successful as "Nabucco" and "I Lombardi" were in Milan. . . .

Guasco had no voice at all and was so hoarse that it was frightening. It is impossible to flat worse than Loewe did last night. Every number, great and small, was applauded, excepting Guasco's cavatina. But the ones that made the biggest effect were Loewe's cabaletta, the cabaletta of a duet that ends as a trio, the whole finale of the first act, all of the act of the conspiracy, and the trio in the third act.

There were three curtain calls after the first act, one after the second, three after the third, and three or four at the end of the opera. This is the true story.

Within a week I shall be in Milan.

To Vincenzo Flauto   *Milan, March 21, 1844* (A)

Vincenzo Flauto was impresario of the San Carlo Theatre in Naples. Salvatore Cammarano wrote four of Verdi's libretti, among them "Il Trovatore."

Certainly, the advantage of writing an opera to a poem by the famous poet, Signor Cammerano, and with such executants, as well as the great prestige which redounds to any competent composer, when he is performed at the Teatro Massimo—all these things together make me lose no time in accepting the offer you make, on the following conditions:

    1. The opera company will pay me 550 (five hundred and fifty) gold *napoléons* of twenty francs apiece, payable

in three equal installments. The first as soon as I arrive in the city, the second at the first orchestra rehearsal, and the third on the day immediately after the first performance.

2. The company shall forward Signor Cammerano's libretto to me in Milan by the end of this year 1844.

3. I shall not be obliged to produce the opera before the end of June.

4. The singers will be selected from the personnel of the company according to my choice, always provided that this personnel includes Tadolini, Fraschini and Coletti.

To Antonio Barezzi   *Milan, April 22, 1844* (E)

Emanuele Muzio, a young musician of Busseto, who was sent to study in Milan by Verdi's father-in-law, Antonio Barezzi, became Verdi's pupil, assistant, and faithful apostle, and finally a conductor in his own right. From his copious correspondence with Barezzi, a few of his early letters are given here for the light they throw on Verdi. They are touching documents from the pen of a young provincial, still amazed by everything he sees and hears, written in the scarcely literate style of an Italian peasant to whom the standard tongue is almost a foreign language.

Maestro Verdi has been giving me lessons in counterpoint for several days because no foreigner nor any one from the Milanese province can attend the Conservatory; and if eventually I am able to attend, it will be through a special favor which the Viceroy and the Governor of Milan grant to Signor Verdi. Furthermore, he will be so kind as to make out a recommendation for me, which I shall send you just as soon as I receive it. Many students would pay as much as two or three talers a lesson if Signor Verdi would give lessons, but he does not give any to any one, except a poor devil like me, whom he has already done a thousand favors, now in addition is giving him lessons, not once or twice a week but every morning. It amazes me. And very often when he asks me to do something for him, he even offers me lunch. My Maestro has such greatness of soul, generosity, and wisdom and such a heart, that to find its match, I would have to place yours next to his, and then I could say: these are the two most generous hearts in all the world.

EMANUELE MUZIO

To Antonio Barezzi   *Milan, May 29, 1844* (E)

I have finished the books on harmony by Fenaroli. Now I am doing a general review. When I begin the lesson, the Maestro tells me: "Remember, I am inexorable." You can imagine how frightened I get, but I overcome it little by little when he says, "Well done!" Bear in mind, Sir, that he doesn't let a single note get by that might stand; he wants things perfect. He doesn't want hidden consecutive fifths or octaves; or to have all the melodic parts like a scale with never a jump; or to have them all ascend together in parallel motion; and none of these parts, in whatever key, should ever pass this note: ♯ The conditions are few, but the difficulty is to put them into practice. I shall preserve all these writings like a precious jewel. Now, having finished the exercises on the scale, I am studying something else. Instead of that, I put eight consonant parts under a single note of the scale; then one note against one, two against one, etc. This is really counterpoint; the notes, being so many points, are placed one against the other; and from this has come the name

Counterpoint, that is a point against a point, note against note. (This was yesterday's explanation.)

Until now I have studied harmony, and be assured that if I had been studying with another teacher, apart from the fact that he would not have taught me so well, so perfectly, at least one year would have been required, since Corbellini (I tell you this confidentially), in the six months he has been studying, is not yet half-way through the same study that I have covered in so short a time. This depends also on one's will to study. Of course the teacher has a great influence. Mercenary teachers don't teach with Signor Verdi's love and zest. If I write even more bass parts than he tells me to, he is pleased and happy about it and tells me to write as many as I like, provided only that they're well done. And then other teachers don't explain so well, or in such detail as Signor Verdi does. With such teaching the student learns to love his work.

I can truthfully say that I was born most fortunate; first, for having found an unparalleled Maecenas who helps me, second for having a teacher of such distinction and of European fame as Signor Verdi, who is the idol of the Milanese people. [. . . .]

My teacher wants me to begin to go to the theatre. This involves expense, but he says not to worry and to go only when he himself tells me to, and there will be good music. When he tells me to go to the theatre, it's a command; and in the morning at the lesson he wants me to be able to tell him many things which I am to pay attention to; and thus the money isn't spent in vain.

EMANUELE MUZIO

To Antonio Barezzi   *Milan, June 24, 1844* (E)

He is pestered by every one. He says he doesn't want to receive any one, but he's so kind that he'll never stick to it.

A composer, whose name I don't remember, wrote Signor Verdi a letter in which he begged and even implored him not to put "I Due Foscari" to music, because he too had set it to music and feared that the same thing would happen to it as happened to Mazucato's "Ernani." Signor Verdi answered that he had already proceeded too far with the work so that he couldn't grant him his ardent request. [. . . .]

I have already come to Corelli's famous Opus Five, the most beautiful, the most difficult, and the longest of all. This morning I began the imitations. My teacher used the same studies which he used under Lavigna, but which he has improved upon. He guides me with his knowledge and clears the road along which I have started. The lesson lasts only a quarter of an hour; I'll leave it to you to guess what the reason may be. My funds are low; I added up my expenses and find I have money enough to live until the middle of July, but on the 15th of that month I must pay for the rent of my room and the piano, and that will take all my money. Please help me at your convenience. My teacher tells me that when I'm in need I must tell him freely; but I haven't the courage, because already he does too much by teaching me so well and so willingly. This morning he asked me, "How do you feel after studying with me?" I told him, "I'm a new-born person." I continue to live as economically as possible. I don't spend a cent uselessly, but the expense of paper, light, etc., is so great that it seems impossible. The

Maestro says that if I don't write a great deal and well, I'll never learn. I must do all these things and study very hard.

EMANUELE MUZIO

To Gaetano Donizetti   Milan, May 18, 1844 (G)

"Ernani" was performed by an Italian company in Vienna under Donizetti's direction shortly after the first performance at Venice.

Esteemed Maestro: It was a delightful surprise to read your letter to Pedroni, in which you kindly suggest attending the rehearsals of my "Ernani." I have not a moment's hesitation in accepting your amiable offer with profound thanks; of course it cannot but be of great advantage to my music for a Donizetti to interest himself in it.

In that way I dare to hope that the spirit of the work will find its due expression.

Would you be so kind as to keep an eye on the direction in general, and on the changes which may be necessary, especially in Ferretti's part?

To you, *Cavaliere,* I have no need to sing paeans. You are one of that little band who are geniuses in the highest sense, and need no praise for themselves.

The favor you are showing me is too great for you to have any doubt of my gratitude. With profound admiration, I am your humble servant.

To Francesco Piave   May 22, 1844 (A)

Francesco Maria Piave was librettist and régisseur *at the Teatro Fenice of Venice. He was the author of the libretti of "Ernani," "Macbeth," "Rigoletto," "La Traviata," "La Forza del Destino," and other Verdi operas. This letter*

[107]

shows how early Verdi began to take great pains with his texts, often to such a degree that all the librettist had to do was to put Verdi's words into verse.

So far everything is going marvelously, except for one little thing. I notice that up to here nothing has been said about the crime for which Foscari is sentenced. It seems to me that ought to be emphasized.

In the tenor's cavatina there are two things which are bad. First, Jacopo remains on the stage after he has sung his *cavatina,* which always weakens the effect. Second, there is no contrast in idea to set off the adagio. So do just a bit of dialogue between the soldier and Jacopo, and then have an officer say: "Bring in the prisoner!" Follow this with a cabaletta—but make it a good rich one, for we are writing for Rome. And then, I repeat, the character of Foscari must be made more forceful. The woman's *cavatina* is excellent. At this point, I think you ought to do a short recitative and then a solo for the *Doge* and a grand duet. This duet should be rather short, for it is the finale. Put yourself in a really inspired mood: write some beautiful verses. In the second act do Jacopo's romanza, and don't forget the duet with Marina, then the great trio; after that, the chorus and finale. In the third act do just as we agreed, and try to make the gondolier's song join with a chorus of the people. Couldn't it be arranged for all this to happen toward evening, and thus have a sunset too, which is always so beautiful?

Certainly, agree to write for Pacini. But try not to do the "Lorenzino," because you and I want to do it together some other time. But if you can't get out of it, then do "Lorenzino" too. Do what is best for you.

To Salvatore Cammarano   *May 23, 1844* (A)

I have received the outline of "Alzira," and I am satisfied with it in every respect. I have read Voltaire's tragedy; in the hands of a Cammarano it will make an excellent libretto. I am accused of liking a lot of noise and neglecting the singing. Pay no attention to such talk. Just put plenty of passion into it, and you will see that I write quite passably. I am surprised that Tadolini isn't singing. For your own information, paragraph three of my contract reads: "The singers to be engaged for the opera which Signor Verdi is to write will be chosen by him from those who are under contract to the management." So if Tadolini is under contract, Tadolini will have to sing. I certainly shall not give up my rights, for anything in the world.

To Giovanni Ricordi   *Milan, July 3, 1844* (A)

Dear Ricordi: Having carefully considered the contract for Naples I find that I absolutely cannot accept it. You know the management there invited me to write one opera for which I asked 550 gold *napoléons*. Since you were going to Naples, I entrusted you with the task of arranging the affair; always provided the sum was not reduced below 12,000 Austrian lire. The sum which is now offered me is even less than 12,000; but I don't want to spoil everything you have done. So I agree to write the opera for the 1845 season. The other is neither possible, nor would it be worth my while.

I am new to Naples so don't be surprised if I am a little particular about some clauses in the contract which must be changed; Clause 4—"the cast of the opera for 1845 is to be chosen by Maestro Verdi from the company's personnel, always provided that it includes Tadolini, Coletti, and Fraschini."

Clause 1—"In compensation for the opera which Maestro Verdi is to write for the San Carlo Theatre of Naples, the company will pay to the above-mentioned Maestro, two thousand three hundred ducats in three equal installments; the first on the arrival of the Maestro in town, the second at the first orchestral rehearsal, the third on the day immediately after the first performance."

Clause 2—"Signor Cammarano's libretto must be handed over to Maestro Verdi, in Milan, by the opera company, four months before the performance."

If during the current month of July, the contract is corrected as I have indicated, I am ready to accept it. By the end of this month, I shall consider myself free from any obligation whatsoever. Believe me, always yours affectionately.

To Antonio Lanari   *Milan, July 22, 1844* (A)

. *Antonio Lanari was impresario of the Teatro Pergola in Florence.*

Regarding the opera, "Due Foscari," I conclude from your letters that it still stands to be produced about October 22. I shall use three principal singers: La Barbieri, Roppa, De Bassini, and three secondary singers—a basso profundo, a tenor, and a soprano.

I shall also use a woman's chorus, a small stage orchestra, and I shall include a harp. The librettist will come to put on the opera for 40 scudi. Sketches for the costumes will be sent you from Venice. I definitely cannot use Selva, but I will use the basso profundo whom you told me you have.

So now we understand each other perfectly, and I have only to remind you to take particular pains with the *mise-en-scène*. This is a subject which requires careful handling and which offers infinite possibilities. With all esteem.

To Giuseppina Appiani *Venice, December 26, 1844*
          One hour after midnight (A)

You are impatient for news of "I Lombardi," so I am sending it promptly: it is hardly a quarter of an hour since the curtain fell. "I Lombardi" was a grand fiasco: one of the really classic fiascos. Everything displeased or was simply tolerated, except the cabaletta of the vision. That is the simple but true story; and I tell it without joy, but without sorrow either.

To Antonio Barezzi   *Milan, April 28, 1845* (E)

Leidesdorf (?): probably the friend of Beethoven and Schubert, who was himself a composer and publisher.

My Maestro continues in good health. He is not doing anything yet about the opera at Naples. At present he is busy only with me, giving me lessons from ten in the morning until two in the afternoon. He has me read all the classical music of Beethoven, Mozart, Leidesdorf, Schubert, Haydn, etc.

EMANUELE MUZIO

To Antonio Barezzi   *Milan, July 9, 1846* (E)

Today I received a letter from the Maestro, saying he arrived happily and is well but bored: that he likes the waters and is not bothered by them, and hopes they will give him back strength.

[111]

Is it possible that the Maestro's father believes all that gossip? Set his mind at ease by assuring him that the Maestro left Milan in good health and that if he'd been ill he wouldn't have undertaken that trip, and not to pay attention to the gossip of idle people. Now they say he died of poison, then of gastritis; now they claim he's dangerously ill, or dying of consumption, or sick in many other ways; but he always ends up by being well, and I hope he will always remain so.

I tell you these things so that you can communicate them to the Maestro's father, since he asked me to do so. The letter which his father wrote him in Recoaro was *filled with much agitation over the state of his health. "You, too, write to my father-in-law to tell my father that I'm well, and hope to bring some added weight to Milan."* Those are his words.

EMANUELE MUZIO

To Salvatore Cammarano   Milan, June 2, 1845 (A)

The Marchese Imperiale di Francavilla was supervisor of the theaters of Naples.

Dear Cammarano: We artists are never supposed to be sick. We shouldn't always be such gentlemen. Impresarios believe us or don't believe us as it happens to suit them. I don't like the way Signor Flauto wrote me. Even after talking with you, he still doubts that I really am sick and distrusts my medical certificates.

The Duke of San Teodoro, whom I met here, has added a few lines to a letter I am writing to the Imperial Marquis of —— which you will hear about. In this letter, I am trying to get him to persuade the company to grant me the month's postponement I asked. As soon as I have secured this postponement, I shall leave immediately for Naples.

OIL PAINTING BY GAIBAZZI   *Courtesy Musical Courier*

ANTONIO BAREZZI
VERDI'S FATHER-IN-LAW

Dear Cammarano, thank you for all the trouble you have taken for me; please excuse me for having been such a nuisance; and assure the company that the sooner they allow me the postponement, the sooner I shall leave for Naples. For the rest, I wish (and you must wish too) that these bickerings would stop and that we wouldn't have to discuss the matter any more, for to tell the truth, I can't stand it any longer. Believe me, your devoted servant.

To Antonio Barezzi   *Milan, June, 1845* (A)

The project for a theater in Busseto mentioned in the following letter, was not taken up again until twelve years later. In spite of Verdi's initial protestations, the theater was named after him, and he even contributed ten thousand lire to its construction.

I have read over the project for a theater and with my usual frankness, I will tell you that I don't think much of it. It really wasn't very tactful to air the whole business and compromise my name with the authorities, just because of a word I said to a friend or a confidential letter I wrote. Everywhere in the world people have built theaters, without having anyone in advance to write and sing the opera for their openings; and if Busseto has that advantage over the others, they should avail themselves of it, but not depend on it. I am not taking back my word, but you know that in 1847 I have to write two operas for Naples and for the publisher, Lucca, and I am not made of iron, to be able to stand any further exertion. As for the two singers, how can I promise anything about them? I said these exact words to your brothers: "It is just possible that we might have Frezzolini and Poggi." In a moment of enthusiasm (for

I admit I liked the idea of the theater) I took pleasure in saying this because, aside from my friendship with the two artists, the last time I took leave of Frezzolini, she said: "This fall we shall take a rest, you come and spend a fortnight in the country with us, and then we will visit you in Busseto and do a benefit there for the poor." I answered: "I take you at your word. But not for this year because I have no home. So I expect you next year without fail." But if Frezzolini should have a contract in hand (which means forty or fifty thousand francs) for the year that they want to open the theater, who would be fool enough to suggest she come to sing *gratis* at Busseto? . . .

I repeat, I should not have been named at all in their petition, all the more because it gives me the appearance of being ambitious to have a theater named after me and a bust of myself put up in it, while most Italians know by experience how strongly I combat such *réclame*, whenever I can.

Please avoid having the project sent to me to *indorse as security for them,* for I should reply that it is now my custom simply to put my name beside a figure of twenty to thirty thousand francs.

To Jacopo Feretti   November 5, 1845 (A)

"Alzira" is considered, perhaps wrongly, one of the lesser of Verdi's operas. The performances in Naples and Rome were not very successful. The libretto of "Attila" pleased Verdi and his friends better than it did the broad public, though the line: "Avrai tu l'universo, resti l'Italia a me!" (You may have the universe, but let me keep Italy!) gave rise to further political demonstrations.

I am very thankful to you for your news about poor, unfortunate "Alzira," and even more for the suggestions you are kind enough to make. In Naples, I too saw those weaknesses, before the opera was put on, and you can't imagine how long I thought them over! The ill is too deep-seated, and retouching would only make it worse. And . . . how could I? I hoped that the overture and last finale would compensate to a great extent for defects of the rest of the opera, but I see they failed me in Rome. Well, it wasn't to be!

I have read your sonnet. Beautiful! I am really quite confused by all the nice things you say to me, the more so since I should never be able to show my gratitude as I should like to.

"Attila" keeps me very busy! What a wonderful subject! The critics can say whatever they like, but I say: "What a wonderful, musical libretto!"

To Sofia Loewe   *Venice, December 19, 1845* (A)
"Giovanna d'Arco" (Jeanne d'Arc) had a similarly cold reception in Venice in 1845.

Here is your new cavatina. I leave it to you whether you want to take over the rights to it or leave them to me. In the latter case, you will understand if I beg you to guarantee that my rights will be respected, and that, therefore, no copies of any kind will be made by anyone. You may use it this season, only on nights when "Giovanna" is being given. Write me a line and let me know. Forgive me for not being able to come personally, and believe me, affectionately yours.

To Vincenzo Luccardi   *February 11, 1846* (A)
This letter shows again what great pains Verdi took with the production of his operas. "Caro matto" (dear crack-brain) was one of Verdi's favorite nicknames for Vincenzo Luccardi.

I owe you an answer to a very charming letter and am sending it very tardily; but you probably know that I have been ill ever since the second of January, and it was only a few days ago that I began to go out and to write again. I have a great favor to ask. I know that in the Vatican, either in the tapestries or in one of Raphael's frescos, there must occur the meeting of Attila and St. Leo. Now, I need a costume sketch of the Attila. Jot it down for me with a few strokes of the pen, and then make a note for me of the colors, with words and numbers. Above all, I need the hairdress. If you do me this favor, I shall bestow upon you my holy benediction. Nothing new here. "L'Elisir," the other night, made a furore as usual. I am tired of being in Venice. This dull, melancholy quiet sometimes puts me in an insufferable mood now. Farewell dear crack-brain! Give my regards to all our friends.

To Vincenzo Flauto   *Milan, August 2, 1846* (A)

Verdi's irritation with Naples dated from the performance of "Alzira" in that city. Later it disappeared. See his letters to the De Sanctises.

I am deeply touched by the affectionate solicitude you show in asking about my health. I am perfectly well. Of course, I don't know how my enemies will feel about this news; as for my friends, I will take advantage of your kindness and ask you to let them know.

In regard to the alteration or change of date that you would like to make for the opera which I am to write for the San Carlo, you know I have engagements both before this one and after, and at the moment I can't give you a definite answer. But there is plenty of time, and we can talk about this several months from now.

I thank you for your assurances of friendship, and as for your wish that I be good-humored with the Neapolitans, I don't know what you mean, but I assure you I am absolutely bursting with hilarity. Why should I be ill-disposed toward the Neapolitans or the Neapolitans toward me? Are colors so lacking in their prism that they have need of Verdi? As for me, I don't despair of finding some poor little second-rate theatre for the present. If all else fails, at least the Grand Opéra of Paris would not desdain to open its doors to me, as I can show you by a letter from Pillet. Meanwhile, let me hear from you often and command me if I can be of use to you. Believe me, yours affectionately.

To Benjamin Lumley   *November 11, 1846* (A)
Benjamin Lumley was manager of the opera at His Majesty's Theatre in London.

If the Directors of Naples allow me to postpone till fall the opera which I was supposed to write for them in June of next year, 1847, I, for my part, am ready to write an opera for His Majesty's Theatre in London, which could be produced about the end of June. I must have the right to choose the singers who are to be in the company, which must include Lind and Fraschini. You know, furthermore, that the opera which I am to write for you, belongs to the publisher, Francesco Lucca, with whom you will have to make all arrangements. With all esteem, I am devotedly yours.

To Antonio Barezzi   *November 23, 1846* (E)

As for the contest, you must tell me what you think about it, without regard for any one, as soon as you know the conditions, and when it will take place. But I am telling you the truth when I say that it would be a very painful thing for me to have to leave the Maestro, after he has given me a new lease on life, and is always trying to have me make a good impression in society, in the company of all fashionable people. Now he's planning to do something for me before he leaves Italy that will climax all the services he has done me and will place me before the whole musical world at the beginning of my career. If you could only see us together, I don't seem like his pupil but like more than a friend. We are always together at dinner, at coffee, at a game (for only one hour from 12 to 1). In short, he goes nowhere without me. At home he has chosen a large table which both of us use for writing, and so I always have his counsel. As for me, I absolutely couldn't leave him. Remember, he has done so much for me that I'm afraid to appear ungrateful. If it hadn't been for the Maestro, what would have become of me, poor, ignorant devil that I am? And now that he has taught me and that, thanks to his teachings, I can live honorably, and in due time accomplish something more, should I leave him? No—I'll never, never do that. Let people say what they like, I don't care. It's enough for me to be with my Maestro. May he never have to say to me, *"Now that I've taught you, you leave me, ingrate."* I'd die of remorse, if I gave him cause to say that to me. I haven't yet spoken of this at length with the Maestro, and I shall avoid speaking of it. If he should speak to me about it himself, I would tell him the same as I have written you, and something more which the Maestro's modesty doesn't permit me to say or to write. Please think this all over carefully and you will see that I'm right. Some will say the needs of my family are great, I understand that myself.

But they've been patient for two years now and I hope that for another year at most they won't die of hardship. Please tell my mother about all these things, because I haven't the heart to write them to her. She is good and all the others are good too, and they'll understand my reasons. And I hope they will think them good reasons and that they won't say that I'm wrong. I, on my part, will do everything possible to help my family, to be a credit to you, to my Maestro, and to my country.

Thursday, I shall write you again. For the present I write no more because my mind needs to be distracted and not filled with such unpleasant thoughts.

The Maestro definitely is going to London. In my first letter I shall tell you how things have gone.

EMANUELE MUZIO

To Francesco Lucca   *Milan, December 3, 1846* (A)

"I Masnadieri" was based on Schiller's play, "Die Räuber."

When you write, be sure to remind Lumley of the stipulation I called to his attention in my letter of the 11th of November, namely that he give me the singers he promised in a confidential conversation. Mr. Lumley must now write me a letter specifically assuring me those singers, and at the same time giving me the right to choose from his company.

As far as the subject is concerned, you know that I have changed my opinion of "Il Corsaro" and have had a new libretto written, "I Masnadieri," of which almost one-third is already composed. You know this very well, and I am amazed that you broach the subject to me at all. Here are the conditions which have been agreed upon: I write "I Mas-

[119]

nadieri" and Lumley binds himself to give me the two members of his company he has already promised me.

To Antonio Barezzi   *Milan, December 19, 1846* (E)

"Macbeth" is going better and better. What sublime music! I can tell you that there are things in it that thrill you. It costs him a great deal of hard work to compose music like that, but he succeeds very, very well. The first acts are almost finished except for the arias, the rest is already at the copyist's and next week it will be sent to the respective performers.

EMANUELE MUZIO

To Giovanni Ricordi   *December 26, 1846* (A)

At this time La Scala was still an Austrian Imperial Court Theatre.

Dear Ricordi: I approve the contract you have drawn up for my new opera, "Macbeth," which is to be produced during the next Lenten season in Florence. And I give my consent to your using it, on the condition, however, that you allow no performance of "Macbeth" at the Imperial Theatre of La Scala. I have too much evidence to convince me that they either don't know how or don't want to produce operas properly, especially not mine. I cannot forget the terrible performances they gave of "I Lombardi," "Ernani," "I Due Foscari," etc. . . . Another example is right before my eyes: "Attila" ! . . . Just ask yourself: in spite of the good cast, could this opera have been given a worse performance? . . .

I repeat, therefore, that I cannot and must not allow a performance of "Macbeth" at La Scala, at least not until there has been a change for the better. I felt obliged to let you know for your own guidance, that this stipulation which I now make for "Macbeth" goes for all my operas from now on.

To Antonio Lanari   *January 21, 1847* (A)

When you receive the music you will see there are two choruses of the utmost importance, so don't be economical about the number of singers and you will be pleased with it. Be sure and notice that the witches are always to be divided into three groups, the best way being in groups of six, six, and six, eighteen altogether. Take particular pains with the tenor who is to sing Macduff. See that the second singers are good too, because the ensemble needs good voices. And I am much concerned about these ensembles.

I can't tell you exactly when I shall be in Florence, because I want to finish the opera here in peace. Be assured, I shall arrive in time. Pass out the solo and choral parts to everybody so that when I arrive we can begin with the orchestra after only two or three rehearsals . . . for we shall need many orchestral and stage rehearsals.

I am annoyed that the singer who is to do Banquo doesn't want to do the ghost. Why so? Singers must be engaged to sing and to act, and furthermore it is high time to do away with such leniencies. It would be monstrous for someone else to play the ghost, for Banquo must preserve exactly the same appearance when he is a ghost.

Farewell! Write me at once. I repeat, I expect to send you more music. Meanwhile, give my regards to Romani. I shall write him soon.

Florence, Tuesday, March 16, 7 A. M. (E)

This letter is from Antonio Barezzi to his family.

My dear Ones: I didn't write yesterday for lack of time, because we had to see so many things that would amaze any great man; and I shall relate them all in person.

Last night was the first performance of "Macbeth," which, as is usual with Verdi's works, produced immense enthusiasm. He had to appear on the stage 38 times in the course of the performance. I can assure you that "Macbeth" is a great opera, extremely great and magnificent.

Many good wishes to all, and longing to embrace you, I am yours.

ANTONIO BAREZZI

To Antonio Barezzi   *March 25, 1847* (A)

I have long intended to dedicate an opera to you, who have been father, benefactor, and friend to me. It was a duty I should have fulfilled sooner if imperious circumstances had not prevented me.—Now I send you "Macbeth," which I prize above all my other operas, and therefore deem worthier to present to you. My heart offers it; may the heart receive it, as testimony of my eternal gratitude and love for you.

To Francesco Lucca   *April 10, 1847* (A)

I am very glad Jenny Lind is going to London; though it seems to me that she is going very late, and I should not like the season to be too far advanced when my opera goes on.

Remember, I shall not put up with such a thing, nor am I disposed to tolerate the slightest slip-up. I have been pretty poorly treated in this whole business; and if the opera is not

[122]

performed at the proper time and in the proper way, I tell you quite plainly that I shall not have it given.

To Giovanni Ricordi   *May 20, 1847* (A)

Dear Ricordi: In answer to your letter of April 26, as I am now freed from the contract for the opera I was supposed to write for Naples, I am willing to compose it for you instead. It must be done by a company of high standing in one of the first theatres of Italy, with the exception of the Imperial Theatre of La Scala; and in order that you should not bear the entire loss in case of an unsuccessful outcome, I wish to assume part of the expenses. Here are my terms for the contract:

1. The opera shall be given in the year 1848 in one of the first theatres of Italy (other than La Scala) by a company of high standing. The libretto will be my business.

2. You will pay me for the printed matter of every kind, 12,000 francs cash in 600 *napoléons d'or,* immediately upon delivery of the orchestral score, that is, on the day on which the dress rehearsal of said opera takes place.

3. During the first season, when the opera is performed under my direction, you will pay me 4,000 francs in 200 *napoléons d'or.*

4. Each time that the above-mentioned opera is performed in countries where a copyright law exists for literary and musical works, you will pay me 300 francs for each theatrical season, continuously for ten years. After the first ten years have passed, you will retain complete ownership of the score.

5. For all other countries which are not included in the

copyright convention, you will transfer to me a share of the 300 francs of the rental you receive.

6. If you sell the rights to the score of the above-mentioned opera in France, you pay me 3,000 gold francs in *napoléons d'or*. If you sell it in England, likewise, 3,000 francs. In all other countries, it may not be sold without my consent, as I wish to have a part in the sale, too.

7. This opera may not be performed at La Scala without my express permission.

8. In order to prevent the changes which theatres make in musical works, it is forbidden to insert anything into the above-mentioned score, to make cuts, raise or lower a key, or in general make any alteration which would entail the slightest change in instrumentation, on pain of 1,000 francs fine, which I shall demand of you for every theatre where a change is made in the score.

If these terms look all right to you, I shall hold myself bound to them through Saturday, the 22nd instant.

To Antonio Barezzi   Paris, June 1, 1847 (E)

Dear Signor Antonio: This morning at 7 o'clock we arrived in Paris, after having travelled more than one thousand miles. We had a delightful trip, with no mishap.

Wednesday we left Milan in a suffocating heat. When we arrived at Como we no longer felt it so much because we skirted the Lake, and as it's in the midst of the mountains, we always had a little breeze. At four on Thursday we arrived at Flüelen in Switzerland, and crossed the Lake in a steamboat which took us to Lucerne.

From Lucerne we took the diligence to Basel. From Basel

we went to Strasbourg by railroad. When we reached Strasbourg we missed the diligence which would have enabled us to leave at once for Paris, and the Maestro, not wanting to wait, got the whim to go to Paris by way of Brussels. Instead of continuing through France, we crossed the Rhine River and entered the Grand Duchy of Baden-Baden. On the other side of the river an omnibus took us to Kehl, from Kehl we went by locomotive over land to Karlsruhe, from Karlsruhe to Mannheim, from Mannheim to Mainz, from Mainz to Coblenz, from Coblenz to Bonn, from Bonn to Cologne, from Cologne to Brussels, and from Brussels to Paris.

The beautiful part of the trip started in Switzerland. There are unbelievably picturesque views, stupendous waterfalls. We ascended the St. Gothard; there was so much snow that we had to put on our overcoats and cloaks. At some points, tunnels had been dug and we drove through them in our carriage.

At Lugano we crossed the Lake, which is delightful. At Lucerne we covered more than fifty miles of the Lake, called "the Four Cantons," and we saw William Tell's Chapel and the house where he lived, the place where he killed Gessler, the man who oppressed the Swiss.

We rode by night from Lucerne to Basel, but we saw some beautiful sights because the moon was out.

From Basel to Strasbourg, by the railroad; here are some fine tunnels, beautiful bridges, and above all, a country-side so prosperous that it seems incredible.

At Strasbourg we saw the celebrated Cathedral, which is one of the most famous in the whole world. We saw the monument to Kléber, Napoleon's general; the monument to Desaix on the plains outside Strasbourg, near the Rhine, because Desaix was general of the famous army of the Rhine under Napoleon; and the monument to Gutenberg, inventor of the printing press.

Outside Strasbourg, which is the principal fortress of France, flows the Rhine, one of the largest rivers of Europe, in the plains of which Napoleon had an army of three hundred thousand men—that being considered the key to France. Here we passed into the Grand Duchy of Baden-Baden and went to Kehl by omnibus.

From Kehl to Karlsruhe, our train passed through a tunnel three miles long. Karlsruhe is an entirely new city, so beautiful, so well-planned, the factories so well placed, that it seems a painted city; here we spent the night.

From Karlsruhe we went by rail to Mannheim.

At Mannheim we embarked on a steamboat on the Rhine and went to Mainz, where we spent the night.

The Rhine is the most delightful river there is, for its views as well as its vineyards. There are large numbers of ruined castles, with which the people associate frightful stories of devils and witches.

At Coblenz there is a very respectable fort that looks out over almost the whole Rhine River. At Bonn we visited the monument they built last year to Beethoven, who was born there; at Cologne we saw the great Cathedral which was ruined by an earthquake and which they have begun to rebuild.

From Cologne to Brussels we went by railroad, and from Brussels to Paris, likewise, by locomotive.

At Brussels, we were unable to see anything because we stopped for only a half-hour, and during that time we dined, for we were as hungry as wolves.

I forgot to tell you that from Cologne to Brussels, inasmuch as it's all mountainous country, we passed through twenty-four tunnels. In the cars the lights were always on because these tunnels are very long, some five miles, others three.

We passed from Lombardy to Switzerland, from Switzerland to France, from France to the Grand Duchy of Baden-Baden, then to the free cities of the Rhine, then to Prussia, then to Rhenish Austria, then to Prussia again, then to Belgium, and from Belgium to France. And we passed through all these provinces and kingdoms without being asked for our passports, which we still have in our portfolios. Moreover, our trunks were examined only once, in Belgium. What a difference from traveling in Italy, where it's so inconvenient that you have to be showing your passport every minute, and always have your trunks open to show what's inside.

Here is the list of hours that we spent in carriage, steamboat and locomotive.

From Milan to Fiora by diligence	30	hours
" Flüelen to Lucerne by steamboat on the Lake	2	"
" Lucerne to Basel by diligence	11	"
" Basel to Strasbourg by rail	5	"
" Strasbourg to Kehl by omnibus	¾	"
" Kehl to Karlsruhe by rail	2	"
" Karlsruhe to Mannheim by rail	3	"
" Mannheim to Mainz by steamboat on the Rhine	4	"

"	Mainz to Coblenz, Bonn, Cologne on the Rhine	9	"
"	Cologne to Brussels by rail	11	"
"	Brussels to Paris by rail	13	"

91¾ hours

The expense was quadrupled because, though the trip from Strasbourg to Paris cost 60 francs, we spent more than four times that going by way of the Rhine.

EMANUELE MUZIO

To Antonio Barezzi   *London, June 4, 1847* (E)

Steam by land and by sea. The steam engine flew over the earth, and the steamboat flew over the sea. What chaos in London! What confusion! Paris is nothing in comparison. People shouting, the poor weeping, steam engines, steamboats flying along, men on horseback, in carriages, on foot, and everybody howling like the damned. My dear Mr. Antonio, you can't imagine!

Milan is nothing. Paris is something in comparison with London. But London is unique in the world. It's enough to imagine almost two million inhabitants, and you can picture what an immense city it must be. To go from one end of the city to the other you have to pass three horse posts and change horses three times.

EMANUELE MUZIO

To Clarina Maffei   *London, June 9, 1847* (A)

Verdi's friendship with the Countess Clarina Maffei began in 1842, and lasted until her death in 1886. Her salon in

[128]

*Milan was a favorite meeting place for Italian nationalists.
In his letters to her, Verdi disclosed, as to few other people,
his inmost thoughts and feelings.*

I have been in London for hardly two days. I had a terrible
trip, but it was very amusing. When I arrived in Strasbourg,
the "mallepost" had already left, and rather than wait 24
hours, I took the Rhine trip and so did not tire myself out. I
saw the enchanting landscapes; I stopped in Mainz, Cologne,
Brussels, two days in Paris and now at last I am here in London. In Paris I went to the Opéra. I have never heard worse
singers or a more mediocre chorus. The orchestra itself (if
our "lions" will permit me) is hardly more than mediocre.
What I saw of Paris I rather liked, and I like particularly the
free life one can lead in that country. I can say nothing about
London, for yesterday was Sunday and I haven't seen a soul.
But this smoke, this coal smell plagues me; I feel as if I were
on a steamer all the time. I am going soon to the theatre to
find out how matters stand with me there. Emanuele
[Muzio], whom I sent ahead, found me such a homeopathic
apartment that I can hardly move about in it. But, like all
houses in London, it is very clean.

Jenny Lind is arousing a fanaticism here which simply cannot be described. They are already selling boxes and seats for
tomorrow night. I cannot wait to hear her. I am in fine health.
The trip tired me very little because I took my time about it.
It's true I arrived late and the impresario could complain,
but if he says a single word that doesn't suit me, I shall give
him back ten for an answer and leave immediately for Paris,
whatever happens.

To Giuseppina Appiani   *London, June 27, 1847* (A)

All hail to our sun, which I have always loved so much, but which I now worship, since I have been living in this fog and smoke, which chokes me and blinds my spirit! On the other hand, what a magnificent city! There are things that make you stand petrified . . . but the climate spoils all the beauties. Oh, if there were the Neapolitan sky here, you wouldn't have to wish for Paradise. I haven't yet begun the rehearsals for my new opera, because I have not yet had time to do anything. Understand me: *to do anything.* That tells the whole story! By the way, Jenny Lind still makes the same impression on me; I am the very essence of loyalty! . . . Do not laugh, by Heaven, or I shall fly into a rage.

The theatres are crowded to overflowing, and the English take pleasure in performances which—and they pay so many lire!! Oh, if I could stay here a couple of years, how I should like to carry away a bag of these *most holy* lire! But there is no use getting such ideas into my head, because I couldn't stand the climate. I can't wait to go to Paris, which has no especial charm for me, but which I shall enjoy immensely because there I shall be able to live as I like. What fun to be able to do as you please!! When I think that I shall be several weeks in Paris without getting mixed up in musical affairs, without hearing anyone talk about music (I shall throw all publishers and impresarios out the door), I almost lose my senses, so consoling is the thought.

My health is really not bad in London, but I am always afraid that some misfortune may descend upon me. I stay home a lot, to write (or at least with the intention of writing) ; I go very little in society, very little to the theatre, to spare myself annoyance. . . . Oh, if I had time, I should like to write you so many things. But now I can only press your hand warmly and tell you that I am your friend for life.

To Emilia Morosini   *Paris, July 30, 1847* (A)

I am sure you must be angry with me and you will receive this letter with God knows what disdain. This time you are right, and my work, the London climate, my poor health, my bad moods, are all no excuse. I am wrong, I am wrong, and if you offer me your hand in reconciliation, I shall be happy.

Although the London climate was horrible, I took an extraordinary liking to the city. It isn't a city, it is a world. Its size, the richness and beauty of the streets, the cleanliness of the houses, all this is incomparable; you stand amazed and feeling very small, when in the midst of all this splendour, you look over the Bank of England and the Docks. Who can resist this people? The surroundings and the countryside about London are marvelous. I do not like many of the English customs, or rather, they do not suit us Italians. How ridiculous it looks when people imitate the English in Italy!

"I Masnadieri" didn't make a furore, but was well received, and I should have returned to London next year to write another opera, if the publisher, Lucca, had accepted ten thousand francs to release me from the contract I have with him. As it is, I can't return for another two years. I am sorry for it, but I cannot go back on my contract with Lucca.

I have been here two days, and if I keep on being as bored as this, I shall be in Milan very, very soon. The July festivities seem to me to be a very bad business!

[131]

If you wish to give me the pleasure of a letter, address it to *Paris, poste restante.*

To Francesco Lucca   *Paris, August 2, 1847* (A)

"L'Avola" was to have been based on "Die Ahnfrau," a ghost-drama by the Austrian poet, Grillparzer. The libretto and sketches for the music are preserved at St. Agata.

I feel it my duty to inform you that, according to the contract between us by letter of October 16, 1845, I shall write the opera for one of the first theatres of Italy for the Carnival season of 1848.

So far I have the following plots in view: "Il Corsaro," "L'Avola" (a fantastic German drama), or else "Medea," in which case I would use Romani's old libretto. If you have anything better to suggest, I give you liberty to do so, provided you do it within the current month of August.

I beg you to let me have an answer, and sign myself your servant.

To Giuseppina Appiani   *Paris, August 22, 1847* (A)

I owe you a great many letters, but I am sure you will forgive me when I tell you all the things I have had to do here. The Opéra here is nothing like the opera in London!! Imagine finding oneself all day long between two librettists, two impresarios, two music editors (here they always go by twos), having to see that a prima donna gets her contract, having to concoct a subject for a libretto, etc., etc. Isn't it enough to drive you crazy? However, I have no intention of going crazy and I defy the whole theatrical outfit, all the Parisians, all the newspapers, both pro and con, and the funny articles in "Charivari" and in "Entre-Acte." Apropos

of "Entre-Acte," there was a very funny article in it about me.
I think Emanuele Muzio has taken it to Milan. Have him give
it to you.

I shall be here until about the 20th of November, and at
the end of that month, I shall be admiring the dome of the
Duomo.

As for my health, I am feeling better than in London. I
don't like Paris as much as I do London, and I have a deep
dislike for the boulevards (shhh, let no one hear me pronounce such blasphemy).

You ask me about Donizetti and I shall give you the real
facts, although they are not pleasant ones. I have not seen
him yet because I have been advised not to, but I assure you
I have a strong desire to do so; and if the opportunity presents
itself, without letting anyone know it, I shall certainly see
him. He looks well excepting that he always holds his head
bent over his chest, and his eyes closed; he eats and sleeps
well and almost never says a word, or, if he does, very indis-
tinctly. If anyone approaches him, he opens his eyes a moment; if he is told "give him your hand," he extends it, etc.
. . . It seems this is a sign that his mind is not completely
gone. In spite of this, a doctor, who is a very dear friend of
his, told me that he does these things out of habit and that it
would be better if he were animated or even violent. One
might hope, then; but in his present condition, only a miracle
would help. On the other hand, he is now just the same as he
was six months ago, a year ago, no better, no worse. This is
Donizetti's real condition. It is dreadful; it is just too dreadful! . . . If there is any change for the better, I shall write
you immediately.

[133]

To Giovanni Ricordi   *Paris, October 15, 1847* (A)

"Jérusalem" was an adaptation for Paris of "I Lombardi."
The first performance there took place on November 26,
1847. The first Italian performance of this version was at
La Scala, December 26, 1850.

Dear Ricordi: I shall not make any long explanations or excuses for not having written sooner, because I have no time; but I shall come directly to the point, concerning the opera "Jérusalem" which I was asked to write and which will be put on here at the Académie Royale probably before November 15.

I shall then make over to you the above-mentioned score, for all the musical world except England and France. For the score, you are to pay me 8,000 francs in 400 gold *napoléons,* to be paid either in Paris or Milan, whichever I designate, as follows: 100 gold *napoléons* on the first of December, 1847; 100 on January 1; 100 on February 1; and the other 100 on the first of March, 1848.

For the first ten years, you will pay me my royalties as follows: for the first five years, 500 francs on each rental fee; and for the next five years, 200 francs on each rental fee.

If I can find an Italian librettist here, I will have the Italian translation done myself; if not, I will send you the French score, but on the condition that you have Emanuele Muzio do the translation. With the exception of the ballet music, which may be omitted, it is forbidden to add anything or cut anything whatsoever out of the score under penalty of 1,000 francs, which I shall collect from you every time the opera is given in a theatre of the first rank. In theatres of secondary rank, this clause will also hold good, and you will have to study all possible means of collecting the fine in case of infringement. However, if you are unable to collect it, you shall not be obliged to pay it to me. Farewell.

To Giuseppina Appiani   *Paris, March 9, 1848* (A)

I see from the few lines you have written me that you didn't receive my last letter. This is already the third or fourth letter which has been lost, and I can't understand why! I know very well that there is a revolution, but what has that to do with letters? [. . . .]

You probably know all about the happenings in Paris. The funeral procession that accompanied the victims to the memorial column of the Bastille was imposing, magnificent. And though there were neither troops nor police guards to maintain order, not the slightest incident occurred. The great National Assembly which is to choose the government, is set for the twentieth of April. I still can't understand why it wasn't called earlier; I am too hard-headed, or perhaps too cynical. You hear absolutely nothing about Thiers, perhaps he will show his claws all of a sudden!! . . .

I can't conceal from you that I am having a wonderful time and that nothing has disturbed my sleep so far. I do nothing, go walking, listen to the most ridiculous nonsense, buy nearly twenty papers a day (without reading them, of course) to avoid the persecutions of the vendors, for when they see me coming with a whole bundle of papers in my hand they don't offer me any. And I laugh, and laugh, and laugh. If nothing more important calls me to Italy, I shall stay here for the rest of April to see the National Assembly. So far I have seen everything that has happened, serious and comical (please believe me that "seen" means *with my own eyes*) and I don't want to miss the twentieth of April.

Paris, August 8, 1848 (A)

To General Cavaignac and Minister Bastide

The wave of revolution which was sweeping across Europe had stimulated Lombardy to revolt, and it was hoped that France would lend its help in abolishing Austrian rule in Italy. The original of this letter, written in French, was signed by the most eminent Italians in Paris. It was composed at the request of the Milanese Foreign Minister to assist him on his mission of appeal for French assistance.

Gentlemen: We have just received news from Milan of the fourth of August. Preparations are being made for a desperate defense. General Radetzky's proclamation only shows what fate is in store for the inhabitants of Lombardy. They will die, with the cry: "Long live Italy,"—their glances turned toward that France whose noble assistance they await in calm and faith. For they cannot confuse the memory of the France of Louis-Philippe with the feelings of the French Republic.

Gentlemen, can you continue as indifferent witnesses to the spectacle offered by the martyrdom of so noble and so unfortunate a people?—This people which calls out to you, as to its brothers, which has given you so many proofs of its sympathy in the most glorious epochs of your history, and whose gratitude you might win forever? Every moment of delay may decide the fate of thousands of victims! Every instant lost for the freedom of Italy is a gain for despotism in Europe! If France were still to hesitate, it would be better for France itself, for us, for all the world that such great words as *nationality* and *human progress* had never been uttered! Her hesitation would be a further dishonor, which would not damage the cause of freedom, but would discourage many and call forth much recrimination.

Gentlemen! A great responsibility rests upon you at this moment. They talk about England and refuse to see that England is negotiating with Austria, without France, and against France! They talk about money and seem not to know that the Kingdom of Lombardy-Venice was an inexhaustible gold mine for Austria, and that it could be the same thing for the cause of freedom. They talk about a European war and forget that war is already here, war between two irreconcilable principles! But of justice, of truth, of the new Europe, which alone can be the friend of France, there is no mention!

No, you will not practice petty politics, you will not practice the old diplomacy! You will not talk about your *union with the cabinets* now, since the union of all noble, free men has been achieved.

Do not permit the cry to arise from the madness of suffering, and with a semblance of reason: "Unhappy are the peoples who put faith in the promises of France!"

A. Guerrieri, member of the Provisional Government of Lombardy; A. Aleardi; Tom. Gar, Ambassador of the Provisional Government of Venice; S. Trivulzi; G. Carcano; A. Mora; F. Foresti; G. Verdi; Frappelli; De Filippi.

To Clarina Maffei   *August 24, 1848* (A)

Your letter gave me great pleasure, for I didn't know what to think about you. Now that I know you are safe and sane, I am happy.

You want to know the French opinion about things in

[137]

Italy? Dear God, what should I say to that? Those who are not opposed to us are indifferent. And I must add that the idea of a united Italy frightens the petty, little, insignificant people who are in power. France will certainly give no military aid, if it is not swept along against its will by some unforeseen event. Anglo-French diplomatic intervention can be only unjust, shameful for France, and ruinous for us. . . . Indeed, such intervention would tend to make Austria abandon Lombardy and content itself with Venetia. Supposing that Austria could be induced to give up Lombardy (at present she looks as if she might, but perhaps she would sack and burn down everything before leaving), that would be one more dishonor for us: the devastation of Lombardy, and still another prince in Italy. No, no, no! I have no hopes of France, nor of England. If I have hopes of anybody, it is— what do you think?—of Austria; I have hopes of internal confusion in Austria. Something serious must be happening there, and if we use the opportunity and wage the war that should be waged, the war of insurrection, then Italy may yet be freed. But God forbid that we should rely on our kings or on foreign peoples!

Italian diplomats are arriving here from every direction, yesterday Tommaseo, today Picciotti. They will have no success; it seems impossible that they should still have hope in France. There you have my opinion. Please don't attach any importance to it, for you know I don't understand politics.

For the rest, France herself stands before a catastrophe and I don't know how she will surmount it. The investigation of the events of May and June is the most despicable, repulsive thing in the world. What a pitiful, puny age. Nothing great happens—not even great crimes. I believe that a new revolution is coming, you can smell the *odor* of it everywhere. And the next revolution will overthrow this poor republic completely. Let us hope it will not happen, but there is reason enough to fear it will.

To Salvatore Cammarano   *Paris, September 18, 1848* (A)

Dear Cammarano: I can't believe your letter of the 9th was written seriously. What do you mean? I am always obliged to write the music and hand it in four months after I receive the libretto? So if the opera company in Naples should take a notion to give my opera a year from now, two, three, ten years from now, I am always to be their very humble servant at the disposal of the opera company? I am to give up all other engagements until the company deigns to send me the libretto? Oh, own up! You were not writing seriously! Do you know what the first clause in my contract says? *The music will be performed in October 1848, the complete score to be handed in by Sig. Verdi by the end of August, on condition that he has received the complete libretto four months earlier.* Then they talk about litigation . . . recourse to the law . . . very well. Such threats don't frighten me.

Because of my friendship for you, I am sincerely sorry you have to suffer, and I assure you that so far as it depends on me, I shall do all I can to get you out of this mess, although I myself am in a worse mess than you. You know I had made other arrangements for this opera in case it were not given in Naples at the time agreed upon. I have engagements here at the Opéra which are impossible to postpone for a single hour. If you hadn't left me with nothing to work on for two months, I should have finished the opera by this time. But now that it is almost impossible to fulfill this engagement, I find even greater difficulty in accepting the project which you now propose. In spite of this, I shall make every effort to adjust things amicably, but you must not delay a moment in sending me the rest of the libretto.

To Salvatore Cammarano   Paris, September 24, 1848 (A)

Dear Cammarano: By means as lacking in humanity as they are in legality, the opera company of Naples wishes to obtain the strict fulfillment of the terms of the contract. You, an honest man, father of a family, and a distinguished artist, would be the victim of all these ignoble intrigues. Secure in my contract, I could afford to laugh at the opera company and forget the whole business, but for your sake and only for your sake, I shall write the opera for Naples next year, even if I have to steal a couple of hours every day from my rest, from my health.

I can't exactly say when I shall give the opera in Naples (that will depend on how I can either postpone or free myself from other engagements) but you can assure the opera company of the date next year which they themselves asked for, on the condition that you have nothing to suffer, because it is for you alone, and only for you, that I make this sacrifice. Otherwise, this letter is not binding.

In closing, I might say that from his keen wits, his knowledge of affairs, and I may even say, from the poor style of Flauto's negotiations so far, I should have expected a different sort of procedure from him. Farewell, my dear Cammarano. Send me more text as soon as possible. Always yours.

To Salvatore Cammarano   Paris, September 24, 1848 (A)
The opera which Verdi discusses in the following letter is "La Battaglia di Legnano." This work, too, had its patriotic

implications: Legnano was one of the strongest Austrian fortresses in Lombardy.

In case you have adjusted things in the meantime with the opera company, do not use my letter, I beg of you in the name of friendship, for I am extremely hard put to find time to write this opera.

If you cannot do without it and if I am obliged to write it, at least keep in mind that I need a short drama, interesting, swift-moving and full of passion, so that it will be easier for me to set it to music. I rely on you. Meanwhile, keep on sending me the drama which you have begun and let me know the following: in case the censorship should not permit the story as it stands, do you think that by changing the title, scene of action, and so forth, one could retain all or most of the text? For the present, we must go ahead and develop it as it stands.

May I ask a favor of you in connection with the last act? At the beginning in front of the temple of Saint Ambrose, I would like to bring together two or three different melodies; for example, I would like both the priests inside and the people outside to have a text in the same poetic metre, and Lida a song with a different metre. Leave the task of putting them together to me. You might even (if you think right) give the priest some little Latin verses. Do whatever you think best, but be sure that this situation makes a dramatic effect.

To Clarina Maffei   *Paris, October 2, 1848* (A)

I have nothing of comfort to say about our poor Italy. You are fortunate, that you still have hopes. I have none left. What can we possibly hope of all these diplomatic intrigues, of the extension of the armistice? When it is over, it will be winter and then they will say: nothing can be undertaken during the winter. Meanwhile Lombardy will have become a desert, a graveyard. And then they will argue that the nation, which they have used every means to exhaust, is lucky to be subject to the paternal Austrian government. God protect it!

Yesterday in the National Assembly the government was questioned about the Italian affair. They wanted to know how it stood, how far the negotiations had progressed, and what they had achieved. Cavaignac gave the answer which used to be given by Guizot: that he could not and would not talk. A fine Republic!

To Giuseppe Mazzini   *Paris, October 18, 1848* (A)

In London, in 1847, Verdi had made the acquaintance of Mazzini who was in exile because of his fearless advocacy of the Italian revolution of independence. The music for the poem, "Suona la Tromba," by Goffredo Mameli, was to have been a battle hymn, but it was not completed until the days of battle were past.

I am sending you the hymn, and though it is a little late I hope it reaches you in time. I have tried to be as popular and understandable as I could. Do whatever you like with it. Throw it in the fire if it doesn't seem worthy to you. If you publish it, have the poet change a few words and the beginning of the second and third strophes. [. . . .] I could have composed it as it stands, but then the music would have been difficult, hence less popular, and we would not have achieved what we set out to do.

May this hymn, amid the music of cannon, soon be sung on the Lombardian plains.

Accept the most heartfelt greetings of a man who holds you in great honor!

P. S. If you decide to print it, you can apply to Carlo Pozzi in Mendrisio who is affiliated with Ricordi.

To Vincenzo Flauto   *Paris, November 23, 1848* (A)

I am sorry it looks as if I were being touchy and precious, whereas I am extremely frank, decided, sometimes irascible, even savage if you like, but never touchy or precious; and if I seem so it is not my fault but that of the circumstances. You paint me a flattering picture of the reception I should find in Naples now. But asking your pardon, might it not be that you, with your nervous affliction, are subject to visions and excite yourself to the point where you see rose color where there is only black? Certainly, I should be lying if I were to tell you I was satisfied with Naples the first time. But believe me, the outcome of the opera was not what disgusted me, but the endless foolish tattle that had nothing to do with any opera. Why blame me, either because I went to a big café, or because I was on Tadolini's balcony, or because I wore light colored shoes instead of black ones, or a thousand other petty matters which were certainly unworthy of either a serious public or a great city?

You think that my presence might influence the success? Do not believe it! I repeat what I said to you at the beginning, that I am a sort of savage, and if they noticed so many defects about me in Naples the first time, it would be no different the second time. It is true I have been in Paris now for a year and a half (in the city where one is supposed to acquire good manners) but I must confess I am more of a bear than before. I have been working constantly now for six years, and wandering from country to country, and I have never said a word to a journalist, never begged a friend, never courted rich people to achieve success. Never, absolutely never! I shall always despise such methods. I do my operas, as well as I can: for the rest, I let things take their course without ever influencing public opinion to the slightest degree.

But let us leave this exordium, which has nothing to do with our business. I should like to persuade you now that if I do not come to Naples it does not depend on me. I would sincerely like to prove to the Neapolitans that I really can do something which would not be at all unworthy of their theatre. But listen and then say, yourself, whether I should be able to take on new obligations. [. . . .]

Frankly, that is how matters stand, but don't make them known except to those persons who you think should know. For the rest, carry on your affairs freely. This correspondence is to be no tie either on you or on me. If the future changes, I shall change, myself.

I am writing to Cammarano about various things in "Macbeth." You should be present too at the rehearsals, and don't grudge an extra one. This opera is a little more difficult than my others and its *mise-en-scène* is important. I confess, I am more attached to it than the others and I should be sorry to see it ruined. Tell them it belongs to a genre with which you generally achieve either a great success or break your neck. That is why the greatest pains must be taken for the performance.

To Salvatore Cammarano   *Paris, November 23, 1848* (A)

I am still waiting for an answer to my letter acknowledging receipt of the third act. I particularly asked you in that

[144]

letter to add a scene for the prima donna. I still hope you will be so friendly as to do me this favor. In case you didn't receive the letter, I repeat my wishes here. Since the lady's role doesn't seem to me to have the importance of the other two, I would like you to add, after the death-chorus, a great, agitated recitative, in which she expresses her love, her despair at Arrigo's being doomed to die, her fear of being discovered, and so on. After a beautiful recitative, have the husband arrive and do a moving little duet. Have the father bless his son, or something of the sort. And so on.

One more last, tiny, favor I want: at the end of the second act I should like four verses between Arrigo and Rolando (together) before: ["La Battaglia di Legnano"]

| *Infamati e maledetti* | "Dishonored and accursèd |
| *Voi sarete in ogni età.* | Ye shall be forever more." |

I would like to lend this passage, before the finale, a certain significance and I shouldn't want to repeat words here. I want these verses powerful and vigorous. I should like them to express the following idea: "A time will come when your descendants will shrink in horror from bearing your name" and so on. Then, "Dishonored and accursèd," etc.

If you can write them and send them immediately you will be doing me a great favor, for I have no time to lose.

And tell me too: (don't be frightened!) I need another voice in the ensemble of the introduction, a tenor. Could we put in one of Arrigo's shield-bearers? I should think we could use him in the last finale too. He could support Arrigo when he is wounded. Answer me this too.

I know you are rehearsing "Macbeth," and since it is an opera which interests me more than all my others, you will permit me to say a few words about it. They gave the role of Lady Macbeth to Tadolini, and I am very surprised that she consented to do the part. You know how much I admire Tadolini and she knows it herself; but in our common interest I think we should stop and consider. Tadolini has too great qualities for this role! Perhaps you think that a contradiction!! Tadolini's appearance is good and beautiful, and I would like Lady Macbeth twisted and ugly. Tadolini sings to perfection, and I don't wish Lady Macbeth really to sing at all. Tadolini has a marvelous, brilliant, clear, powerful voice, and for Lady Macbeth I should like a raw, choked, hollow voice. Tadolini's voice has something angelic, Lady Macbeth's voice should have something devilish. Pass on these reflections to the management and Maestro Mercadante: more than anyone else he will approve my ideas. Pass them on to Tadolini herself, and then do what you think best, according to your own lights.

Tell them that the most important numbers of the opera are the duet between *Lady Macbeth and her husband* and the Sleep Walking scene. If these two numbers are lost, then the opera falls flat. And these two numbers absolutely must not be sung:

> They must be acted and declaimed
> With very hollow voice,
> Veiled: otherwise it will
> make no effect.
> The orchestra *con sordini.*

The stage extremely dark.—In the third act the apparitions of the kings (I have seen this in London) must take place behind a special opening at the back with a thin, *ashen col-*

ored veil before it. The *kings* must not be dolls, but eight men of flesh and blood. The place they pass over must be like a mound, and you must be able clearly to see them ascend and descend. The stage must be completely dark, especially when the cauldron disappears, with light only where the kings appear. The music underneath the stage must be reinforced for the big San Carlo house. But take care there are no trumpets or trombones. The sound must seem far away, muffled, therefore it must be composed of bass clarinets, bassoons, contrabassoons, and nothing else.

To Filippo Colini   *Paris, November, 1848* (A)

The directors who had accepted "La Battaglia di Legnano" were those of the Teatro Argentina in Rome.

I don't know how these arrangements about the opera have been handled, but I do know that I have received various letters that are extremely mortifying for me. It seems that they have been to enormous pains; that these directors have conferred a great favor in *accepting* this score. Dear Colini, you know that I have never put myself under obligation to anyone; I have never asked to have my scores "accepted" nor have I ever received *favors* or *charity* from anyone, not even six years ago, when I needed them and needed them badly. And you can imagine whether I should be willing to submit to any humiliation now, however small!

To Carlo Verdi   *Paris, April 19, 1849* (A)

Dearest Father: As I wrote you in my letter of the eleventh, Ricordi will send you the money you need for the payments. You will receive either 271 silver *napoléons* or 67 gold

[147]

napoléons. Ricordi will write you when you must be in Piacenza, and at the same time you will pay Signor Bonini.

Give this letter to Emanuele and he will tell you what it's all about. Try to adjust the accounts with Merli and send me a note after May 11 of all the expenses incurred.

Farewell. A kiss to Mother.

To Vincenzo Luccardi   *Paris, July 14, 1849* (A)

On the second of July, 1849, the French had taken Rome for the purpose of supporting an already established power, the Papacy. This was a very different sort of intervention from what Verdi and the Italian patriots had looked for.

Dear Luccardi: For three days I have been awaiting your letters impatiently. You can imagine how heavy my thoughts are at the catastrophe of Rome, and it was wrong of you not to write me immediately. Do not let us speak of Rome! What good would it do? Force still rules the world! Justice? What can justice do against bayonets? We can only bewail our misfortune, and curse those who have brought about so much disaster. . . .

So talk to me about yourself, tell me about your affairs! What are you doing now? Tell me everything our new masters will let you tell. And tell me too about my friends!

Write quickly, quickly, don't lose a minute. I bear an inferno within me.

To Vincenzo Flauto   *Busseto, September 7, 1849* (A)

"Eloisa" is "Luisa Miller," an opera based on Schiller's play, "Kabale und Liebe." This letter contains the first reference to the opera which finally became "Rigoletto."

Dear Flauto: I haven't time for a long letter and I only

want to tell you that I shall follow your suggestion and write another opera after "Eloisa," to be performed the day after Easter, 1850. So send me the contract on the basis of the suggestions in my last letter of July 26. . . .

As to the opera I am now writing, I shall be in Naples by the eighth or tenth of October to put it on by the end of the month. Arrange everything so that I can begin rehearsals the day after my arrival, for I shall bring the score finished, except for the instrumentation. As to the payment for this opera, guide yourself by my very first contract.

It is time now to consider seriously the libretto of the opera to be produced on the day after Easter. Because in order to do things properly, Cammarano should have the sketches ready and give me the first numbers by the end of October, when "Eloisa" will have been produced. I shall leave Naples for a while then, and would like to take the text with me to compose. As a subject, suggest Victor Hugo's "Le Roi S'Amuse" to Cammarano. A wonderful play, with tremendous dramatic situations and two magnificent roles in it for Frezzolini and De Bassini. Farewell.

P. S. It is understood that for the opera which is to be written for the day after Easter, I must have the right to choose the singers from among the company's personnel. Don't forget to insert this point into the contract.

To Salvatore Cammarano   *January 2, 1850* (K)

Dear Cammarano: The subject I should like and which I suggest is "El Trovador," a Spanish drama by Gutierez. It seems to me very fine, rich in ideas and in strong situations. I should like to have two feminine roles. First, the gypsy, a woman of unusual character after whom I want to name the opera. The other part for a secondary singer. So be up and doing, young man, and on with the work. It can't be hard to find the Spanish drama. . . . Farewell. I am yours sincerely.

To Giulio Ricordi   *Busseto, January 31, 1850* (A)

"L'Assedio d'Arlem" (The Siege of Haarlem) is the title which the Austrian censor gave to "La Battaglia di Legnano" (The Battle of Legnano) after having had the scene of action shifted to Holland.

Dear Ricordi: I haven't the slightest doubt that everything you say in your letter of the twenty-sixth is true. I know very well that times are difficult, that you have enormous expenses, that you have lawyers working everywhere (though not only for my scores). But you know too that I have ten years ahead of me, and during that time theatrical affairs may take a turn for the better, as I have reason to believe from various letters I've received. Incidentally, without reserving these rights for myself, I might, at one time, have made different stipulations for "Jérusalem," and "Battaglia di Legnano." But I don't want to bore you with the thousands of arguments I could advance on my side; only, I am surprised that after Emanuele wrote me you had agreed to 50%, you now want to put me down to 30. That is too much!! Nevertheless, I don't want to insist and I accept your proposal to pay me 30% of all rental fees you receive and 40% on all sales in all countries for 10 years, provided you include "Luisa Miller" in this arrangement and handle it as you do "Jérusalem" and the "Battaglia di Legnano" or the "Assedio d'Arlem." Thus, it seems to me, I have divided the burden, and you see how fair I am and how much I believe in the arguments you advance. If this suits you, we will have to adjust our accounts up to now. Then you will draw up a list of all the rental agreements and sales you undertake, which either I or someone delegated by me will go over twice a year. At the end of June and December you will remit the sums due me.

This agreement is to go into force today and my rights will subsist for ten years, beginning with the date on which the aforementioned three operas had their first performances.

As for the other opera I was to write for Naples, I freed myself from the contract, disgusted by the disgraceful methods of procedure of the Opera Company and the directors. However, since Cammarano and I had already agreed upon the subject, I shall write it anyhow, and it will be finished, I hope, in four or five months. I shall turn it over to you willingly, together with the responsibility of having it performed some time in November of the current year, 1850, in one of the leading theatres of Italy (except La Scala of Milan) by a company of high standing, and with the pledge that I myself will be present at the rehearsals. In recompense you are to pay me 16,000 (sixteen thousand) francs in 800 gold *napoléons* of 20 francs each, either on the day of the first performance or in monthly installments which we will arrange by common consent, as soon as you have accepted the principal conditions. In addition you will pay me 30% of all rental fees you receive and 40% on all sales in all countries for ten consecutive years, beginning with the day of the first performance of said opera, which must be, I repeat, within the month of November, 1850. These conditions regarding the rental fees of the opera to be written will go into effect as soon as you have accepted those concerning the other three operas, and thus all four will be bound together by the same arrangement.

[151]

To Salvatore Cammarano   *Busseto, February 28, 1850* (A)

For the opera, "King Lear," which was never completed, see Verdi's later correspondence with Antonio Somma.

Dear Cammarano: At first glance "King Lear" is so tremendous, so deeply involved that it would seem impossible to make an opera out of it. However, after examining it closely, it seems to me that the difficulties, great as they are, are not insuperable. You know, we need not turn "Lear" into the usual sort of drama that has been customary up to now. We must treat it in a completely new way, on a grand scale, without any regard for convention. It seems to me that the principal parts could be reduced to five: Lear, Cordelia, the Fool, Edmund, Edgar. Two secondary parts: Regan and Goneril (perhaps the latter would have to be made a second prima donna). Two secondary bass parts (as in "Luisa Miller"): Kent, Gloucester. All the rest minor parts.

You say that the reason for which Cordelia is disinherited is a little childish for our day? Of course we would absolutely have to cut certain scenes, such as the blinding of Gloucester, the scene in which the two sisters are carried onto the stage, and many others that you know better than I. The number of scenes can be reduced to eight or nine. I call your attention to the fact that there are eleven in "I Lombardi," and that that has never yet been an obstacle to performance.

ACT I, SCENE I   *Great throne-room in Lear's palace*

Lear on the throne. Division of the Kingdom. Objections of the Earl of Kent. Rage of the King. He banishes the Earl. Cordelia's farewell.

SCENE 2

Edmund's soliloquy. Gloucester enters (*without seeing Edmund*) and bewails Kent's banishment. Edmund, meeting Gloucester, tries to hide a letter. Gloucester forces him to show it. He believes in Edgar's plot. Enter Edgar. The father, blind with rage, draws his sword against him. Edgar flees, after trying to soothe his rage with pleading words.

SCENE 3   *Hall (or environs) of Goneril's castle*

Kent is seen in beggar's clothes. Lear enters and takes him into his service. Lear has his arrival announced to Goneril. Meanwhile the Fool chaffs Lear, with his mad songs, for having trusted his daughters. Goneril enters, complains of the shameless behavior of her father's knights and refuses to receive them in her castle. The King bursts out, realizing his daughter's ingratitude, and fears he will go *mad*. But he thinks of Regan and calms himself, hoping for better treatment from her. The arrival of Regan, who has been invited by her sister, is announced. Lear turns to her and relates the wrongs of Goneril. Regan cannot believe him and says he must have offended her. The sisters unite to make Lear dismiss his followers. Thereupon Lear realizes the heartlessness of his daughters and cries: "You think I'll weep; no, I'll not weep." He swears vengeance, vows he will do terrible things; he does not know what, "but they shall be the terrors of the earth." (The beginning of a tempest is heard.) The curtain falls.

ACT II, SCENE 1   *Heath—the tempest continues*

Edgar in flight. Banned for the alleged attempt on his father's life, he laments his unjust fate. He hears noises, and hides in a hut. Lear, Fool, Kent. "Blow, winds, and crack your cheeks. Rumble thy bellyfull! Spit, fire! Spout, rain! Nor rain, wind, thunder, fire are my daughters. I tax you not, you elements, with unkindness; I never gave you kingdom, called you children!" The Fool (*still chaffing*) : "O nuncle, court holy-water in a dry house is better than this rain-water out o' doors." He enters the hut and is frightened at the sight of Edgar, who pretends to be mad, howls with anguish. Lear cries: "What, have his daughters brought him to this pass? Couldst thou save nothing? Didst thou give them all?" (*Magnificent quartet.*) Somebody comes with a torch. It is Gloucester, who has defied the command of the daughters and seeks the king.

SCENE 2 *Hall in Goneril's castle*

BIG CHORUS (*must have various types of verse*) : "Have you not heard? Gloucester transgressed the command. Terrible punishment awaits him! What? He is to be blinded. Horror, horror! Acccurséd age, in which such crimes are done." The fate of Lear, Cordelia, Kent, and Gloucester is told again. At the last, all fear a terrible war which France will wage against England to avenge Lear.

SCENE 3

EDMUND: "To both these sisters have I sworn my love; each jealous of the other, as the stung are of the adder. Which of them shall I take? Both? one? or neither?" And so on. Goneril enters, and after a short dialogue, she entrusts him with the command of the army and gives him a token of her love.

SCENE 4 *Poor room in a farmhouse*
(LEAR, KENT, EDGAR, THE FOOL, PEASANTS)

The Fool asks Lear "whether a madman be a gentleman or a yeoman?" Lear answers, "A king, a king."—Song—The delirious Lear, still possessed by the fixed idea of the ingratitude of his daughters, wishes to arrange a court of judgement. He calls Edgar "most learned justicer," the Fool "sapient sir," and so on. Very singular, moving scene. Finally Lear tires and gradually falls asleep. All beweep the unfortunate King. End of the second act.

ACT III, SCENE 1 *The French camp at Dover*

Cordelia has heard her father's misfortune from Kent. Great anguish of Cordelia. She sends out messenger after messenger to see whether he has been found. Is ready to give all her possessions to whoever can restore his reason. Invokes the pity of nature, and so on. The doctor announces that the King is found and he hopes to heal him. Cordelia, intoxicated with joy, thanks the Heavens, and longs for the hour of vengeance.

SCENE 2 *Tent in the French camp*

Lear on a couch, sleeping. The doctor and Cordelia enter very softly. "He sleeps still." After a short dialogue, soft music is heard behind the scene. Lear wakens. Magnificent duet, as in Shakespeare's scene. The curtain falls.

ACT IV, SCENE 1 *Vast plain near Dover.*
Trumpet blasts from afar

Edgar leads Gloucester. Touching little duet, in which Gloucester recognizes his injustice to his son. Finally Edgar

[155]

says, "Here, father, take the shadow of this tree for your good host; pray that the right may thrive." (Exit.) Trumpets nearer. Noise, attack, finally the signal to assemble is blown. Edgar returns: "Away, old man; give me thy hand; away! King Lear hath lost, he and his daughters ta'en." (March.) Enter in triumph Edmund, Albany, Regan, Goneril, officers, soldiers, etc. Edmund gives an officer a letter: "If thou dost as this instructs thee, thou dost make thy way to noble fortunes." An armed warrior (Edgar) enters unexpectedly with lowered visor and accuses Edmund of treason. As proof he shows the letter to Albany. They fight. Edmund is mortally wounded. Before his death he confesses his crime and bids them hurry to rescue Lear and Cordelia: "For my writ is on the life of Lear and on Cordelia; nay, send in time."

LAST SCENE *Prison*

Moving scene between Lear and Cordelia. Cordelia begins to feel the effect of the poison. Her agony and death. Albany, Kent, and Edgar rush in to save her. Too late! Lear, oblivious of their arrival, raises Cordelia's corpse in his arms and cries: "She is dead, dead, dead. She's dead as earth. Howl! Howl! Howl!" Ensemble in which Lear must lead. The end.

To C. D. Marzari   *Busseto, April 18, 1850* (A)

From your esteemed letter of the 10th, I see that the basic terms have been agreed upon and it only remains to draw up the contract, in which I must ask you to have the article concerning the actual production couched in more or less the following terms:

"Maestro Verdi pledges himself to be on hand toward the end of January in order to begin rehearsals on the first of February, 1851, and bring out the production as soon as possible. During that time the management is to put at Maestro Verdi's disposal the artists who are to take part in the new opera."

I lose little time in orchestration or rehearsals, therefore, the management can be assured that if things go regularly, the opera can be performed on the 20th of February.

To Guglielmo Brenna   *Busseto, April 18, 1850* (A)

The Spanish drama mentioned in this letter is "El Trobador" by Gutierrez.

Dear Brenna: You will see from the letter to Signor Marzari that everything has now been arranged. I only ask a few days postponement of the performance, because I shall not be able to begin rehearsals before February 1. For the rest, if the singers are good and willing, you can be sure things will go quickly; certainly there will be no delay on my account.

In "Luisa Miller" there is a part for a contralto, but a very small one. I can make no promises, nor on the other hand have I any objection to writing for a contralto. It will depend on circumstances, and the subject that we may be obliged to choose.

If you draw up the contract, make it brief and clear. Do not include the clause on the dress rehearsal, costumes, lights, etc.

If the management is sending me the contract, tell Piave, in order to spare time, that if he hasn't been able to find the Spanish drama I indicated, I suggest "Kean," one of Dumas' best dramas. So many fine things can be done with this play without losing time. I could begin work in a month. Farewell, always devotedly yours.

[157]

To Giulio Carcano   *Busseto, June 17, 1850* (A)

My dear Carcano: How many doleful, tender memories are contained in the few lines you were moved to present me with!

My dear Carcano! We cannot forget the past. And the future? What will it bring?

I would give a great deal to associate my name with yours. I know that if you suggest my composing "Hamlet," the adaptation will be worthy of you. Unfortunately this great subject demands too much time, and for the time being I've had to renounce "Lear" too, which I commissioned Cammarano to adapt for some more convenient moment. But if "King Lear" is difficult, "Hamlet" is even more so. And since I am pressed by two commissions, I have had to choose easier, shorter subjects to be able to fulfill my obligations. But I still hope that some day when we meet, we can find a way to do this masterpiece of the English stage together. I should be proud to clothe your verses with my tones and thus present the operatic stage with a beautiful poetic work.

To C. D. Marzari   *Busseto, December 5, 1850* (A)

"La Maledizione" (The Curse) was the original title of "Rigoletto." "Stiffelio," a little known opera of Verdi's, had just been performed in Trieste. It was revived later as "Aroldo," and is totally forgotten today.

The letter with the decree banning "La Maledizione" was so unexpected it almost made me lose my mind. This is really Piave's fault—all his fault! He assured me in several letters, written as far back as May, that he had obtained approval for it. Thereupon, I set a good part of the drama to music, working with the greatest assiduity in order to finish it according to schedule. The decree refusing it drives me to desperation, because it is too late now to choose another libretto: it would be impossible, absolutely impossible for me to set it to music this winter. This is the third time I have had the honor of writing for Venice, and the Board knows with what conscientiousness I have always fulfilled my duties. It knows that when I was almost on my deathbed I gave my word to finish "Attila," and I finished it. Now, I repeat on my honor, it is impossible for me to compose a new libretto even if I were to work so hard as to sacrifice my health. But to show you my real good will, I offer the only thing I can do. "Stiffelio" is new for Venice. I propose giving this, and I myself would come to Venice to put it on, at whatever time during the Carnival season of 1850-1851 the Board thinks opportune. There is one great draw-back to this opera (also on account of the censor) : the final scene. It cannot be done as it stands. But if it should be impossible to obtain permission from Vienna to do it as I conceived it, I should be disposed to change the denouement, which thus would have its première in Venice. I beg the Board to accept this proof of good will and to believe that the displeasure and damage I suffer from this bann are greater than I have words to tell.

To C. D. Marzari   *Busseto, December 14, 1850* (A)

The central figure of "Rigoletto" was originally called Triboletto (Triboulet) in Victor Hugo's play, "Le Roi S'Amuse." This play had been badly received even in France, for it was considered immoral. The Austrian censors in Venice were at first beside themselves; objected both for this reason and be-

cause it tended to undermine the institution of monarchy. A compromise was reached by changing the scene of action and the names of a few characters. Bianca was changed to Gilda, Francis I to the Duke, Magellona to Maddalena.

I have had very little time to examine the new libretto. But I have seen enough to tell that in this garbled form it lacks both character and significance, and, finally, its most dramatic moments now leave one completely cold. If the names of the characters had to be changed, then the scene of action should have been changed too, with a duke, or prince of another locality, for example a Pier-Luigi Farnese or some such person, or put the plot still further back in the time before Louis XI, when France was not yet a united kingdom, and have a Duke of Burgundy or Normandy—in any case, an absolute ruler. In the fifth scene of Act I, all the rage of the courtiers against Triboletto doesn't make sense. The old man's curse, so terrible and sublime in the original, is made ridiculous here, because the motive which drives him to utter the curse no longer has the same importance, and because it is no longer a subject who speaks so daringly to his king. Without this curse—what point, what meaning is left to the drama? The Duke has no character: the Duke must absolutely be a libertine. Otherwise there is no reason for Triboletto's fear that his daughter might leave her hiding place, and the whole drama is impossible. What would the Duke be doing in the last act in a lonely tavern, alone, uninvited, and without a rendezvous? I don't see why the sack has been eliminated. What difference could a sack make to the police? Are they afraid it won't be effective? But may I say this: Why do they think they know more about it than I?

Who can be sure? Who can say this will be effective and that not? We had just such a difficulty with the horn in "Ernani." Well, and did anyone laugh at the horn? If there is no sack, then it is improbable that Triboletto would talk to a corpse for half an hour, before a lightning flash reveals that it is his daughter. Finally, I observe they have avoided making Triboletto ugly and hunchbacked. A singing hunchback? Why not?. . . Can it be effective? I don't know. But if I don't know, then neither, I repeat, does the person who proposed the change. That is just what seemed so wonderful to me: to portray this ridiculous, terribly deformed creature, who is inwardly filled with passion and love. It was precisely because of all these original traits that I chose the subject, and if they are cut out I shall no longer be able to compose the music. If I am told I can leave my music as it is, for this drama too, I reply that I don't understand such reasoning. And I declare quite plainly that my music, whether beautiful or ugly, is never written at random, and that I always try to give it character. All in all, a powerful, original drama has been turned into something completely ordinary and cold. I regret extremely that the Board did not answer my last letter. I can only repeat and beg them to do what I said there, because my artistic conscience will not permit me to put this libretto to music.

Busseto, December 30, 1850 (A)
At the residence of Maestro Giuseppe Verdi

In accordance with the contract received on December 27 from the President of the Board of Proprietors of the *Teatro La Fenice,* the undersigned Secretary of the President invites

Maestro Verdi to specify the changes which he consents to make in the libretto presented under the title of "La Maledizione," in order that this libretto may be composed for the current season, Carnival and Lent, 1850-51, according to the contract of April 23. These changes are to remove the objections which the State authorities place in the way of its performance.

In consultation therefore, with the poet, Francesco Maria Piave, the following is agreed:

1. The scene shall be shifted from the French court to that of an independent Duke of Burgundy or Normandy, or to the court of a minor absolutist Italian state, preferably that of Pier-Luigi Farnese, and in the period most favorable for scenery and dramatic effect.

2. The original characters of the drama, "Le Roi S'Amuse," by Victor Hugo, shall be retained, but other names shall be found for the dramatis personae, according to the period chosen.

3. The scene in which Francesco appears determined to use the key in his possession to let himself into the room of the abducted Bianca shall be omitted. It shall be replaced by another, which preserves the proper decencies, but does not make the play uninteresting.

4. The King or Duke shall come to the rendezvous in Magellona's tavern because of a pretended invitation brought to him by the figure who replaces Triboletto.

5. In the place where the sack with the corpse of Triboletto's daughter appears, Maestro Verdi reserves for himself the right to make such changes as he deems necessary.

6. The above-mentioned changes demand more time

than was originally supposed. Therefore Maestro Verdi declares that he cannot bring out his new opera before February 28 or March 1.

Accordingly this protocol has been signed and agreed upon by those present.

G. Verdi—F. M. Piave—G. Brenna, Secretary

To Giovanni Ricordi   *Busseto, January 5, 1851* (A)

Dear Ricordi: I hear with displeasure that they want to give "Stiffelio" at La Scala, because, ordinarily, operas which are not written expressly for that theatre are too badly neglected there. "Jérusalem" is a new proof of this. Why do they take out the little duet at the beginning? Why (aside from the insipid performance of chorus and orchestra) do they take out the "Ave Maria"? If they don't like a score, it's better not to give it at all! To return to "Stiffelio," if it absolutely must be given, the censors must convince themselves that the libretto contains nothing contrary to politics or religion. They should leave the libretto as it is planned, with all the text and the staging that belongs with it. Nothing should be changed, nothing emasculated, and everybody should put his best into it. It should be observed especially that the effect of the last scene depends on how the chorus is arranged on the stage. There must not be just one stage rehearsal, as usual, but ten, twenty if necessary. Otherwise I cannot permit "Stiffelio" to be given at La Scala. And remember that if it should fail of its effect because of poor execution, I shall hold you, Signor Giovanni Ricordi, responsible for any damage which may arise from it.

P.S. I cannot possibly come to Milan to put on "Stiffelio."

To Doctor Ercolano Balestra

Busseto, January 21, 1851 (A)

From a reliable source it has come to my knowledge that my father goes about saying matters have been arranged through you in one of the two following ways: namely, that I have accorded the administration of my properties to him, or that I am going to lease them to him. I do not believe there can be any misunderstanding between you and me, Doctor, nor do I believe that you have proposed any of these things. Nevertheless I should like to repeat for my own peace of mind, that I do not intend to comply with either of these two projects. I intend to keep entirely separated from my father in domestic as well as financial affairs. And finally, I can only repeat what I told you yesterday; in so far as the world is concerned Carlo Verdi and Giuseppe Verdi must remain two distinct and separate persons. I have the honor to sign myself, with much esteem, devotedly yours.

To Salvatore Cammarano   *Busseto, April 9, 1851* (A)

Dear Cammarano: I have read your sketch. As a gifted and very superior man, you will not be offended if I humbly take the liberty of telling you that it's better to give up this subject, if we can't treat it with the boldness and novelty of the Spanish drama. [. . . .]

It seems to me, if I am not deceived, that several situations no longer have the force and originality they had, and above all, that Azucena has not retained her strange and novel character. It seems to me that this woman's two great passions, *filial love* and *maternal love,* are no longer present with all their original force. For example, I shouldn't want to have the Troubadour wounded in the duel. There is so little to this poor Troubadour—that if we take away his courage, what will he have left? How could he possibly interest such a high-born lady as Leonora? Nor do I want to have Azucena address her narrative to the gypsies, to say in the ensemble of the third act: "Your son was burned alive," etc. . . . "but I was not there." And finally I should not like her to be mad in the last act. I wish you would leave the big aria!! Leonora takes no part in the *Miserere* and the Troubadour's canzone, and this seems to me one of the best places for an aria. If you are afraid of making Leonora's part too big, leave out the cavatina.

To express my thought more clearly, I shall explain in detail how I should have liked to treat the material.

PART ONE—PROLOGUE

First number—The chorus and introductory narrative are good. Cut out Leonora's cavatina. Do a magnificent

2. Trio, which begins with a recitative of De Luna; canzone of the Troubadour, Leonora's scene, trio and challenge, and so on.

PART TWO

Gypsies, Azucena, and the Troubadour who is wounded in the battle.

3. Gypsies sing an exotic, fantastic chorus. While they are drinking, Azucena begins a somber song. The gypsies interrupt her because it is too ominous. "As ill-omened as its story . . ." "You know her not. . . ." ("You shall be avenged!") These words grip the Troubadour, who should stand deep in thought up to this point. Morning dawns and

[165]

the gypsies disperse in the mountains, repeating a stanza of the chorus, etc. The Troubadour remains alone with his mother and begs her to tell him the story which horrified him so. Narrative, etc. Duet with Alfonso: it must keep to new, free forms.

4. Duet with Alfonso—It doesn't seem right to me for Azucena to tell her narrative in the presence of the gypsies, during which a hint escapes her that she abducted the son of De Luna and that she has sworn to avenge her mother.

5. Scene of the investiture as a nun, etc., and finale.

PART THREE

6. Chorus and romanza of De Luna.

7. Ensemble. The dialogue, question and answer in the Spanish drama, show the character of the gypsy very well. On the other hand, if Azucena reveals herself for what she is, she puts herself instantly into the hands of her enemies and robs herself of the means of revenge. It is good to have Fernando make the Count suspicious, and also good to have the Count, who calls himself De Luna, upset Azucena. Thus she is recognized by Fernando but does not betray herself, except perhaps with the exclamation: "Be still . . . if he knows it, he will kill me!" Very simple and beautiful are Azucena's words: "Where are you going?" "I do not know. I lived in the mountains and had a son. He deserted me: I go to seek him . . ."

8. Recitative of Leonora. Recitative of dream-narrative of Manrique, followed by

9. The duet between him and Leonora. He reveals to his affianced that he is the son of a gypsy. Ruiz brings the mes-

sage that his mother is in prison. He rushes away to save her, etc.

PART FOUR

10. Leonora's big aria, through which are interspersed the *Miserere* and the Troubador's canzona.

11. Duet: Leonora—De Luna.

12. Don't have Azucena go mad. Exhausted with fatigue, suffering, terror, and sleeplessness, she speaks confusedly. Her faculties are weakened, but she is not mad. *This woman's two great passions,* her love for Manrico and her wild thirst to avenge her mother, *must be sustained to the end.* When Manrico is dead, her feeling of revenge becomes stupendous; and in the utmost agitation she cries "Yes, he was your brother! . . . You fool! . . . Mother, you are avenged!!"

Please excuse my presumption. I'm probably wrong, but at least I had to tell you how I felt about it. Incidentally, my first suspicion that you didn't like this play, now seems confirmed. If this is the case, we still have time to think of a substitute. Rather that, than have you do something that doesn't appeal to you. I have prepared another subject, simple and passionate, and which can be said to be almost finished. If you wish, I'll send it to you, and we'll forget "Il Trovatore."

Write me a word about it. And if you have a subject, tell me what it is. A heartfelt farewell, my dear Cammarano! Write me speedily, and believe that I'm devoted to you for life.

To Antonio Barezzi   *Paris, January 21, 1852* (A)

Giuseppina Strepponi, a prima donna of La Scala, shared Verdi's life with him from at least 1849 on, at which time she was with him in Paris. She had encouraged his first works and helped him to success by appearing in them. Then she left the stage to join her life to Verdi's. Barezzi gave voice to the disapproval of the small town of Busseto, because Giuseppina was living at St. Agata without having been married to Verdi. But a reconciliation with Barezzi soon followed. They were not married until April 29, 1859. Giuseppina ("Peppina") was a solicitous and understanding helpmate, and even carried on part of Verdi's correspondence for him. In her letters she emphasized again and again Verdi's greatness as a human being. She lived until 1899 and Verdi survived her by only a year and a half.

Dear Father-in-law: After waiting so long, I hardly expected to receive such a cold letter from you, which, if I am not mistaken, also contains some very biting words. If this letter were not signed Antonio Barezzi, my benefactor, I should have answered very violently or I should not have answered at all. But since it bears that name, which it will always be my duty to honor, I shall do my best to convince you that I do not deserve such reproof. In order to do this I must go back to past matters, I must speak of other people, of our home. The letter will be a little long and irksome, but I shall try to be as brief as possible.

I don't think that you would have written a letter which you knew could only anger me of your own accord. But you live in a neighborhood that has the bad habit of frequently butting into other people's affairs and disapproving of everything that doesn't square with its own way of looking at things. I am not accustomed to interfere in other people's business, unless I am asked to, because I demand that no one interfere in mine. Hence the gossip, the grumbling

[168]

prattle, the disapproval. This freedom of action, which is respected even in less civilized communities, I claim as my own good right at home. Be the judge yourself, be a strict judge, but cool and dispassionate. What harm is it if I keep apart, if I see fit not to visit titled people? If I don't take part in the festivities, the pleasures of others? If I manage my property myself, because it is a pleasure and a recreation for me? I repeat, what harm is it? Certainly it hurts no one.

This said, I now come to the sentence of your letter: "I understand very well that I am not a man for commissions, because my time is already past, but I am still good enough for little things." If by that you mean to say that I once used to give you important commissions and that I now use you for little things, alluding to the letter which you enclosed in yours, I can find no excuse for it, and though I should do the same for you in similar cases, I can only say that this will be a lesson to me for the future. If the sentence is meant as a reproof for my not having entrusted you with my affairs during my absence, permit me to ask you: How could I ever have been so presumptuous as to charge you with such a heavy burden—you, who never set a foot into your own fields because the burden of your own business is already so great? Or should I have commissioned Giovannino? But isn't it true that last year, during the time that I was in Venice, I gave him ample power of attorney in writing, and that he never even set his foot in St. Agata? Nor am I reproving him for it. He was perfectly right. He had his own business which is important enough, and therefore he could not take care of mine.

This reveals my opinions, my actions, my wishes, my so-to-say public life to you. And since we are making revela-

[169]

tions, I see no objection to raising the curtain which hides the mysteries hidden within my four walls, to speaking to you about my home life. I have nothing to hide. In my house there lives a free, independent lady who loves seclusion as I do, and possesses a fortune which puts her out of the reach of care. Neither she nor I owe any account of our action to anyone. On the other hand, who knows what our relations are? Our business? Our connection? Or what claims I have on her and she on me? Who knows whether she is my wife or not? And who knows in this special case, what our thoughts and reasons are for not making it public? Who knows whether this is good or bad? Why mightn't it be a good thing? And even if it were bad, who has the right to hurl the ban against us? Indeed, I tell you that in my house she is paid the same or rather greater respect than I am, and no one is allowed to fail in that regard for any reason whatsoever, and, finally, she has every right to it, as much for her dignity as for her intelligence and her unfailing graciousness to others.

With this long chatter I have meant only to say that I demand my freedom of action, because all people have a right to it and because my whole being rebels against conforming to other people. But you, who are at bottom so kind, so just, and so good-hearted, don't let yourself be influenced, don't take on the ideas of a community which, as far as I am concerned, you must admit, would not deign to accept me as their organist a little while ago, and now are always grumbling and gossiping about me and all my doings. It cannot go on like this. But if it should, I am man enough to defend myself. The world is big—and the mere loss of twenty or thirty thousand francs, would never prevent me from seeking a home elsewhere. There can be nothing offensive to you in this letter. But in case any of it should displease you, then consider it unsaid. I swear to you by my honor that I have no intention of hurting you in any way. I have always considered you and still consider you my benefactor. I regard it as an honor. I boast of it! A hearty farewell in old friendship!

To Cesare De Sanctis   *Busseto, May 24, 1852* (B)

Cesare De Sanctis was a Neapolitan merchant and music-enthusiast, who enjoyed Verdi's friendship from 1849 on. His son, Giuseppe, was Verdi's godson. The elder De Sanctis was a sort of representative for Verdi in Naples. He was a member of a circle of Verdi's admirers there, which included the painter, Morelli; Vincenzo Torelli, chief editor of the "Omnibus" and father of the dramatist, Achille; Francesco Florimo, secretary of the Conservatory.

Verdi received the Legion of Honor later, in 1874, after a performance of his Requiem in Paris.

In heaven's name, what have you got into your head about the Legion of Honor? I know nothing about it. You know how these things are done; ordinarily people go after decorations, and you think I'll never go after them.

To Cesare De Sanctis   *Busseto, August 5, 1852* (B)

Cammarano had died suddenly in July in Naples. He left the almost completed libretto for "Il Trovatore."

I was thunderstruck at the sad news of the death of our Cammarano. I simply can't tell you how grieved I am! And I read of his death not in a friendly letter but in a stupid theatri-

[171]

cal magazine! You who loved him as I did, will understand
all that I can't express. Poor Cammarano!

What a loss!

To Cesare De Sanctis   *Busseto, January 1, 1853 (which
                            I wish may be happy for you and
                            as you wish it to be)*   (B)

Then we are agreed on the finale of the second act, which I
shall have printed in the form in which I rewrote it. I should
like nothing better than to find a good libretto and with it a
good poet. We need one so much! But I cannot conceal from
you that I read all the libretti that are sent to me with
considerable dissatisfaction. It is impossible, or almost impossible, for anyone else to guess just what sort of thing I
want. I want plots that are great, beautiful, varied, daring
. . . daring to an extreme, new in form and at the same time
adapted to composing. If a person says I have done thus and
so because Romani, Cammarano, and others did so . . .
then we no longer understand each other.

Precisely because of the fact that those great men did it that
way, I should like to have something different done.

I shall have "La Dame aux Camélias" performed in Venice.
It will perhaps be called "La Traviata." A subject from our
own time. Another person would perhaps not have composed
it because of the costumes, because of the period, because of
a thousand other foolish objections.

I did it with particular pleasure. Everybody cried out when
I proposed to put a hunchback on the stage. Well, I was over-
joyed to compose "Rigoletto," and it was just the same with
"Macbeth," and so on. . . .

[172]

To Clarina Maffei   *St. Agata, January 29, 1853* (A)

Dear Clarina: Here I am back in my desert again. I'm tired enough from the trip and now I have to work again!

You've probably heard about "Il Trovatore": it would have been better if their company of singers had been complete. People say the opera is too sad, and there are too many deaths in it. But after all, death is all there is in life. What else is there? . . . [. . . .]

My dear Clarina, I have to leave you now. I have to go back to my sharps and flats, which are a real torture for me.

To Emanuele Muzio   *Venice, March 1, 1853* (A)

Dear Emanuele: "Traviata" last night—a fiasco. Was it my fault or the singers'? . . . Time will tell.

To Tito Ricordi   *March 7, 1853* (A)

Dear Ricordi: Unfortunately I have to send you sad news, but I can't conceal the truth from you. "Traviata" was a fiasco. Don't try to fathom the reason; that's the way it is. Farewell!

I leave day after tomorrow. Send any letters to Busseto.

To Cesare De Sanctis   *Busseto, March 12, 1853* (B)

Domenico Bolognese was one of the librettists of the circle in Naples, who sought to become Cammarano's successor.

I have read Signor Bolognese's lines. The point couldn't be put better and I'm entirely of his opinion, only I'm not attracted to such subjects. I adore "Faust," but I shouldn't like to treat it. I've studied it a thousand times, but I don't find Faust's character musical . . . musical (understand me well) in the way I feel music. Frankly I don't like the other subjects. There's nothing extraordinary about them.

[173]

To Cesare De Sanctis   *Busseto, May 16, 1853* (B)

Well, frankly, this "Beggar Woman" is still not the subject
for me. It's certainly very beautiful, but not for me. Tell this
to Mr. Bolognese, and if he perseveres, he'll certainly succeed
in finding something.

To Antonio Somma   *St. Agata, April 22, 1853* (D)

*In Venice, from the 1850's on, Verdi had three enthusiastic
champions: the music merchant, Gallo; the psychiatrist,
Vigna; and the lawyer and playwright, Antonio Somma, who
was only 54 years old when he died in 1864. Not until after
Somma's death was it known that he had written the libretto
of "A Masked Ball," which up to then had been published
as anonymous. He had not signed his name to it, not only
because the text had been badly mutilated by the censor but
also because it was closely modeled on a play by Scribe.
This play had already been composed as an opera by Auber;
Bellini wanted to do the same; and Mercadante wrote a similar work, "Il Reggente." At Verdi's suggestion, Somma wrote
a libretto, "Re Lear." Though the subject had an irresistible
fascination for him, Verdi seems nevertheless to have been
overawed by the greatness of certain scenes and never completed the score, of which only sketches exist. The following
letters have been chosen as examples of Verdi's shrewd and
meticulous collaboration with his librettists. The history of
"Lear" is told in imaginary detail in Franz Werfel's novel,
"Verdi."*

Dear Somma: I'm ashamed of not having answered your
very good letter sooner. A million little details I had to attend to, and in particular the need to think over carefully the

subjects you proposed, were the reasons for my delay. Nothing could suit me better, nothing would give me greater pleasure, than to join my name to your great name. But in order to set the very great poetry, which you couldn't fail to write, to music worthy of it—or at least to the best music I can compose—allow me to point out to you some of my own ideas, for whatever they may be worth. My long experience has confirmed me in the beliefs I've always held concerning dramatic effect, though in my youth I didn't have the courage to put them wholly into practice. (For instance, ten years ago I wouldn't have risked composing "Rigoletto.") To me, our opera nowadays sins in the direction of too great monotony, so much so that I should refuse to write on such subjects as "Nabucco," "Foscari," etc. They offer extremely interesting dramatic situations, but they lack variety. They have but one burden to their song; elevated, if you like, but always the same. To be more explicit, Tasso's work may be better, but I prefer Ariosto a thousand times. For the same reason I prefer Shakespeare to all other dramatists, including the Greeks. As far as dramatic effectiveness is concerned, it seems to me that the best material I have yet put to music (I'm not speaking of literary or poetic worth) is "Rigoletto." It has the most powerful dramatic situations, it has variety, vitality, pathos; all the dramatic developments result from the frivolous, licentious character of the Duke. Hence Rigoletto's fears, Gilda's passion, etc., which give rise to many dramatic situations, including the scene of the quartet which, so far as effect is concerned, will always be one of the finest our theatre can boast. Many operas have been written on "Ruy Blas," eliminating the character of Don Cesare. But if I were to put that subject to music, I should be attracted above all by the contrast which that most original character produces. Now you will have understood what my feelings and thoughts are, and since I know I'm writing to a man of sincere, frank character, I take the liberty of telling you that though the subjects you propose are eminently dramatic, I don't find in them all the variety my crazy brain desires. You may say that you can insert in "Sordello" some festivity, a banquet, or even a tournament, but even so the characters would still produce the same impression of gravity and austerity. On the other hand, there's no particular hurry. If I should have to write for one of the coming seasons, I could content myself with a libretto put together as well as possible, while awaiting the good fortune to clothe in music one of your works, which would be a real event for the whole literary world. While poor Cammarano was still alive, I suggested *King Lear* to him. Take a look at it, if you don't mind, and tell me what you think of it. I shall do the same, since I've not read it for a long time.

Forgive me for this mad chatter, and believe me your sincere friend and admirer.

To Antonio Somma   *Busseto, May 22, 1853* (D)

Dear Somma: I have read "King Lear" again. It's marvellous, only I'm appalled by the need to span such a tremendous canvas in a narrow frame without detracting from the originality and grandeur of the characters. But courage, perhaps we shall still be able to achieve something above the usual with it. However I think that the drama should be limited to three, or at most four, acts.

In the first act, the division of the kingdom and the departure of Cordelia (this would furnish an aria): then, fol-

lowing each other, the scenes at both Courts. For the close
I imagine Lear's curse, where he says:

". . . I will do such things,—
   What they are, yet I know not, but they shall be
   The terrors of the earth."

The second act I would begin with the storm, then follow
with the next scenes, among them the judgment scene (un-
speakably original and touching), and would end with Cordelia's sending for her father, who flees at the sight of the
officers, etc., etc.

I would begin the third act with Lear's slumber. Cordelia
is with him (lofty duet!), etc., etc. Battle, final scene.

Leading roles: Lear, Cordelia, the two brothers, Edgar and
Edmund, the Fool, which I shall perhaps write for contralto.
—Secondary roles: Goneril, Regan, Kent, etc. The others,
very subordinate roles.

Already I think that the following will be the principal
numbers of the opera: Introduction, with Cordelia's aria;
storm; judgment scene; the duet between Lear and Cordelia,
and the closing scene.

This is the way I see it, but you do what—in your judgment—seems right to you. Only keep your eye on the need
for absolute brevity. . . .

I have always felt, and I still feel, that to our theatrical
public, Lear's reason for disinheriting Cordelia in the first
scene is childish, indeed ridiculous. If we can't find anything
weightier than that, we should be detracting from Cordelia's
character. In any case, this scene has to be handled with the
utmost care. So I shall wait for the outline, which you will be
friendly enough to write; and since you allow me, I shall

then tell you my opinion quite frankly (of course from the point of view only of dramatic effectiveness). As soon as we are agreed on the skeleton of the plot we have the main work behind us. Meanwhile I remain devotedly yours.

P.S. I especially commend to you the role of the Fool—it is deep and original. Be sure that Lear's part is not too exhausting!

To Antonio Somma   *Busseto, June 29, 1853* (D)

Dear Somma: Do whatever you think right with the notes I jotted down on your outline. There are two things about this project that worry me. First, it seems to me that the opera is turning out to be too long, especially in the first two acts. Therefore if you can find anything to cut out or to shorten, do so; the effect can only benefit from it. If this can't be done, do your best to say things as briefly as possible in the less important scenes. Second, it seems to me there are too many changes of scene. The only thing that has always prevented me from treating Shakespearean subjects oftener has been precisely this necessity to change scenes at every moment. When I used to go to the theatre it annoyed me greatly: I felt as if I were watching a magic lantern. In this the French are right: they plan their dramas so as to need only one scene for each act; thus the action flows freely without hindrance, and without anything to distract the attention of the public. I understand very well that in "Lear" it would be impossible to have only one scene for each act; but if you could manage to do without some of them, it would be excellent. Think it over, and when you've put a few scenes in verse send them to me. Meanwhile I press your hand affectionately. Farewell.

My dear Somma: I meant to write you two weeks ago, but
I've always been interrupted by some boring detail or some
business. At last I have an hour of leisure! I have received
the rest of the first act. I shall say nothing of the verses, which
are always beautiful and worthy of you, but with all due
respect for your talent, I must tell you that the form does not
lend itself very well to music. No one loves novel forms more
than I do, but only such novelties as can be put to music. Of
course, anything can be put to music, but not always with
good effect. In composing music you need stanzas to write
cantabiles, stanzas to write ensembles, stanzas for largos, for
allegros, etc., etc., and all varied enough so that none of it
turns out cold or monotonous. Let me analyze this poetry of
yours. I shan't speak of Edmund's aria, though it passes too
abruptly from the adagio to the allegro; it can remain as it is.
In the following little duet, there is really no place for a melody or even a melodic phrase, but since it's brief it can stand,
if you add at the end a four-line stanza in the same meter for
Edmund, and another four-line one for Edgar.

The following part which, musically speaking, would be
the finale of the act, is very confusing. The stanzas of the
Fool are very good, but from the moment Goneril enters I'm
at a loss to know what to do. Perhaps you intended the six-
line stanzas as an ensemble. But those stanzas are written as
dialogue, the characters must answer each other back and
forth, and consequently their voices can't be united. So there
would have to be another ensemble with stanzas of eight
lines when Regan enters. At the end you have Goneril and
Regan go off stage and Lear closes the act alone. This is all

right in tragedy, in spoken drama, but in music the effect would be cold, to say the least. If you glance through Romani's best dramas (from which certainly you have nothing to learn) perhaps you'll admit I'm right. It seems to me, however, that with little effort this scene could be better adapted to music and made more effective without taking away from the interest of the drama. We could leave the first six stanzas of six lines, and put the whole passage from *Lasciero le tue soglie* ("No, rather, I abjure all roofs") up to *Dileguisi da te* ("May it vanish from thee") in the same meter. It isn't necessary for all the characters to have stanzas of six lines each; on the contrary, that would be monotonous. It's enough for the meter to continue so that I can give the music a measured flow. After Regan has said *la villana porta si deve dileguare,* Lear bursts out into a declamatory passage (which would be the ensemble) where we could use *Ohimè de' nembi.* But we would need similar stanzas in this meter for all the other characters, each one expressing his own feelings. After finishing this passage, Regan ought to say (changing the meter), "Lear can make use of the Duke's servants and dismiss all his own knights." Long pause. Lear looks for his crown, then bursts forth: *Voi antri cupi.* ("Ye dark dens.") No one should leave the stage, and every one should say (always expressing his own feelings) at least one little six-line stanza in the same meter. Excuse this long drawn-out prattle. Write me immediately, and believe me as always yours.

To Antonio Somma   *Busseto, September 9, 1853* (D)

Dear Somma: I have received the second act and your very welcome letter of the second of the month. Even in this second act there are things that don't lend themselves to the music, but as you very rightly say, it's better to wait to adjust them until you've finished the drama completely. As for the recitatives, if the scene is interesting, they can be even rather long. I've done some very long ones, for example: the soliloquy in the duet of the first act of "Macbeth" and the other soliloquy in the duet of the first act of "Rigoletto." In haste, yours affectionately.

To Antonio Somma　　　　　*Paris, November 19, 1853* (D)

"Trema Bisanzio" is a famous aria from Donizetti's opera, "Belisario."

Dear Somma: The other night, as soon as I had mailed my letter, I received your very welcome letter of November 12. By this time you should have received a letter of mine, containing a check for Ricordi which was sent eight or ten days ago. My motive in coming here is to fulfill a promise I made the Opéra many years ago. You see that I have nothing to do with the Théâtre-Italien; and on the other hand "King Lear" would be too vast a subject and its form too novel and daring to risk it here, where they only understand melodies which have been repeated for twenty years.

Let us speak of our own affairs. I wrote to you about the second act in my last letter. In the third act you need adjust only two stanzas so that (since the situation requires it) I can compose two clear-cut, forthright melodies, with a good rhythm. [. . . .] The stanzas are: *Ti sien grazie* ("Receive my thanks") and the other *Deh non volermi illudere* ("Ah, seek not to beguile me"). For the first, you wrote two lines, then five, then three, etc. With this irregularity the musical

[181]

phrase is bound to be halting. The same can be said of the endless line: *Non ti far gioco!* . . . ("Pray, do not mock me. . . .) and of the other which is too prolonged: *Varcato ho l'ottantesimo anno* ("I am a very foolish fond old man, fourscore and upward"). Think of the most popular arias of our Italian operas and you'll note how the stanzas are composed. For example: *Casta Diva* . . . etc., *Meco tu vieni o misera* . . . . . . *etc. No, non ti son rivale,* etc. There is never any interruption, any break in the line. So please fix the aforementioned stanzas because, I repeat, their place in the drama calls for two clear-cut melodies, impassioned and popular. [. . . .]

After the last words of the drama, there should be added an exclamation, a phrase, a line for the whole ensemble. Then, if you can shorten and reduce those seven lines of the recitative, it will be fine. The drama, the action, ends with Cordelia's death, therefore the sooner the curtain goes down, the greater the effect. [. . . .]

This is all. In these last acts you have but little to do.

It may happen that I shall need some little change here or there to get in a cantabile or a phrase, but never anything that mars the dramatic interest. Moreover, this will never be because of a mere artist's whim, but because art itself requires it. Do you remember Belisario's aria, *Trema Bisanzio?* Donizetti did not scruple to attach the word *"sterminatrice"* to Bisanzio, thus producing a horrible contradiction, but the musical rhythm absolutely required it. Following the meaning of those lines it would have been impossible to create a phrase. So wouldn't it have been better to ask the poet to adjust that stanza? . . .

And now I must say good-bye.

Send me "Lear" fully adjusted as soon as possible, for we shall give it in some big theatre in Italy. For this opera we need a public, capable of enthusiasm and understanding and able to judge according to the impressions received.

A hearty farewell.

To Antonio Somma   *Paris, February 6, 1854* (D)

Dear Somma: I am pleased that you touched up the passage referred to in the duet of the third act. It's a place worth while bringing to perfection, because it's among the most beautiful scenes of the drama, and it should also be one of the best numbers of the opera.

The changes of a line or a phrase, which I might eventually need, are trifles that I can only suggest here and there while I am writing the music. I repeat they will only be little things, such as an accent to which the note might not be suited, or a word that sounds bad in music. Make all the changes that you deem necessary "to improve the phrase here and there," as you say. The more beautiful and sonorous the line is, so much the better for me.

It's a good thing that you've removed all doubts concerning the pronunciation of Lear and Gloucester.

For many years I've had a contract with the Opéra, and now I've received an entirely finished libretto by Scribe. I hoped first to put "King Lear" to music for Italy, but it was impossible. Perhaps it's just as well, for I shall be able to devote myself later to this opera with all the necessary leisure and make of it, I don't venture to say something new—but something a little different from the others. Therefore you have all the time you need for the changes you wish to make.

You haven't answered me regarding what I said about Cor-

[183]

delia's character. Perhaps I'm mistaken, please persuade me that I am. Convince me as you did when I told you that the reason for disinheriting Cordelia seemed to me childish for our times: as soon as I read the first words of your answer, I quickly recognized my ignorance and my mistake.

I told you also that the libretto has turned out a bit too long, and, I repeat, if you could cut a line or a stanza here and there, it would be a good thing. There are also some words missing in a few of the lines, as I told you in my last letter. . . .

Answer at your convenience. Give my greetings to Vigna, who is really an excellent person, and believe me, for life, yours affectionately.

To Antonio Somma   *Paris, March 31, 1854* (D)

Dear Somma: I am very late in replying to your letter of the 18th of last month!

As to "La Traviata," I think Gallo and Ricordi have decided to do what they found expedient, since I gave Ricordi liberty to do so.

In order to shorten "King Lear" a bit, I should think we could take the finale of the first act, from the line *Padre, angusto e il mio castello* ("Father, narrow is my castle") up to *O ciel, de' nembi il tuono* ("O Heavens, the thunder of the clouds") and change these forty lines into twelve or fifteen or twenty lines of recitative, with very animated dialogue and some witty jesting on the part of the Fool.

In the second act, it might be possible to reduce the first part of the chorus *Ricca Albion* ("Rich England") to just a few lines.

Then part of the first scene of the first act up to Lear's entrance could be cut out. At most, if the drama needs any explanation, put in five or six lines of recitative for Glouces- ter and Kent. If we let the chorus be, I shall have to compose an orchestral number, and an orchestral number always takes time. I also feel that to begin the opera immediately at the rise of the curtain with trumpet flourishes (not modern band trumpets but long, antique, straight trumpets) would be much more impressive and characteristic. But do as you like.

If there are any lines in the recitatives that you can shorten or cut out, it will be so much gained for the whole opera. In the theatre lengthy is synonymous with boring; and of all styles, that of boredom is the worst.

Farewell, my dear Somma. I can't wait to get to work on "King Lear," which pleases me tremendously and with which I hope to accomplish something not quite as bad as my other works.

My greetings to Vigna and to Gallo. Tell the latter to think over "La Traviata" so as not to be sorry later. Farewell.

To Antonio Somma   *May 17, 1854* (D)

Sophie Cruvelli (originally Crüwell) was a famous opera star, who sang principally in Paris and London.

Dear Somma: You can work quite at your ease, because the winter and my indisposition have prevented me from finish- ing the French opera in time, and the date for Cruvelli's leave of absence is here. The rehearsals will begin in Sep- tember, and the opera will not be ready for production until next winter, so I am forced to deprive myself of the pleasure of having you in my cottage, as I had hoped. That must be put off for another year, and if by then you haven't finished a libretto for "King Lear" that you can bring me, then you shall bring me your own very dear person.

I hear marvelous things about La Spezia. Do you think she would make a good Cordelia? Tell me. Would her voice be suitable for a big theatre? It doesn't matter whether it is big or little, it's enough that it should be heard. Some intelligence and soul she must have.

To Antonio Somma   *Paris, January 4, 1855* (D)

Dear Somma: I am entirely of your opinion. The whole thing gains one hundred percent by cutting out the two Gloucesters. The plot not only becomes more unified and clearer, but it gains by its brevity, and we get rid of two or three ineffective numbers. Only I don't understand how you can manage to reveal the evil doings of Edmund. Who will fight the duel? Albany perhaps? or will you think of something else? I also think it should be possible to eliminate one setting, the second: the castle of the Gloucesters. Since Edmund has already committed the double assassination and is a duke, he can very well be in Lear's court in the introduction, or in the park of Goneril's palace, and in one of these two scenes sing his aria and reveal his character.

Be sure to develop this aria well and give it a new turn by alternating recitative with rhymed stanzas, etc. It needs the greatest variety of mood: irony, contempt and rage, all thrown into sharp profile, so that in as much as I can't give a cantabile to such a character I may have varying moods.

I only regret that we shan't have Edgar in the scene of the tempest, and I regret even more that he isn't in the trial scene. That fourth character went very well in the scene with the shepherds. Perhaps it would be possible to put a poor old man in Edgar's place, a beggar who has taken refuge in the hut on account of the tempest. Lear then would bring him with him in the following scene of the trial. This poor man might also be an old servant, a steward or a knight of the Gloucester family, who by some sign might reveal all Edmund's foul play to Albany and might even fight the duel! What do you say? . . . In this do what you think best for the drama.

In my other letters you will find remarks on the form of certain numbers, the introduction for example. I still feel that in the duet between Lear and Delia the recognition does not come about naturally, and after a long cantabile that *Delia tu sei?* ("Cordelia, is it thou?") is a little too abrupt and ineffective.

So work on these things, that I can start on "Lear" as soon as I finish the French opera.

Now and always yours with affectionate.
P.S. A thousand greetings to our very dear Vigna and to that terrible Gallo.

To Antonio Somma   *January 8, 1855* (D)

Dear friend: I hasten to answer yours of the third of the month, and hope you've received my answer to your last letter by now.

It seems to me that the new aria you intended for Edmund is too pretentious, too obviously seeking for effect. I have the feeling that such a ballet, such a chorus, would lead to monotony instead of variety. The whole act would be too full; that is, so many numbers would give the eye no rest. The ear, too, would be sadly strained in this act; for we would have in it an introduction in which the whole company has to sing, an aria with double chorus for the ballet and the singers, a finale of the most violent passion, etc., etc. I shall probably have to compose another solo number for the scene with Edmund. Be sure and draw this character sharply, take great pains with it, and don't be afraid that it will be too long, for now that we're taking out the two Gloucesters, the opera will be of the right length. As for me, I should contrive Edmund free of all remorse, a ruthless rascal; not a repellent gallows-bird like Franz in Schiller's "Die Räuber," but a person who laughs at everything, despises everything, and commits the most horrible crimes with the greatest equanimity. But here I bow to your superior knowledge, so do what you think is right. [. . . .]

The second act we shall cut extensively, and it will be very good. [. . . .]

In the third act, I repeat, I wouldn't have Cordelia appear in armor, but rather, as throughout the drama, as a woman and angel. Reading through this scene, I find that the prayer ("It is thy gift") like all prayers, is cold in its effect. If she is to thank Heaven, have her say two or three verses after Kent's recitative (in any case it's advisable that she should end the recitative). Then try to write two beautiful stanzas, passionate, deeply felt, so that we can insert a fine *andante cantabile* here.

I hope to be through here at the end of February. After that I should arrive in Busseto at the beginning of March. I wish very much that "Lear" could be finished by then. . . . Yes indeed, "Trovatore" is going well in the Théâtre-Italien. Unfortunately Boucardé is not very well, but the others are liked and the whole opera is good. . . .

A thousand greetings to you and Vigna.

Farewell. I am, and will always remain devotedly yours.

[188]

P.S. Reading through your postscript, I think you're right to put two little stanzas into the mouth of the Fool at the beginning of the second act. But try to write four-line stanzas, and if the lines are short—that is, five, or six, syllables, instead of twelve or sixteen—then you can write twenty or twenty-four of them if you want to. But don't have any officers' chorus in Cordelia's tent.

To Antonio Somma   *Paris, January 24, 1855* (D)

Dear Somma: That sestina which you sent me is good; only, if you do four sestinas of ten syllables, the aria, or rather its rhythm, will be monotonous. If you need twenty-four or thirty lines to develop your idea, use them, but alternate the meter. Retain that first sestina and write another too, if you wish, but after them, change the meter. The more variety of meter there is, the more variety there will be in the music. If this aria had even three or four different meters, it would not be bad: the more originality in the form the better.

As for the trial scene, I have nothing to say. It is good as you sent it to me.

In great haste I press your hand.

To Antonio Somma   *Paris, March 10, 1855* (D)

Dear Somma: Send the libretto of "King Lear" to this address because I shall be here until the opening of the Exposition; also because the opera cannot be produced until near the end of April. Now that you have finished "Lear," could you find another subject which you could do for me at your leisure? A beautiful subject, *original*, interesting, with fine situations, and impassioned; passions above all! . . .

In haste, farewell, farewell. If you have any time to spare, search, search, search.

[189]

To Antonio Somma   *Busseto, April 7, 1856* (D)

"La Sonnambula" was one of Bellini's best known operas.

Dear Somma: I read very carefully the outline which you had the kindness to send me. I shall say nothing of the merits which are always present in everything you write. But it seems to me that the characters are a bit too wicked and ferocious for a musical drama, nor is there enough variety. Admitting that I may be mistaken, let me remind you that when I had the pleasure of seeing you and speaking to you *en passant* about this, I explained that I wanted to write a quiet, simple, tender drama, on the order of "Sonnambula," but without imitating "Sonnambula." This is a million miles away from it. I return it to you, so you can use it for something else.

I am not sure the fourth act of "King Lear" is good in the form in which you just sent it to me, but I do know that you can't impose so many recitatives one after another, on the audience, especially in a fourth act. These are not a composer's whims. I would be willing to set even a newspaper or a letter, etc., to music, but in the theatre the public will stand for anything except boredom. All those recitatives, even if composed by Rossini or by Meyerbeer, could only turn out to be long and consequently boring. To tell the truth, I'm very much afraid of this first half of the fourth act. I don't know exactly what it is, but there's something that doesn't satisfy me. It certainly lacks brevity, perhaps clarity, perhaps truth. I can't say what. So I ask you to think it over, and see if you can find something more dramatic. Farewell. Think of me kindly, and believe me affectionately yours.

To Cesare De Sanctis   *Busseto, September 9, 1853* (B)

The lady who was to accompany Verdi to Naples in secret
was his future (second) wife, Giuseppina Strepponi.

Are you good at keeping a secret? I think you are, and
that's why I'm writing you.

If I were to decide to come to Naples to spend the winter,
tell me:

First. Whether I could find a comfortable little apartment
well situated, facing the sea, in case it were not convenient
for me to remain at the hotel. It should be furnished for two
people, besides one or two servants.

Second. Whether I could find one or two servants.

Third. Whether, coming to Naples just for a pleasure trip,
with only a regular passport, I should have trouble with the
police. They are so strict, people say! . . .

Fourth. Whether a lady who came with me, with an equally
regular passport, would have such trouble.

Answer all these questions quickly. I repeat: it must be
kept a secret. Your answers will determine my decision.

If I should come, I shall be Mr. Giuseppe Verdi in Naples,
and not Maestro Verdi. I don't want to hear any operas, nor
proposals for operas, etc.

Farewell, and Hush!

To Cesare De Sanctis   *Paris, January 18, 1854* (B)

The information you sent concerning Palermo is more than
sufficient, and I thank you. Now I'm going to give you more
trouble, and you'll have to confer with Contreau about this.
I should like to know whether the Tarantella is always in
minor and in 6/8 time. If there is any example of one in a

different key or measure, let me know; and if there should be a tarantella in major and in a measure other than 6/8, send me a copy. I should also like to know if there is any other popular dance in Sicily beside the Tarantella. If there is, send it to me. I know that a ballet divertissement called "Vespri Siciliani" or "Giovanni da Procida" has been given in Naples. Send me a libretto of this too, and address it all to 4, Rue Richer, Paris.

What a lot of bother! Poor De Sanctis!! . . .

I wish I could tell you the title of Scribe's libretto which he has finished, but I don't know it. This will surprise you, but it's the truth. I can tell you only that the setting must be Naples or Sicily, more probably the latter; and since the story is fictitious, I plan to call it later either "Paolo," or "Pietro," "Maria," or "Posilippo," or "Saint Rosalia's Grotto." I can't say. They could have given a good many other names to "La Muette de Portici."

You can see for yourself that with such an undertaking on hand, I couldn't accept any others, and as for the proposal made me to write for Naples, I can only answer, as I have done to Milan, to Rome, to Venice, to Turin, etc.

As for the subject of "Paolo," I can't do it, because, beside the French libretto, I possess another Italian one; also because it seems to be one of the usual things without novelty or variety.

Novelty, novelty, the rock on which all young poets founder! They think they are touching the Heavens with their finger when they can say: "I write as Romani, as Cammarano did," etc. . . . Great Heavens, precisely for that reason, they should do otherwise. . . .

When will the poet come who will give Italy an operatic

text that has scope, power, freedom from convention, variety, that unites all these elements and is above all new! Who can tell?

Meanwhile farewell, and forgive me for so much bother. Give my very best to all who send me their good wishes. I haven't been able to come this year, but I hope to spend at least a part of next winter with you, for I'm tired of this fog and cold.

How lucky you are, and how I envy you! But the time will come, I hope, when I too, can send all musical notes to the Devil, and can enjoy life a little more than I have until now, for I certainly have been working very hard. Farewell.

To Giuseppina Appiani   *Paris, February 25, 1854* (A)

I have read "Graziella." It is a little play in only one act. In my opinion there is little interest to it and no dramatic movement. It was about five years ago that I read "Les Confidences" and I seem to remember that that story pleased me very much. Here, the style and language are everything; but style and language are worth nothing in a play without action. The climax of interest lies in the final scene, but it is too heroic and tragic and horribly out of tune with the preceding scenes. In short, I don't like it; but Eugenia must not pay any attention to my opinion. Most advice is a mistake, for just as no two mouths, noses, or faces are the same, so each heart is different, and therefore no two people see or feel the same way. The artist must give himself up to his own inspiration, and if he has true talent, he feels and knows better than anybody else what he needs. I should feel perfectly confident in composing any subject that moved me, even if it were condemned by every other artist as unsuitable for music. For

[193]

these reasons, I repeat, let Eugenia pay no attention to my advice and if she likes the subject, let her do it without hesitation. If she wishes, I shall send it to her.

I am very sorry to say that I shall not write for La Scala!

Of course, if I find a subject I like, I shall send it, with whatever notations I think necessary; but I always advise people not to pay too much attention to them.

I write very slowly; as a matter of fact I may not write at all. I don't know why, but I do know that the libretto is there, still there in the same place.

To Clarina Maffei   *Paris, March 2, 1854* (A)

The opera Verdi was writing was "Les Vêpres Siciliennes," to a libretto by Scribe.

[. . . .] You ask whether I shall write for La Scala? No. If I were asked why, I would hardly know what to say. I could say that I lack desire to write; or better, that I hate to sign a contract. But it is not as people have said, because of obligations I have contracted here through 1856 and after. I have no other obligations after the opera which I am writing now. Nor is it (as has also been said) any desire to *grow roots* here. *Grow roots?* Is that really possible? And what would be the use of it, anyhow? For what purpose? For fame? I don't believe in it. For money? I make just as much and perhaps more in Italy. And I repeat, even if I wanted to do so it would be impossible. I am too fond of my seclusion, my little piece of sky at home, and I refuse to doff my hat to any barons or counts or anyone else. Finally, I don't have millions, and I shall never spend my hard-earned couple of thousand francs for publicity, claques, and such vile horrors. And it seems that they are necessary if you want to achieve success. Even Dumas wrote a few days ago in his paper, apropos Meyerbeer's new opera: "What a shame Rossini didn't give us his masterpieces in 1854! Of course, we must admit that Rossini never had that German zeal which contrives to bring a success to the boil six months beforehand in the witches' cauldron of the newspapers—and thus time the explosion of interest exactly for the evening of the première." That is true. I was at the first performance of his "Etoile du Nord" and understood little or nothing, while the good public here understood everything and thought it all beautiful, marvelous, divine! And yet this same public, even after twenty-five or thirty years, still doesn't understand "William Tell"; and so this opera is performed completely mutilated, in three acts instead of five, and with unworthy *mise-en-scène!* And that is supposed to be the first theatre of the world. . . But I am talking to you, without realizing it, about a lot of things that can't possibly interest you. So I shall close by saying I have a ferocious desire to go home. This I tell to you, *sotto voce,* because I know you will believe me. Others would think it an affectation on my part. I have no interest in saying what I don't feel. But our Milanese *lions* have such an exaggerated idea of everything that is and is done in Paris! . . Well, so much the better. I wish them much joy!

To Louis Crosnier   *Paris, January 3, 1855* (A)

The original of this letter is written in French. Crosnier was director of the Opéra in Paris.

I feel it my duty to let no more time pass without making a few observations concerning "Les Vêpres Siciliennes."

It is both distressing and mortifying for me that M. Scribe

will not take the trouble to improve that fifth act, which everybody agrees is uninteresting. I know very well that M. Scribe has a thousand other things on his mind, which are perhaps more important to him than my opera! But if I had been able to foresee the indifference on his part, I should have stayed in my own country, where I really was not doing so badly!

I had hoped that M. Scribe would have contrived for the end of the drama one of those touching pieces which move one to tears, and whose effect is almost always sure, since, in my opinion, the situation seems to lend itself to that. And please observe, my dear Sir, that this would have improved the entire work, which has nothing touching about it, except the romanza in the fourth act.

I had hoped that M. Scribe would be kind enough to appear at rehearsals from time to time, to be on watch for certain less happy words, lines that are difficult to sing, in short, to see whether there was anything to be touched up in the numbers, the acts, etc. For example, the second, third, and fourth acts all have the same form; aria, duet, finale.

Finally, I expected that M. Scribe, as he promised me from the beginning, would change everything that attacks the honor of the Italians. The more I consider it, the more I am convinced that there is a danger here. M. Scribe injures the French because Frenchmen are killed; he injures the Italians because he turns Procida, whose historical character he changes, into a conventional conspirator, according to his beloved system, and presses the inevitable dagger into his hand. Good Lord! There are virtues and vices in the history of every people, and we are no worse than the rest. In any case, I am first of all an Italian, and I will not make myself an accomplice to an offense to my country at any price.

It remains for me to say a word about the rehearsals in the foyer. Here and there I hear words and remarks which, if not actually wounding, are, to say the least, inappropriate. I am not accustomed to such things, and I shall not tolerate them. Possibly there are people who think that my music is not on a par with the eminence of the Grand Opéra; possibly there are others who judge their roles unworthy of their talent. It is possible that I, in my turn, find the performance and the style of singing different from what I might have wished! . . . In short it seems to me (or I am strangely deceived) that we are not at one in our way of feeling, of interpreting the music, and without perfect accord there can be *no possible success.*

You see, Sir, that everything I have just said to you is serious enough for us to stop and consider how to turn aside the catastrophe with which we are menaced. For my part, I see but a single means which I do not hesitate to propose. *It is the dissolution of the contract.*

I know very well you will answer that the Opéra has already lost time and had some expenditures! . . . but that is little in comparison with the year I have lost here, during which I could have made a hundred thousand francs in Italy.

You will say further, that it is all very well to annul a contract, when there is a deficit. To that I reply that I should already have paid it if my losses and expenses here were not excessive!

I know you are too just and reasonable not to choose the lesser of two evils. Believe my experience of music: under the conditions in which we find ourselves, *a success is very difficult!* A half-success profits no one. It is best to close the matter. Each of us will try to make up for lost time. Let us try, Sir, to arrange everything quietly, and we shall perhaps both gain by it.

Accept, Sir, the assurance of my high esteem.

P.S. Excuse my bad French; the important thing is that you understand.

To Cesare De Sanctis   *Paris, February 17, 1855* (B)

Just one more word about "La Traviata." You find the second act is weaker than the others. You're wrong. The second act is better than the first. And the third is best of all, and so it should be.

I should only like to produce the duet of the second act, which seems long to you, with two suitable artists, and then you might find it very effective, equal to any other duet of mine, as far as the thought is concerned, and superior in respect to form and sentiment.

To Tito Ricordi   *April 4, 1855* (A)

[. . . . Toselli] asks me too whether, after all, the poem is really as terrible as everybody says. This seems already to have become "public opinion." How stupid! I think the poem is better than many other libretti by Piave. But it's enough for a libretto to bear that poor devil's name to make people assert that it is wretched, even before anyone has read it. I must tell you a little story. It was ten years ago that I conceived the idea of composing "Macbeth." I did the sketch for the libretto myself. More than that, I wrote out the whole drama in prose, with the division into acts and scenes, indicating the vocal numbers and so on. Then I gave it to Piave to put into verse. Since I had reservations about what Piave wrote, I asked Maffei, with Piave's permission, to go over it, and particularly to rewrite the chorus of the witches in the third act and the sleep-walking scene. And then—would you believe it?—although the libretto did not mention the author's name people thought it was by Piave, and that chorus and the sleep-walking scene were the most bitterly abused and ridiculed of all. Perhaps both pieces could have been better done, but as they stand they are still verses by Maffei, and the chorus particularly bears the stamp of true individuality. There you are: that is public opinion.

To Clarina Maffei   *Paris, June 28, 1855* (A)

It seems to me that "Les Vêpres Siciliennes" is not going too badly. You sympathize with my weal and woe (if a bit of opera can be weal and woe)—I am more than convinced of that, for I know you too well. Hence my gratitude and the affection I shall always feel for you.

The critics here have been either non-committal or favorable, excepting three, who are Italians: Fiorentini, Montazio and Scudo. My friends say: "What injustice!" "What a vile world!" Not at all! The world is too stupid to be vile.

Ristori is making a furore and I am delighted. She has completely annihilated Rachel. As a matter of fact, she is far superior to Rachel and the French themselves—an unheard-of thing—agree. The difference is that Ristori has a heart, while Rachel in the same place has a piece of wood or marble.

I haven't looked over the Exposition carefully, yet. I have skimmed through the rooms where there are Italian things. I must admit, reluctantly, that I would have wished for something better. Nevertheless there is one beautiful, sublime thing: Vela's *Spartacus*. Glory to him!

Farewell, my dear Clarina. I hope to be in Italy a fortnight from now.

To Ercolano Balestra   *Paris, October 21, 1855* (A)

At this time there was no Kingdom of Italy, and Verdi was a citizen of the Duchy of Parma.

Dear Doctor Balestra: I have not answered your very kind letter because I hoped to be home before now, but since I have to put on "Il Trovatore" at the Théatre-Italien, I must stay here another fortnight. Meanwhile, may I speak to you again concerning the famous English affair? At one time there existed in that country a copyright for the works of composers, artists, writers, etc. That is, if I, for example, wrote an opera, no one in England could either publish or perform it without my permission. Thus I was naturally able to sell my opera to a publisher. Now, a recent law of the House of Commons denies the copyright to any foreigner who does not belong to a country which has an international agreement with England. So now the editors find it more convenient to appropriate our operas for themselves without buying them from the composer, which is perfectly natural. During my two visits to London I was advised to apply for either English or French or even Piedmontese citizenship (because France and Piedmont have international agreements with England) but I wish to remain what I am, a peasant of Le Roncole, and prefer to ask my government to make an agreement with England. The Government of Parma has nothing to lose in a treaty like this which is purely artistic and literary. It would only have to take the trouble to apply for it through its representative in England who I believe is either the Austrian or the Spanish ambassador—and it would be done. When you go to Parma, will you be so kind as to arrange matters so that when I return I can tell whether or not this is practicable. May we meet soon again, and believe me, with esteem and friendship, I am affectionately yours.

To Tito Ricordi   *Paris, October 24, 1855* (A)

Dear Ricordi: I wish to lodge a bitter complaint about the printed editions of my last operas, which were very carelessly prepared and full of mistakes; and above all because the first edition of "Traviata" was not withdrawn. That is inexcusable negligence! If the merest accident had not taken me one day into the shop of the Escudiers, this edition would have gone all over France. Who knows whether it isn't going now through Germany, Spain and other countries in the same way! You know that this edition should have been out of the trade two years ago!! It was only on that condition (a condition in my contract, I asked you no money for it!) that I made the arrangement for Coletti. But who has ever cared about the reputation of an artist? I can't help making a reflection that I find very discouraging. In the course of my already long career I have always found all impresarios, publishers, etc., hard, immovable, implacable, with the law books at hand if need be. Fine words and very bad deeds. I've never been regarded as anything more than an object, a tool, to be used as long as it brings in anything. That's very sad, but it's true.

To Vincenzo Torelli   *Busseto, April 22, 1856* (A)

[. . . .] For a production of "King Lear" the following artists would be necessary:

[201]

A big baritone, for the part of King Lear.

A soprano prima donna, not necessarily with a big voice, but deep feeling, for Cordelia.

Two excellent supporting artists.

A very good contralto.

A tenor with a big, beautiful voice (but the part is not particularly important).

As for the soprano and contralto, I hear Piccolomini and Giuseppina Brambilla very well spoken of. Both sing with feeling and are young!

I wish and must ask you kindly to preserve the completest secrecy in this matter. It will make it easier to smooth out difficulties.

To Ercolano Balestra   *Paris, August, 1856* (A)

I've been in Paris for three or four days, and as usual I need your help. First, to find out whether the government of Parma has finally asked for the copyright treaty. Second, to entrust you with a commission for Piccolomini.

You know I have long desired to compose "King Lear." There have been great difficulties in the way of finding a proper cast. But the company in Naples now offers me what I need. As you can imagine, I've had my eye on Piccolomini, who is to be the Cordelia. I wrote her to this effect, and she answered with such kindness, such self-abnegation that even a less conscientious person than I am would have been much embarrassed. I am and will remain eternally thankful to her for so much trust, but my sense of delicacy won't allow me to take such a great responsibility upon myself. I know what's in her best interests, I foresee her future, and not for all the money in the world would I want her to suffer for this, or say

[202]

to herself some day: "The sacrifice I made was too great."
You know that my eye is sometimes sharp enough to read
people's hearts.

So ask her to tell me her conditions in advance (in order
that they may be transmitted to Naples), absolutely freely
and openly, as if I had nothing to do with the whole matter.
Tell her that I will arrange for her to make her debut in
"La Traviata"; but that she must play the part for the first
time in the Teatro San Carlo. She would have to bind herself
only from October 15, 1857 to March 15, 1858, since they
will have to engage another prima donna. She should say
how many performances she wants to have a week and how
many ducats she asks a month.

The role I've chosen for her (as I've already told you) is
that of Cordelia in *King Lear*. Perhaps she knows it already,
or she can familiarize herself with it in Shakespeare. But if
she thinks there is the slightest disadvantage for her in the
proposition, she should have no scruples, for I shall not be
at all offended if she refuses.

To Antonio Somma   *Busseto, November 6, 1856* (D)

*The following letters refer to "Un Ballo in Maschera" (A
Masked Ball).*

Dear Somma: I have received your nice letter of November 1st with the rest of the first act. This poetry is quite good;
there are only a few very small things, which you can correct
in a moment.

The scene between Amelia and the Witch is good.

The stanzas *Della citta all 'occaso* ("To the west of the
city") are very beautiful. Also the recitatives which follow.

I find Amelia's, the Witch's, and Gustave's three stanzas a little weak, though I may be mistaken. Perhaps they need to have a little of your powerful inspiration breathed into them.

All the scene of the entrance of the chorus, and Gustave's ballad, are very good; and beautiful above all is the recitative that follows up to *scritto e lassu* ("on high is written").

In the quartet that follows be sure we have a chorus of conspirators. They must have something to say, so write a stanza for them. In this quartet with the chorus too, you can use that fore-mentioned breath of inspiration.

The only place that needs touching up is from *Strega mia* to *ti tradi*. All this is not dramatic enough. You say, I grant, all there is to say, but the words are not vivid. Consequently neither Gustave's indifference, nor the Witch's surprise, nor the conspirators' terror, is brought out sufficiently. Since the scene at this point is alive and important I want it to be well-worded. Is it the meter or the rhyme that hampers you? If it is, turn this passage into a recitative. I prefer a good recitative to a mediocre lyric stanza.

Please change *e desso . . . ad esso* for me. These rhymes coming so close sound bad in music. Cut out also *Dio non paga il sabato.* ("God does not pay every Saturday," i.e., punishment of sin, though it be tardy, is always sure.) Believe me, all proverbs, all colloquialisms are dangerous in the theatre.

At the end of this act you must not forget Oscar and Ankarstroem: they are on the stage and each one must sing a stanza. I await the corrections, and I hope they will be like this last poetry with which I am very pleased. [. . . .]

To Antonio Somma   *Busseto, November 20, 1857* (D)

Dear Somma: I have received the second act. The duet between Ricardo and Amelia is beautiful, marvelous. I find in it all the warmth and agitation of passion. That is what I should have liked the preceding aria of Amelia to be like. Perhaps it is the form that spoils everything; the two stanzas weaken the situation.

The trio after the duet hasn't turned out so well. Above all, you must try to end the recitative with a twelve-syllable line; this is absolutely necessary! In the conversation between Ricardo, Amelia and Ankarstroem there is something hard, distorted, perhaps unclear [. . . .]

To Antonio Somma   (D)

Dear Somma: I have had the last acts of "Lear" in my hands for a couple of days. I think you were wrong to cut the andante out of Cordelia's aria. This way it remains incomplete. It seems to me it should have been changed, but not taken out. I liked that stanza for voices in the distance (after the battle) very much: it had character and color. Albany's *coup d'état* doesn't seem natural to me. How can this Duke, who up till then has been a stupid fool, summon the decision to capture the real queen and her lover, to whom she had given a free hand? Goneril's death and the duel were much more natural! . . . Think it over. However, we can discuss it in Italy.

As far as the "Monk" is concerned (if you mean Lewis' "Monk") I don't think much of him for an opera. If he is of your invention, then I have nothing to say. Only so much, that I don't want a spectacular piece, but rather something

[205]

based on sentiment, a sort of "Sonnambula" or "Linda"; but it would have to deviate somewhat from that style, which is too outworn. At the moment I have no plot to suggest.

If you do find a plot of the kind I have mentioned, then draw up a sketch of it at your leisure, and you can send it to me after I am back home in Italy.

Farewell, in the greatest haste (the hurry-scurry of Paris!), yours devotedly.

To Antonio Somma　　　　*Busseto, November 26, 1857* (D)

Dear Somma: I really think the 12th century is a little too remote for our Gustave. It is such a raw and brutal period, especially in those countries, that it seems a grave contradiction to use it as a setting for characters conceived in the French manner as Gustave and Oscar are, and for such a brilliant drama based upon the customs of our time. We shall have to find a great prince, a duke, some rascal whether of the North or not, who has seen a little of the world and breathed the atmosphere of the Court of Louis XIV. After you have finished the drama you can think this over at your convenience.

I've written you about the second act, now I shall tell you what I think of the third.

The first dialogue between Ankarstroem and Amelia is cold, in spite of the situation which is very much alive. In French there is that *il faut mourir* ("You must die") which occurs from time to time, and which is very dramatic. I know that *Apparecchiati alla morte* ("Prepare yourself to die") and *Raccomandati al Signore* ("Commend yourself to God")

[206]

mean the same thing, but on the stage they don't have the same force as that simple *Bisogna morire* ("You must die"). Then almost all those lines are too hard for music. Furthermore, the words essential to the scene don't stand out strongly enough. The four stanzas of Amelia's cantabile are good, except for the first two lines which seem commonplace:

> *Ah mi concedi in grazia* "Ah grant me, please
> *Ancor una volta almeno* At least once more"

All of Ankarstroem's aria is good. The scene between the latter and the conspirators needs more pace. Cut it down somewhere, and change *Vi dilletta giocar di noi?* ("Do you enjoy fooling us?"). The stanza, *Tutti stretti* ("All bound") is good.

In the French drama the situation where Amelia enters and draws the name of her husband is beautiful and terrible. In the poetry you have sent me it doesn't stir me in the same way. The characters aren't well dramatized, the language is weak, and that great moment passes almost unobserved.

Think it over carefully, because this is a vital point. From the words *Signora, ho un invito* ("Lady, I am bidden") up to the following stanzas, it is all too long.

To Antonio Somma   *Naples, February 7, 1858* (D)

Dear Somma: I'm drowning in a sea of troubles! It's almost certain that the censors will forbid our libretto. Why, I don't know. I was only too right in telling you that we should avoid every sentence, every word, which could offend. They began by shying at certain phrases, certain words, then they went from words to whole scenes, and from scenes to the subject itself. They made me the following suggestions (and that only as a special favor):

1. Transform the hero into some great lord, so that all thought of a sovereign is eradicated.

2. Transform the wife into a sister.

3. Change the scene with the fortune-teller, and put it back into a time when people believed in such things.

4. No ballet.

5. The murder to be behind the scenes.

6. Leave out completely the scene with the drawing of the name.

And, and, and!! . . .

As you can imagine, such changes are impossible; hence no more opera; hence the subscribers won't pay the last two installments of the subscription; hence the government withdraws the subvention; hence the directors are starting suits against all the parties, and threatening me with 50,000 ducats damages! What an inferno! . . . Write me what you think about all this.

To Antonio Somma   *Busseto, August 6, 1858* (D)

Dear Somma: Arm yourself with courage and patience. Above all with patience! As you will see from Vasselli's letter, enclosed herewith, the Censor has sent a list of all the expressions and lines of which he disapproves. If on reading this letter you feel a rush of blood to your head, put it aside and pick it up again after you have dined and slept well. Remember that in the present circumstances our best plan is to give this opera in Rome. The lines and expressions struck out by the Censor are numerous, but there might have been even more. Besides, it is better this way, because now we know what course to pursue, we know what lines to leave in and what to cut out. Moreover, a great many lines would have had to be changed anyway, since the king is now nothing but a governor.

As for the gallows in the second act, don't worry about that, for I shall try to obtain the permit.

So cheer up, fix the lines marked, plan your affairs so as to have fifteen or twenty days free during the Carnival season so you can come to Rome, where I hope we shall have a good time together.

To Antonio Somma   *Busseto, September 11, 1858* (D)

Dear Somma: I have received the libretto which, in my opinion, has lost but little; as a matter of fact, I think it has gained in some points. But you've let some words slip by you which the public may find in bad taste and disapprove. [. . .]

In the third scene I find the expression weaker than before. That *Te perduto* ("If you are lost") was strong and offered an excellent opportunity for the declamation; this was theatrical, and helpful to me. Try to retain it, it shouldn't be difficult to say in two lines: *Te perduto, a questa terra e tolto ogni avvenire* ("If you are lost, all this land's future is cut off").

In the ninth scene the music already composed demands that Amelia should have an entire line: *Lui che su tutti il cielo arbitro pose* ("Whom the heavens gave supreme power over all"), or some other verse. But Ulrica must not interrupt it. *Un pugnale t'aspetta* ("A dagger awaits you") is worse than "l'assassinio" ("the murder"). The Censor will not have it.

So find a phrase, a circumlocution which means the same, such as . . . *da mano amica ucciso sarai* ("by the hand of a friend you shall be slain").

In the third act you have changed *Sangue vuolsi* ("Blood must flow") to *Rea ti festi* ("You were guilty") and it is all right. But further on, the other changes weaken the scene. [. . .] These words indicate a certain something logical and reflective in the characters which, in such a situation, is out of place. In one way, you gained, but you lost in the most important respect. As it stood before, it had more fire and more truth. With the exception of *Sangue vuolsi* I would leave it all as it was before: and above all that *Hai finito* . . . ("You are at the end . . ."), which is so dramatic.

Further on, the stanza *Dunque l'onta* ("Wherefore the shame"), etc., seems to me weak for the situation. The rhyme *lui* . . . *nui* is too hard for music; and to fit the music already composed, the second line must be smooth. At this point another stanza is absolutely necessary.

This is all. With the exception of that last stanza, you see that all the rest amounts to very little; therefore I shall delay sending the libretto to Rome until you have changed those few words. . . . So please hurry.

Furthermore, prepare to come to Rome yourself, for I think everything will go smoothly now.

To Antonio Somma   *Busseto, December 17, 1863* (D)

My very dear Somma: I know the subject of Ivan. It is grandiose, it is beautiful, it is dramatic, but it still isn't a subject I feel. And if I were to put it to music, I should do you a bad service without profiting myself. Besides, I'm not planning to compose at present; and, if later I do plan to, I have several poems in my portfolio, including your magnificent "Lear." Thank you, however, for having thought of me, and forgive me for not being able to accept your flattering proposal.

To Vincenzo Torelli   *Busseto, September 9, 1857* (A)

The Spanish drama was (according to Toye) "El Tesorero del Rey Don Pedro" ("The Treasurer of King Pedro") by the same Gutierrez who supplied the material for "Il Trovatore," and who was Spanish consul in Genoa. This subject was soon discarded, but the order in which the work was done is interesting: translation of the play; plan for the music; and after that libretto!

I am working day and night on the material for the new opera. I have chosen a Spanish drama and already translated it. Now I am arranging it for music, and afterwards I shall have it put into verse. I should have liked to do *Ruy Blas*, but you are right, a brilliant part would not suit Coletti and moreover he could not have taken the leading role.

To Vincenzo Torelli   *Busseto, October 17, 1857* (A)

The poet to whom Verdi refers is Somma. The plot, which was originally supposed to be played at the court of Gustave III of Sweden, was transferred, at the demand of the censors, first to a ducal court and finally to Boston, Massachusetts, under the title of "Un Ballo in Maschera" ("A Masked Ball").

You are right, and I can see that it is difficult to make changes in our contract. In a few days you will have the outline, or rather the whole libretto, completely done out in prose, for the censors to approve. In the meantime I shall have it put into verse by, I hope, an able poet. It will be "Gustave III." "King Lear" is impossible. It would be certain fiasco, because no one—and that includes Coletti—would be in place. With such a certainty in my mind, you in your turn will understand that I could not work at it with much will.

To Cesare De Sanctis   *January 14, 1858* (B)

Dear Cesarino: Shhhh—Don't tell anyone I'm here. Come and see me immediately. Don't ask for me by name, but for number 18.

Hush! Farewell.

To Tito Ricordi   *February 4, 1859* (A)

In this letter Verdi was referring to the failure of his comic opera "Il Giorno di Regno," which he had been obliged to write immediately after his two children and his wife had died within a few weeks of each other.

The fiasco of "Boccanegra" in Milan was inevitable, and so it happened. A "Boccanegra" without Boccanegra!! Cut a man's head off and then try to recognize him, if you can. You're surprised at the *bad manners of the audience?* I'm not surprised at all. Audiences are always happy if they can manage to perpetrate a scandal! When I was twenty-five I still had illusions and believed in their courtesy. A year later the scales fell from my eyes, and I saw with whom I had to deal. Some people make me laugh when they hint reproachfully that I owe a lot to this or that audience! True—at La Scala they once applauded "Nabucco" and "I Lombardi." Whether it was because of the music, the singers, the orchestra, the chorus, or the *mise-en-scène*, the production as a whole was certainly such that no one needed to be ashamed for applauding. A little more than a year before, however, the same public abused the work of a poor, sick young man, who was then in a pitiable plight, whose heart was almost broken by a terrible misfortune! They knew all that, but that did not prevent them from behaving badly. I have not seen "Il Giorno di Regno" since then, and I'm sure it's bad, but goodness knows how many other operas they accepted and perhaps even applauded, that were no better. Oh, if only the public had—I won't say applauded my opera, but at least tolerated it in silence, I should have been inexpressibly grateful! If they now smile on those operas of mine that have made their way around the world, then that balances the accounts. . . . I don't condemn them. Let them be severe, let them hiss, so long as I don't have to be grateful for applause. We poor gypsies, charlatans, or whatever you want to call us, are unhappily forced to sell our hard work, our dreams, and enthusiasms for gold. For three lire the public buys the right to hiss us off the stage or overwhelm us with applause. Resignation is our destiny: that says everything! But my friends and enemies may say what they like, "Boccanegra" is not a bit worse than a whole lot of other operas of mine which were luckier; perhaps it needed only a more careful performance and a public which would have taken the trouble to listen. What a miserable business the theatre is!!

Quite contrary to my custom, and almost without realizing it, I've poured out a lot of useless chatter to you. But I'm going to send it off just the same, so that I won't have to write the letter all over again.

To Vincenzo Jacovacci   *Naples, April 19, 1859* (A)

Civitavecchia is the port for Rome.

Dear Jacovacci: I have not now, nor have I ever had anything to do with the newspapers, and if you knew me better
you would have spared me that long preamble in your next
to last letter.

In Rome "Gustave III" is allowed in prose but a libretto on
the same subject, to be set to music, is forbidden!!! This is
very strange. I respect the will of the authorities and so I say
nothing. But if I didn't want to give the opera in Naples
because they changed the libretto, I can't give it in Rome,
where they also want to change it.

Everything is straightened out here—and the fight is over!

I shall leave Naples on the Wednesday steamer. I shall be
in Civitavecchia Thursday morning. Mail me there, *poste
restante,* the libretto of "Gustave III" which you have in hand
and let no more be said of this affair which is null and void
according to Article 6 of our contract.

Believe me affectionately yours.

To Vincenzo Jacovacci   *June 5, 1859* (A)

*"Nina Pazza" was one of the most famous operas of Giovanni
Paisiello (1740-1816). "Armida" is one of Gluck's masterpieces. Gluck too wrote an "Alceste," but Verdi recommends
the "Alceste" of his compatriot, Lully (1632-1687). Lully
was only fourteen when he went to Paris, and his operas are
accounted among the greatest of the French school.*

Dear Jacovacci: You were wrong to defend "A Masked
Ball" against the newspaper attacks. You should have done as
I always do: not read them, or let them say their little speech

[214]

as they please. That is what I have always done. The real question is this: the opera is either *good* or *bad*. If it is bad and the journalists spoke badly of it, they were right. If it is good and they wouldn't recognize the fact because of their own petty little passions or other people's, or for whatever reason, then one should let them talk and not bother about them. And now you must admit: if there was anybody or anything that really needed defending during the Carnival season, it was that awful company of singers you palmed off on me. Cross your heart, and admit that I was a rare model of self-abnegation for not just taking the score and clearing out in search of dogs, that wouldn't have bellowed as much as those singers. But post factum, and after everything that has come of it, etc.

Excuse me, but I cannot write to Ricordi about reducing the rental fee for the scores—I am not used to taking part in such affairs. Furthermore the prices you offer for "Aroldo," "Boccanegra," and "A Masked Ball" seem to me (however little these operas may be worth) too modest. I don't know whether Ricordi will see it the way I do. If he does he will say what I say and what you too will say: *help yourself elsewhere.* If by any chance you should also find other people's stipulations too high for you, root around in the old classical repertoire, which has fallen into the public domain, and you can fix up everything for a few pennies. You need three operas? Here they are: "Nina Pazza" by Paisiello, Gluck's "Armida" and Lulli's "Alceste." By this means you can, first, save money, and second, be assured that there will be no battles with the newspapers or anybody else. The music is beautiful, the composers are dead, nothing but praise has been spoken of them for centuries and they will continue to receive nothing but praise, if only because people can say nasty things about those who have not yet done them the little favor of dying.

Farewell, my dear Jacovacci, and let us think no more of new works!

To Clarina Maffei   *Busseto, July 14, 1859* (A)

By way of explaining the political events in the following letters: In the war of 1859, France, under Napoleon III, and Piedmont, the most powerful of the Italian states, defeated Austria which then still held half of Northern Italy. The Treaty of Villafranca gave Lombardy to Piedmont but left the Austrians in possession of Venetia. (They retained it until 1866, when they were decisively crushed by Prussia, and Italy, a united kingdom by then, received the province as fruit of her Prussian alliance.) It was in these troubled times that Verdi married Giuseppina.

Emperor Napoleon informed Empress Eugénie of the events at Villafranca in a proclamation issued at Milan. Under the treaty, the citizens of the Grand Duchy of Parma, of which Verdi was one, were to decide by plebiscite whether to continue under the rule of their Austrian Grand Duchess, Marie Louise (the widow of Napoleon I), or to unite with Piedmont. Provisionally, a sort of dictatorship was assumed under Farini and a "National Guard" was established, for which Verdi procured muskets. The people of Parma voted to join Piedmont, and Verdi, a member of the legislative assembly, was one of five delegates who conveyed their decision to Cavour, the Piedmontese Prime Minister and actual author of the union.

Though originally a republican like Garibaldi, Verdi real-

ized that the monarchy was essential to Italian unity. On this point he was in agreement with Cavour, whose acquaintance he had made through the English Ambassador, Sir James Hudson. It was Cavour who induced Verdi, despite his reluctance (cf. the letters to Minghelli Vaini), to stand as a candidate for the constituency.

Dear Clarina: Instead of singing a hymn of praise today, it would seem more appropriate to me to bewail our eternally ill-starred fatherland.

In the same mail with your last letter I received a bulletin of the 12th, which announced: "The Emperor to the Empress. . . . Peace is declared. . . . Venice remains under Austria!"

And where is the long wished for and often-promised independence of Italy? What does the Proclamation of Milan mean? Isn't Venice Italy too? After such a victory, what an outcome! So much bloodshed for nothing! Poor disappointed youth! And Garibaldi, who has sacrificed his long standing convictions in favor of a king, and still has not achieved his goal. It's enough to drive one mad! I write under the impression of the deepest anger and I don't know what you may think of me. Is it really true then, that we can hope for nothing from any foreigner, of any country whatsoever? What do you think? Perhaps I'm wrong again? I wish I were. . . . Farewell.

To the Mayor of Busseto   St. Agata, September 5, 1859 (A)

Dear Mr. Mayor: The honor which my fellow citizens have conferred upon me by appointing me their representative to the Assembly of the Parmesian Provinces makes me proud and grateful. Though my poor talent, my studies, the art which I practice, do not fit me particularly for an undertaking of this kind, may the great love I feel and have always felt for our noble, unhappy Italy, lend me strength.

It's unnecessary to say that, in the name of my fellow citizens and myself, I shall help proclaim:

The deposition of the Bourbon dynasty

Union with Piedmont

A dictatorship of that great Italian, Luigi Carlo Farini

On the union with Piedmont depend the future greatness, the regeneration of our common fatherland. This must be the constant, mighty resolve of all those who feel Italian blood in their veins. Then the day will come when we too can say that we belong to a great and noble nation.

To Count Cavour　　　　*Busseto, September 21, 1859* (A)

Your Excellency: Please excuse my boldness and the inconvenience I may cause you with these few lines. I had long wished to make the personal acquaintance of the Prometheus of our people, nor did I despair of finding an opportunity to fulfill my great desire. But what I had not dared hope for was the frank and kindly reception with which Your Excellency deigned to honor me.

I left deeply moved. Never shall I forget that estate of Leri where I had the honor of pressing the hand of our great statesman, our first citizen, the man whom every Italian will call the father of his country. May Your Excellency graciously accept these sincere words from a simple artist, who can boast of only one virtue: that he loves and always has loved his native land.

To Angelo Mariani   *Busseto, October 25, 1859* (A)

Angelo Mariani was 35 when he conducted Verdi's "Aroldo" at Rimini in 1857. He participated in the 1848 uprising, and became a devoted friend of the Maestro. He was betrothed to Theresa Stolz, the singer; but when he declined to marry her, and also failed to repay a borrowed sum of money, Giuseppina advised her to break off the affair, which she did. Mariani suspected that Verdi himself took a part in bringing this about, and he turned from Verdi. When Mariani conducted the first performance of "Lohengrin" in Italy (at Bologna in 1871), Verdi regarded it, not without reason, as a demonstration. Nevertheless he suggested Mariani, whom he considered the best operatic conductor in Italy, for the opening of "Aida" at Cairo. Mariani declined. He died in 1873.

I've received your kind letter and the *Movimento*. You seem depressed. But I won't give up to despair yet. We shall see! In the meantime, let's discuss other matters. You know that in Turin Sir Hudson gave me a letter for Signor Clemente Corte, one of Garibaldi's officers, to open the way for me to locate some guns. Signor Corte accepted the commission in a very cordial letter of the 28th of September, and at the same time sent me a wire received from the firm of Danovaro in Genoa: "Available perhaps 6000 of various kinds, mostly English, price 23 to 30 francs. 2500 carbines, 60 muskets, etc."

After receiving the letter and telegram I wrote to Corte on October 2nd asking him to order for the time being 100 rifles. In a second letter of October 18th, I ordered 72 more, all to be sent to Castel San Giovanni, where I intended to send someone to receive them. I would have paid the station master for them, or sent a check to Genoa, as the seller preferred.

I received no answer, either to my letter of October 2nd, or to my second of the 18th. I'm sitting on pins and needles, because the mayor of my little town keeps on asking me for them. Tomorrow I'm sending my servant to Modena to find out whether this man Corte is dead or alive. But in the meantime I should like to know:

1. Whether first 100, and then 72 guns were ordered from the firm of Danovaro;

2. Whether they were sent; and if Corte hasn't arranged it, whether the guns are available and at the price mentioned in the telegram;

3. Whether you, Angelo Mariani, would be ready, if necessary, to order these guns, and more guns later if required, to examine them yourself, and to have them examined by a technician to see whether they will suit our purpose. You would be performing a good and worthy service.

Answer me very, very quickly, and carry out this commission with the good sense that you've always had. Farewell!

To Angelo Mariani　　　　　*Busseto, March 15, 1860* (A)

Dear Mariani: [. . . .] They say there are lots of wild ducks in the woods along the Po. I'm going soon to have a look, and then I'll be able to tell you about it. When are you coming? I advise you to wait awhile until the ground, which is still wet from the thaw, has dried.

Peppina sends her greetings. Good-bye, you young scamp! I hope to see you soon, but in the meantime write me often!

To Angelo Mariani　　　　　　　　*March 21, 1860* (A)

While you were still only a composer, I shouldn't have dared write you a letter like this. But now that you're a capitalist, speculator, and usurer, I'm giving you several commissions to pay out a couple of hundred francs for me, but only for a couple of days. You'll get them back immediately with interest, premium, jobber's fee, and similar thieveries, etc., etc.

Above all go and get my picture, and pay for everything, according to the enclosed letter.

Second, have Maestro Gambini take you to that certain gardener and buy ten magnolia grandiflora, about a meter and a half high, but by no means shorter than a meter. They are to be well-packed in straw, and not until one day before you leave.

Third, go to Noledi and ask him whether he will exchange my St. Etienne rifle for his Liège, the one I like of 13/14 calibre. You know it. And I'll give him four *napoléons* into the bargain. You can assure him that my gun is as good as new. I have used it only a while in December, and the wood and iron parts still look brand new. If Noledi should want to see it beforehand, write me, so that I can box it and send it by train. But you must try out the Liège rifle for me. Watch carefully whether it hits the target well and doesn't kick. It must be tried out with five or six bullets.

There is no more snow. But if you wait a few days the ground will be dry and we can go into the woods.

Please take pains with everything. Take care with the gun, and if it proves to be especially good when you fire it, don't mind if it costs a little more money.

To Angelo Mariani   *Busseto, November 25, 1860* (A)

In a similar case Emperor Francis Joseph is said to have told a petitioner that he would give him an introduction to a corporal—his Minister of War was powerless.

Dear Mariani: My carpenter has a nephew who is due for his military service. But since his foot was damaged in a bad fall, he is unable to do any marching. He has been examined but the regimental doctors have passed the decision on to the doctors in Turin. He is going to Turin at the beginning of the month but he ought to have someone there to help him. Do you know anybody there to recommend him to? It ought to be a good man: not an ambassador or a minister. You would be doing a good deed. Write me.

To Angelo Mariani   *Busseto, January 3, 1861* (A)

Thank you ever so much for having found someone to help my poor protégé. His name is Angelo Allegri and he was born in 1840. It would be well to have the person who is writing to Turin compose the letter, which you would then send to me, and I would give it to the above-mentioned Allegri to pass on to the person to whom it is addressed in Turin. And all as quickly as possible, for he may leave on the 8th.

Verdi was urged by Cavour to accept the candidacy for the first Parliament of the now united Kingdom of Italy. He did not campaign, but was elected February 3, 1861 against Minghelli Vaini.

To Angelo Mariani   *Turin, January, 1861* (A)

Don't be surprised if you see me in Turin! Do you know why I'm here? In order not to become a deputy. Other people go to great pains to be one, and I do everything possible to avoid it—but don't say anything about that. I saw Cavour at seven this morning, and Sir Hudson has just left me. He wanted me to take lunch at his house, but I shall go there only for coffee at seven. Greetings to you.

I leave tomorrow and arrive home at four o'clock. Write me. Thank you for the address you sent for my poor Allegri.

I wanted to be in Genoa tonight, but now it's nearly five o'clock and consequently too late.

To Minghelli Vaini   *St. Agata, January 23, 1861* (A)

Dear Minghelli Vaini: It was not between two glasses of wine, but at an hour when one drinks at most a cup of coffee, that the burdensome business of my nomination to Parliament was discussed. The only purpose of my trip to Turin was to free myself from it, as you know. I didn't succeed, and I'm quite desperate about it. The more so since you are so much better prepared for parliamentary battles than an artist, who has only his poor name to recommend him.

I suggested you and spoke warmly for you at Busseto, knowing that I would be giving my fatherland a real Italian, an honorable man, and a deputy whose knowledge and enlightenment would help the good cause. I have not campaigned; I shall not campaign; I shall do nothing to be elected. If I should be elected, I will accept, heavy as the sacrifice will be for me—you know the circumstances that force me to do so. But I am firmly resolved to resign as soon as I can. This letter, which you may show to anybody who dares to cast damaging aspersions upon you, must suffice for your justification and enable you to recover complete peace of mind. As for the way out, which was suggested to me—to have myself put up in another electoral district of the kingdom: it is— forgive me—against my principles. If I did that, then I should be *campaigning* and I repeat for the hundredth time: I am

[223]

forced to accept the nomination but I shall not campaign nor put myself up in any electoral district.

If you succeed in putting me in the minority and getting yourself elected, I shall be inexpressibly grateful to you for so great a service. You would benefit the Chamber, and thereby confer a favor on yourself and an even greater one on me.

To Minghelli Vaini   *Busseto, January 29, 1861* (A)

Dear Minghelli: You write in your letter: "I don't need to tell you that I'm wholly convinced that you have nothing to do with the intrigues against me, and that you despise them." The word "intrigue" does not exist in my dictionary, and I defy anyone in the whole world to prove the contrary.

If I had intrigued, the article in the *Gazetta di Parma* of the 22nd would not have appeared. If I had intrigued, the electoral committee of Parma wouldn't have posted your name on all the walls throughout the country. If I had intrigued, the article in the *Patriota* of the 28th wouldn't have been printed, either. Nor do I need to intrigue now, for if I had had such a crazy idea as to want to be a deputy, no one prevented me from accepting the candidacy in the first place. I told you frankly on the 21st the reasons which compel me to accept if I am elected. But you haven't known me long enough to understand that my feeling of dignity is developed to the point of pride, and my scorn for certain underhand tricks merges into disgust! I have never made a study of politics and I have neither the ability nor the wish to enter on a political career. I have said so, and repeat it for the hundredth time: I will accept, little as I wish to, if I'm elected; but I shall never do a thing nor utter a word to be elected. So let this close an exchange of letters which we should never have entered upon.

Greetings to your wife from Peppina and myself.

To Dr. Giuseppe Chiarpa
                    St. Agata di Villanova, February 6, 1861 (A)

Dr. Giuseppe Chiarpa was president of the electoral college.

Mr. President: The honor which the electoral district of Borgo San Donnino has spontaneously offered me, moves me deeply. It shows me that I enjoy the reputation of an honorable, independent man, and that means much more to me than the bit of fame and fortune which I owe to art.

I thank you therefore, Mr. President, and beg you to thank all the voters who have entrusted this high office to me. Please assure them at the same time that though it is not given me to furnish parliament with the eloquence of a brilliant speaker, I shall bring to it an independent character, conscientiousness, and determination to cooperate with all my strength for the well-being and honor of our fatherland, which has been so long divided and torn by civil strife.

May fortune now fulfill our long and hitherto vainly cherished wish to see our fatherland united, by sending us a ruler who loves his people! Let us rally closely about him. If he is soon proclaimed the first King of Italy, he will perhaps be the only one who has loved the Italian people more than the throne.

To the Town Council of Busseto   (A)

I herewith fulfill my duty as deputy, and as a citizen I submit a plea.

Italy is in great danger, not from any enemy, nor from

civic or party strife, which would be harmless now in any case, but from her lack of money. Heaven forbid that history should one day record that Italy was ruined for lack of money when she had such territorial riches, and at a time when her cities are being beautified, and monuments and theaters are being erected everywhere. Busseto is building a theater. Don't think I condemn this plan, even if it be vain and useless as it seems to me. This is no time for discussions; we must consider higher and more important matters. And so I return to the town council with the plea to suspend this work and follow the noble example of Brescia and many other cities, by employing this money for the restoration of our country's finances.

I have done my duty as a deputy. As a citizen I renew my plea with the greatest earnestness, though that is perhaps unnecessary, for I know that the feelings that inspire me are common to everyone.

To Opprandino Arrivabene

St. Petersburg, February 1, 1862 (c)

This letter was written by Giuseppina Verdi.

So here is Verdi, condemned to face 24, 26, 28 degrees and more below zero, Réamur. And yet this frightful cold didn't bother us in the least, thanks to the apartments: you see the cold, you don't feel it. But don't misunderstand me; this anomaly is a privilege, reserved for the rich who can really shout: "Hurrah for cold, ice, sleds, and other earthly pleasures!" But the poor in general, and coachmen in particular, are the most unhappy creatures in the world! Just think, dear Count; many coachmen have to sit sometimes all day long and a part of the night, immovable on their seats, exposed to deadly cold, waiting for their masters, who are carousing in warm and splendid apartments; and meanwhile, perhaps, some of these poor unfortunates are frozen to death! Such frightful cases happen every year! I shall never grow accustomed to the sight of such cruel suffering.

To Francesco Piave   *Cremona, July 3, 1862* (H)

Dear Piave: Yesterday, on my return home to S. Agata, I found your letter which had been awaiting me for several days. You can't imagine how hard it has been for us at home because of my wife's sickness of almost a month! Didn't you see Ricordi at all during that time? And didn't he ever give you any news? Peppina was confined to her bed at Genoa for eighteen days with a gastric fever: she was able to come home only yesterday. She is now free of the fever, but she is in an exhausted condition, and her convalescence will take a long time, as is always the case with that illness.

Don't rejoice, my dear Piave! It's true, I'm now a member of the Institute of France (great France!). I'm one of the forty Immortals! But that means that I've become a reactionary old fogey.

Please tell Ricordi that I'm expecting an answer to my last letter. Write to me at St. Agata.

To Opprandino Arrivabene   *Busseto, July 20, 1862* (C)

Dear Opprandino: I'm half-sick, and I shan't come to Turin for the present. However, be a good fellow and oblige me by going to the Post Office of the Chamber, and asking the distinguished gentlemen in charge to forward my letters to Busseto—only the letters.

What are they doing in Parliament? I see they are always quarreling and wasting time.

To Tito Ricordi   *Busseto-St. Agata, October 22, 1862* (A)

The publication mentioned by Verdi is "L'Arte antica e moderna."

Dear Ricordi: It is raining, raining, raining! Good-bye to the country, good-bye to the walks, good-bye to the beautiful sun, which we shall only see pale and sickly from now on; good-bye to the beautiful blue sky, good-bye to infinite views, good-bye to the wishes, and the hope that we might go to Lake Como. Four walls will have to take the place of the infinite, a fire at home the place of the sun! Books and music instead of air and sky! And instead of pleasure, boredom! Well then, let us have music in order to . . . to do what so many other people do. They bore themselves to death with so-called classical music. The only difference is that when I'm bored I say "I'm bored"; while other people pretend to be carried away by beauties that aren't there at all, or of which there are really just as many in our own music. This much is true: The present talks a lot, wavers about, spends a lot of energy, produces little, and tries to create a new music out of perfume and dead bones. But if there should be the slightest ray of sunlight in it, then hurrah for the new music! So (not to be different from the rest) I'm asking you to do me the favor of sending me the work that you're having printed now. I don't remember the title, but it's piano music by ancient and modern composers. But please let's have no misunderstanding: I've made a resolution never to spend a penny on music and never to take up with operatic agents again. So if you on your part have resolved never to give away any music (and that would be a very wise decision) then don't send me the above-mentioned work, and we'll be better friends than ever.

I'm going to Turin where I shall stay eight to ten days. Write me there.

To Cesare De Sanctis
                    St. Petersburg, November 14, 1862 (B)

This letter from St. Petersburg was written by Giuseppina. The Russian word, "niett," means "nothing."

[. . . .] The Proverb, "No news is good news," is not always right. This time I send you news, which is good news! "La Forza del Destino" has been given with great success. Good general performance of the singers, the chorus, and the orchestra. The Emperor, who was afflicted with bronchitis and a bad eye-inflammation, was only able to be present at the fourth performance.

Although your godfather waited, he lost nothing, for the Emperor—after applauding him and calling him out by name—wanted him to be presented in his box by the Minister; and there, to put it simply, he was buried under an avalanche of compliments, especially from the Empress, who was very kind and said many nice things. You might think it all ended there with this presentation at the temple. *Niett* (as the Russians say). Saturday, Verdi received the Imperial and Royal Order of Saint Stanislas (Commander's Cross, to be worn around the neck) and this with no suggestions nor recommendations on the part of anyone, but by *motu proprio* of the Emperor of all the Russias. Take off your hat and make a bow to the Emperor, to the cultured audience, to the Illustrious Decoration—and now good-night.

We shall leave soon for Spain, where Verdi, after insistent

[229]

invitations, has agreed to put on the new Petersburg opera. He is, however, tired of these colossal trips, and wishes to return to his retreat at St. Agata for a long, quiet sojourn. [. . . .]

Your affectionate friend,

GIUSEPPINA.

To Clarina Maffei   *St. Petersburg, November 17, 1862* (A)

I'm leaving St. Petersburg in a few days and I have only time to press your hand and tell you that I am still fond of you.

From Paris I shall write you in detail and tell you all about Russia and high society there, and you won't be able to believe your ears: during these two months I have been going to *salons*, I've been to banquets, parties, etc., etc. I've known great people and little people, men and women of enormous charm and exquisite *politesse*—very different from the insolent *politesse* of Paris.

To Vincenzo Luccardi   *Madrid, February 17, 1863* (A)

Many hearty thanks for your telegram and for the letter which I've just received. The opera went very well in Rome, but it could have gone a thousand times better if Jacovacci had been able to get it into his head that to achieve success *you need operas that suit the singers and also singers that suit the operas.* Of course, you don't have to be able to do coloratura to sing "La Forza del Destino," but you have to have a soul, and understand the *words* and express them. With a soulful soprano, the duet in the first act, the aria in the second act, the romanza in the fourth, and above all the duet with Guardiano in the second act, would most certainly have been a success. That makes four numbers to which the performance did not do justice. And four numbers are a lot; they can decide the fate of an opera! The part of Melitone is effective from the first word to the last. Jacovacci has now realized the need to get another artist in the place of the one who sang this part; but as an old impresario, he should have realized it sooner. But let us thank our good fortune that so much negligence on the part of the singers, and above all of the impresario, did not kill the opera. I thank you too for your affectionate friendship and for sending me this report so quickly.

The opera will be produced here on Saturday, and Sunday morning I shall send you the news. The rehearsals are going fairly well.

I shall leave immediately afterwards for a little trip through Andalusia; then I go to spend some time in Paris.

To Opprandino Arrivabene   Madrid, February 22, 1863 (A)

Last night the première of "La Forza del Destino." Success. Admirable performance by chorus and orchestra, Fraschini and Lagrange good, the rest . . . blank or bad. In spite of it, I repeat, a success. Demonstrations of all kinds, etc., etc.

Tomorrow I leave for Andalusia, and in fifteen days I hope to be in Paris. Write me there *poste restante.*

To Clarina Maffei   Busseto, December 13, 1863 (A)

This letter refers to the first performance of the opera "I Pro-fughi Fiamminghi," by Franco Faccio.

Dear Clarina: [. . . .] I know that this opera has been

[231]

much talked about—too much, in my opinion. I've read a newspaper article full of big words about *art, esthetics, revelations, the past, the future,* and so on. I confess that I, gross ignoramus that I am, understood none of it. On the other hand, I don't know Faccio's talent, I don't know his opera, and I don't want to know it, either. So that I shan't have to discuss it and pass judgment, both of which things I hate because they're utterly futile. *Discussions* never convinced anybody; *judgments* are usually wrong. Finally, if Faccio, as his friends say, has found new paths, if Faccio has been called to put that art, which is now as *malodorous as a house of ill-fame,* on a pedestal again, so much the better for him and for the public. If he's *misled,* as others assert, then may he find the right path again, if he believes it is the right path.

To Opprandino Arrivabene

Busseto, St. Agata, March 3, 1864 (c)

Dear Arrivabene: For once you're safe. Yesterday I went to Cremona, where I found all I needed, so for the present I shan't bother you.

Rossini recently has made progress, and obviously has been studying!!! Faugh! Studying what? In my opinion, he should unlearn all this new music, and write another "Barber of Seville." [. . . .] I used to have complete confidence in the name of Rossini, because of the latest things he wrote, but now, if he has been studying, I begin to have my doubts. With this I leave you and say farewell in great haste.

To Opprandino Arrivabene   *April 4, 1864* (A)

[. . . .] You've guessed it. Ricordi never sends me music, because he knows that during all the ten or twelve years of my stay in Milan I didn't once go to consult his music archives. I don't take in music with my eyes; and if you thought that because they are by Rossini, those two compositions would accomplish the miracle of clarifying my spirit so that I could understand their harmonic glories, which are so highly praised by Arcais and Filippi, then you were very much mistaken. Just the same I thank you for your good intentions, and give you an affectionate farewell!

To Tito Ricordi   *St. Agata, September 8, 1864* (A)

Giovanni Pacini (1796-1867) was a well-known operatic composer (he wrote ninety works), as was Saverio Mercadante (1795-1870). Jubal, according to the Bible, was the inventor of music. Guido d'Arezzo was considered the originator of the musical notation still in use. Pythagoras, the philosopher, was also a musical theorist. Of course, Verdi's suggestion is ironically intended.

Dear Tito: When you see Filippi give him my regards and tell him that if I had dreamed he was going to publish my appointment as a member of the commission for the monument to Guido Arezzo, I should have asked him not to. For I refused, though a letter from Arezzo nominated me along with

Rossini as Honorary President
Pacini as President
Mercadante . . . perhaps as adviser.

After that, of course my worthy person, perhaps in the capacity of doorman. If they had put two more names between Mercadante's and mine I might have said modestly with Dante: *Where I was the sixth in so noble an assembly.*

But you must tell Filippi that if I believed it my duty to

refuse the exalted honor, knowing that I could be of no use in this commission, I nevertheless admire the pious enthusiasm of our time which erects monuments to the great men of the past and the present (President Pacini). And later on I shall ask him to publish a proposal of mine (though I don't even want to be president of the commission):

Let us erect a monument to Pythagoras!

If this suggestion has its effect, then afterwards we must propose another monument to Jubal, and we shall summon, through a *medium,* the spirit of Guido d'Arezzo, to have him compose the inaugural cantata. . . . Though I'm not certain whether Guido really knew music.

To Léon Escudier   *January, 1865* (A)

This letter and the next refer to the revision of "Macbeth" for the Paris performance (April 21, 1865). The trompette à pistons *gives more notes per instrument, but alters the tone.*

A little while ago you received the first two acts of "Macbeth." Day before yesterday I sent the third to Ricordi, through whom you will receive it in two or three days. This third act is entirely new, with the exception of a part of the first chorus and the dance of the Elves when Macbeth faints. I close the act with a duet between Macbeth and Lady Macbeth. It seems to me quite logical that Lady Macbeth, who watches constantly over her husband, should have found out where he is. The end of the act is better this way. The machinist and the *régisseur* will enjoy this act! You will see that there is a bit of plot in the ballet, which fits very well with the rest of the drama. The appearance of Hecate, Goddess of the Night, works out well—she interrupts the infernal dances with a sober, severe adagio. I don't need to tell you that

Hecate shouldn't dance at all, but only mime. And I also needn't point out that this adagio must be played by the *bassett horn* or *bass clarinet* (as is specified), so that in unison with the 'cello and bassoon, it produces a hollow, forbidding tone which suits the situation. Please ask the conductor, too, to supervise the work on the dance music from time to time, so that the dancers keep the tempi I have prescribed. You know ballet dancers always change the tempo. (At the Grand Opéra for example, they say the Tarantella can't be danced the way I want it. But a *gamin* of Sorrento or Capua would dance it very well at my tempo.) If the tempi are changed, the witches' ballet will lose all its character and won't produce the effect of which, in my opinion, it is capable. Then I have something to call to the attention of M. Deloffre: during the apparition of the eight kings he must be sure to have the players of the small orchestra grouped under the stage. This little orchestra, two oboes, six clarinets in A, two bassoons, and a contra-bassoon, produces a strange, mysterious, almost quiescent body of sound which no other instruments could duplicate. It must be arranged under the stage, but under an open *trappe* wide enough to enable the sound to spread through the whole theatre—only it must seem to come from a mysterious distance.

Another note on the banquet scene in the second act. I've seen several performances of "Macbeth" in France, England, and Italy. Everywhere they had the ghost of Banquo come out of the wings. It moves nearer, wavers about, menaces Macbeth, and disappears quietly into the wings. This, in my opinion, produces no illusion, inspires no terror, and no one quite knows whether it's supposed to be a ghost or a man. When I produced "Macbeth" in Florence I had Banquo (with a long

[235]

gash on his forehead) come out of a trap-door, precisely at the place meant for Macbeth; he made no motion at all, except to shake his head at the right time. The stage was arranged like this:

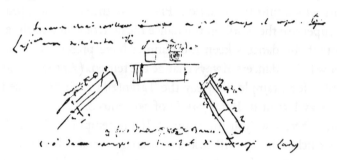

This gives Macbeth room to move around, and Lady Macbeth always stays near him to say, in asides to him, the words that the situation demands.

Is it true that Duprez is no longer to make the translation of "Macbeth"? I am sorry, because it will be hard to find anybody who is himself a composer, understands singing, and knows Italian as well as he. Apropos of this, in the first act duet between Macbeth and Lady Macbeth, the first part always makes a big effect, and there is a line there with the words, *Follie, follie, che sperdono i primi rai del di* . . . The French translator should take over the words, *follie follie;* for it may be that that very word, indicating the secret scorn of Lady Macbeth, contains the whole secret of the effectiveness of this number.

To Léon Escudier   *St. Agata, February 3, 1865* (A)

Today I sent Ricordi the last act of "Macbeth," which is now completely finished. The whole chorus at the beginning of the fourth act is new. The tenor's aria is touched up and re-orchestrated. And all the scenes from the baritone's romanza up to the end are new, that is, the description of the battle and the final hymn of victory. You will laugh when you see that I have written a fugue for the battle!!! I, who detest everything that smells of theory! But I assure you: in this case that form is permissible. The mad chase of subjects and counter-subjects, and the clash of dissonances, can describe a battle quite well. Oh, if you only had our trumpets, that sound so bright and full!! Your *trompettes à pistons* are neither fish, flesh, nor fowl. However, the orchestra will have a good time. At the next opportunity I shall send you my remarks about this whole fourth act.

Have you received the third?

Sunday, I'm going to Turin and Genoa, where I shall stay the rest of the winter. From Genoa I shall write in detail, and you will answer.

I see that the papers have already begun to talk about "Macbeth." For Heaven's sake—*ne blaguez pas trop!*

To Léon Escudier   *Genoa, February 8, 1865* (F)

This beautiful letter was found by Hans Busch at the Teatro Colon in Buenos Aires. The Théâtre-Italien was the Parisian theater where Italian operas were performed in Italian, as opposed to the Opéra and the Opéra-Comique where all performances were in French: "Brindisi" (literally, a toast) is the common term for a drinking song in Italian opera.

Dear Léon: *Ne cherchons pas midi à quatre heures!* We ought not to try for effects with a high C from the chest, or a fresh voice, or a secondary role. But we should try to produce a solid, lasting impression with whatever good there may really be in "Macbeth." Be guided by this: there are three roles in this opera and three roles only: *Lady Macbeth, Macbeth* and the *Chorus of the Witches*. The witches dominate the drama; everything derives from these creatures, uncouth and garrulous in the first act, sublime and prophetic in the third. They are really one of the characters, and a character of the highest importance. You will never succeed in endowing the part of Macduff with any particular significance, no matter what you do with it. On the contrary, the more prominence you give it, the more clearly you will reveal its insignificance. He doesn't become a hero until the end of the opera. He has enough music to distinguish himself, if he has a good voice, but there is no need to give him a single note more. To have him take part in the Brindisi in the big act, would be dramatically illogical and a mistake. In this scene, Macduff is just a courtier like all the rest. The important person, the dominating demon of this scene, is Lady Macbeth, and though Macbeth has to distinguish himself as an actor, Lady Macbeth, I repeat, must appear to dominate and control everything; she reproves Macbeth for being "quite unmanned," she tells the courtiers to pay no attention to her husband's delirium, "the fit is momentary," and to reassure them the better, she repeats her Brindisi with the utmost indifference. This is admirable and coming from her it has the greatest significance; from Macduff it would be absolutely meaningless and dramatically illogical. Is this true or isn't it? Admit that I'm right.

You will receive the fourth act in a couple of days. Tomorrow or the day after I shall write what I have in mind about this act. If M. Carvalho wants to use a hundred voices for the final chorus, so much the better, but I would rather he reinforced the chorus of the witches, especially the contraltos which are always weak. I repeat that the witches' chorus is of the greatest importance; it is a real character. Never forget, either in the musical execution or in the action, that they must be brutal and uncouth from the beginning up to the moment of the third act when they face Macbeth. From this point on, they are sublime and prophetic.

You wrote me once about having a ballet during the witches' chorus in the first act. Don't do it; it is a mistake. First of all, it spoils the effect of the ballet in the third act, and then, the chorus is good as it stands. *Ne cherchons pas midi à quatre heures.* Sometimes, trying to multiply effects ends up with each one killing the other.

I am glad you like what I have sent you; but don't get too excited, so you won't be disappointed at the end.

Now to come to the Théâtre-Italien. One way or another, I may ask Fraschini or Bagier himself to stop the performance of the opera for this year. It can't possibly be successful at the Théâtre-Italien, as it stands. The changes I have in mind absolutely have to be made. And Patti would be out of place in it. Next year, on the other hand, they have a singer, Galetti, who does this opera marvelously. It would be a good thing for the management too, since there are not many operas suited to Galetti. "La Favorita" can't be given at the Théâtre-Italien. "Norma" is too fatiguing for her and she doesn't want to do it any more. Take your cue from what happened at Milan where, after the first evening they gave "Norma," she had to rest for ten to twelve days. She sang it again a second time, and now she has given it up forever, in spite of an immense success. If Bagier knows where his own interests lie, he should do as I suggest. If not, I, G. V., predict a fiasco, and a fiasco with cat-calls.

To Francesco Piave   *February 8, 1865* (A)

Contrary to Verdi's assertion that he was completely out of place in Parliament, it is said by others that he did good work on the various committees. Verdi finally resigned in the course of the year 1865.

You say you want news and details of my political life. My political life doesn't exist at all. To be sure I'm a deputy, but that was by mistake. Nevertheless, I'll tell you the story of my *deputacy*. In September, 1860, I was in Turin. I had never seen Count Cavour, and was very anxious to make his acquaintance, so I asked the English Ambassador to introduce me. Since the treaty of Villafranca, the Count had been living away from all government affairs on one of his estates, I think in the neighborhood of Vercelli, and we went one fine morning to see him. After that I had occasion to write him and to receive a few letters from him, and in one of them he urged me to accept the candidacy for the chamber, which had been offered me by my fellow citizens and which I had refused. The letter was particularly gracious in tone, and I couldn't possibly have answered it with a flat "No." I decided to go to Turin. At 6 o'clock one December morning, when it was from six to ten degrees above zero, I visited him. I had prepared my speech, which seemed to me a masterpiece, and I spoke out my mind fully and freely. He listened very attentively, and when I described my inaptitude to be a deputy, and my outbursts of impatience at the endless speeches you have to swallow from time to time at the sessions, I did it so grotesquely that he burst out into a roar of laughter.

Good, I said to myself, I've succeeded. Then he began to refute my arguments one after the other, and came back himself with counter-arguments, which made some impression on me. Finally I said: "Well then, Count, I accept, but on condition that I may resign after a few months." "So be it," he answered, "but let me know beforehand!" I became a deputy and at the beginning, I went to the sessions of the chamber. Then came that solemn session at which Rome was proclaimed the capital of Italy. I voted, then approached the Count and said: "This seems to me the time to say farewell to these benches."

"No," he said, "wait till we go to Rome."

"Are we going?"

"Yes."

"When?"

"Oh, when, when! For the time being I'm going to the country; good-bye, and take care of yourself."

Those were his last words to me. A few weeks later he died. A couple of months after that I went to Russia, then to London, from there to Paris, back to Russia, to Madrid, traveled through Andalusia, and went back to Paris where I stayed a few months for professional matters. For two years and more I stayed away from the chamber, and afterwards I went very, very seldom. Several times I wanted to offer my resignation, but sometimes they said it would be bad to have new elections now, sometimes there was one reason and sometimes another, so that I'm still a delegate, quite against my wish and desire, without the slightest suitability for it, without any talent, and completely without the patience which is so necessary there. That's all. I repeat: if anyone had wanted to or had to write my biography as a member of Parliament, he'd only need to print in the middle of a beautiful sheet of paper: "There are supposed to be 450 deputies in Italy. This is not true. There are only 449, for Verdi is no deputy."

To Gilbert Duprez   *February, 1865* (A)

I have been so busy these last few days, I hope you will excuse my delay in answering your very kind letter of the 19th of last month.

I know the world in general but the theater in particular, so I am not surprised at any perfidies, great or small, which may be committed there. I am perfectly sure that your brother must have done an excellent translation of "Macbeth," as he did of the others. And if you have approved it and worked on it to adjust it to the music, you, who are a *grand musicien,* a great artist, and a conscientious man, must also have done an excellent piece of work, and there is no need for me to examine the translation to be *absolutely* certain of it. I can only regret that you and your brother have been so badly treated in this whole affair. But all your enemies together (assuming that you have many) could never succeed in reducing by one jot or tittle the profound esteem which I feel for you in every respect.

To Opprandino Arrivabene   *Genoa, March 5, 1865* (C)

In "Macbeth" there is a double bassoon, and it's true that they've sent to Milan to get one. If the producers of "L'Africaine" use it for publicity, they are misguided, because it's known even in Busseto, where I wrote marches for the instrument thirty years ago.

To Léon Escudier   *Busseto, April 28, 1865* (F)

The première of the revised "Macbeth" took place on April 21 in Paris. It had a tepid reception.

Dear Léon: In some French papers I have noticed sentences which would admit of doubt (as to how "Macbeth" went). Some draw attention to one thing and some to another. One finds the subject is sublime and another that it is not suited to music, while another says that I did not know Shakespeare (sic) when I wrote "Macbeth." But in this they are quite wrong. I may not have rendered "Macbeth" well, but that I do not know, do not understand and feel Shakespeare (sic), no, by heavens, no! He is one of my very special poets, and I have had him in my hands from my earliest youth, and I read and re-read him continually.

To Opprandino Arrivabene   *St. Agata, August 28, 1865* (C)

The correspondence between Verdi and Arrivabene was often carried on in jocular fashion between their two dogs.

Black to his brother-dog Ron-ron: Greetings. You did very wrongly, my beloved brother, not to come to see me, for I would have received you with open paws and wide open jaws and my four teeth biting into your hairy cheeks. I'd have shown you, in short, all my fraternal canine affection. Here, too, you wouldn't have run the risk of catching the cholera, nor of meeting with the lunatics of the Capitals. There are instead a lot of imbeciles to whom, from time to time, we give a good paw-slap to keep them on the job. My majordomo, factotum and secretary, the blunderer, provides me with everything. The macaroons continue to rain into my mouth, the large bones are for me, the soup ready on my awakening, the whole house at my disposal, and now that the heat is suffocating, I change room and bed every other minute, and woe to him who touches me. In my happy moments I busy myself with the education of a young kitten, with whose progress I am very well-satisfied; if it doesn't end up by being choked, it will leave behind the reputation of being a very clever thief.

So you see, my beloved brother, everything here is going fine, according to my suggestions and high commands, and if you should come, my paws, my teeth, my tail, are all ready to receive you in a manner befitting a most worthy relative. My male secretary and my lady secretary send you their greetings. Apropos the first, I've read in some newspaper that he's on the verge of making a new blunder. I shall place him on the list of the mad and send him to the Capitals. If I do, I'll inform you. Till then, receive my brotherly canine embrace. Farewell.

BLACK.

To Filippo Filippi　　　　*St. Agata, September 26, 1865* (1)

My dear Signor Filippi: I've been away for five or six days and so I haven't heard anything about the elections here, but I know that Scolari has been put up, and that he has a good chance of winning.

If you give me the pleasure of a visit, you will hardly find much to tell, in your capacity as biographer, about the wonders of Sant'Agata. Four walls to shield me from the sun and bad weather, a few dozen trees planted, for the most part by my own hand, a puddle, which I might dignify with the name of lake, if I had the water to fill it up with. . . .

And all without plan, or architectural arrangement, not because I dislike architecture at all but because it would have been ridiculous to build anything artistic in such an unpoetic spot. So take my advice, and forget for the time being that you are a biographer.

I know that you are a tireless, avid musician. . . . But alas! . . . Piave and Marini have probably told you that we never play or even discuss music at Sant'Agata, and you run the risk here of finding a piano which is not only out of tune, but has missing strings.

Thanking you for the courteous letter you were so kind as to send me, I remain devotedly yours.

To Opprandino Arrivabene
                        St. Agata, November 19, 1865 (C)

Dear Arrivabene: It seems like a century since you've written me, or I you. Tomorrow I shall leave for Paris. Why? I don't know. Enough, the trunks are packed and I must go. Write me there *poste restante,* and tell me in detail about the new Parliament, and about our affairs. I'm in a hurry, so excuse the brevity: the happenings at St. Agata are quickly told.

Black is well, and cordially shakes your hand. Peppina sends her greetings, and I sign myself, yours affectionately.

To Opprandino Arrivabene   Paris, December 10, 1866 (C)

Giuseppe Piroli, Senator, lawyer, and authority on penal law, was born in Busseto. (Died 1890.)

Dear Ron-ron: I'd have written before, if I hadn't had on my fingertips a lot of notes that fell on the score of "Don Carlos," and you ran the risk of receiving a letter full of notes which were worth even less than any of my words. Now that the instrumentation is finished, and there's no longer any danger of my writing you notes instead of words, I can tell you that the opera is completely finished except for the dances, that the rehearsals continue regularly, that the rehearsals for the *mise-en-scène* have begun, and that I hope to give the first performance in the second half of January. What a barracks this Opéra is! There is no end to it! I won't talk about the doings in Italy. I'm displeased and sad about them, but I don't want to depress you with my opinions and my presentiments. Give my best wishes to Piroli, and tell him that I owe him a letter, but to pardon me since I'm so busy.

Peppina sends her greetings.

To Clarina Maffei　　　　　*St. Agata, January 30, 1867* (A)

Concerning the next two letters: Antonio Barezzi, Verdi's patron and the father of his first wife, fell mortally ill in 1867 but did not die until July 20 of that year. On January 15, Verdi had heard the news of his father Carlo's death.

Thank you, my dearest Clarina, for your warm letter.

Oh, this loss will be very hard for me! For three or four days now, he has been better. But I know only too well that it is just a little relief, which may lengthen his life a few days, but no more. Poor old man—he was so kind to me! And poor me, I shall have him only a short time longer, and then shall see him no more!!

You know I owe everything to him, everything, everything. And to him alone, not to other people, as they've tried to make out. I can see him still (and this was many years ago), when I had finished school in Busseto, and my father declared he couldn't support me at the University of Parma, and I had just decided to go back to the village where I was born.

[246]

When the good old man found it out he said to me: "You were sent into the world for something better than to sell salt and work as a farmer. Ask the Monte di Pietà for the little stipend of 25 francs a month for four years, and I'll undertake the rest. You shall go to the Conservatory of Milan, and shall pay me back the money I've spent for you when you're able."

And so it was! You see, he was a generous, good, loving man. I've met all kinds of men, but never a better one! He loved me as much as his own son, and I loved him like a father.

To Clarina Maffei   *Paris, February 26, 1867* (A)

Dear Clarina: I didn't receive your letter, but only two notes, one from Piave and the other from Ricordi.

You have been seriously ill, my poor Clarina. But your misfortune was the less, because you found so many proofs of affection and solicitude among your friends. You must get completely well again and keep yourself for those friends (since you are fortunate enough to have them) who love you so dearly.

Venturi is dead too!

This is an ill-fated year for me, like 1840!! For two months I have heard of nothing but deaths and misfortunes of every kind. They are all the harder for me to bear here, in this country which, to be sure, is the greatest in the world, though I can't ever stand being here for long. I can't wait to leave and get home, where my poor father has left a sister of 83, and a granddaughter of 7. And these two poor creatures are in the hands of two servants!!!

You can just imagine whether I, who have so little faith in

anything, can have faith in the reliability of two servants who are now practically masters in my house. . . .

To Opprandino Arrivabene Paris, March 12, 1867 (C)

Dear Arrivabene: Last night "Don Carlos." It was not a success! I don't know what the future may hold, but I shouldn't be surprised if things were to change. Tonight I shall leave for Genoa. Write me there. Always keep your regard for me, and believe me, affectionately yours.

To Opprandino Arrivabene Genoa, March 16, 1867 (C)

Dear Arrivabene: I just received your letter and I thank you. I leave immediately for St. Agata, but I shall return here to fix up an apartment which I haven't bought, but rented in the Palazzo Carignano Santi Pallavicino. The apartment is magnificent, and the view stupendous, and I plan to spend about fifty winters in it. I have received letters and telegrams about the second and third performances of "Don Carlos." It is going well. They write me as if it were a real success. May it be so.

Wish me well. I am leaving. Farewell.

To Léon Escudier Genoa, April 1, 1867 (F)

My dear Léon: We really are a lot of lunatics! I ask you, was it necessary to travel up and down the railway in order to relieve one's mind after *eight months at the Opéra!* In short, one never comes to the end, and one would never find a minute to write operas again if it were not for rehearsals!

I have read in Ricordi's "Gazetta" the account of what the

chief French papers say of "Don Carlos." In short, I am an almost perfect Wagnerian. But if the critics had only paid a little more attention they would have seen that there are the same aims in the Trio in "Ernani," in the sleep walking scene in "Macbeth," and in other pieces. But the question is not whether "Don Carlos" belongs to a system, but whether the music is good or bad. That question is clear and simple, and, above all, the right one to ask. Good-bye, my dear Léon.

From Giuseppina Verdi to Clarina Maffei
June 4, 1867 (A)

Many years ago (I dare not say how many) I was so fond of the country that I asked Verdi most insistently to come out under the canopy of the open sky and take some of those healthful air- and light-baths that give as much vigor to the body as they do calm and tranquility to the spirit. Verdi, who rather resembles Auber in this, had almost a horror of staying in the country; after many prayers he consented to take a cottage not far from Paris. Among the pleasures of life, I venture to say that this new existence was a revelation to Verdi. He began to love it so warmly, with such passion, that I found myself outmatched, and my prayers but too well answered, in this cult of the sylvan gods. He bought the estate of Sant'Agata, and I, who had already furnished a home in Milan and another in Paris, had to arrange a *pied-à-terre* on the new property of the illustrious musician of Roncole. We began with great delight to plant a garden, which was in theory called "Peppina's garden." Then it grew, and was called *his* garden. And I can tell you he plays the czar in that garden of his now until I am reduced to a few feet of ground, where he is forbidden, on stated terms, to show his nose. I cannot conscientiously say that he always lives up to those terms, but I have found means of bringing him to order by threatening to plant cabbages instead of flowers. This garden, which went on growing bigger and handsomer, demanded a somewhat less countrified house. Verdi became an architect, and I can't tell you the promenades and dances of beds, bureaus, and other furniture that we went through. Suffice it to say that with the exception of the kitchen, cellar, and stables, we have slept and eaten in every nook in the house. When the fate of Italy was at stake, and Verdi and some of the other gentlemen were carrying King Victor's States in their pockets, Guerrieri, Fioruzzi, and others came to Sant' Agata, where they had the honor of dining in a sort of hall or corridor, in the presence of various nests full of swallows, which calmly came and went through a grating to take food to their little ones. When the Lord pleased, the house was finished, and I can assure you that Verdi supervised the work perhaps better than a real architect. Here, then, was the fourth apartment that I had to furnish. But the sun, the trees, the flowers, and the immense variety of birds that make the country so beautiful and so alive most of the year leave it sad, speechless, and desolate in winter. Then I don't like it. When the snow covers these immense plains, and the bare branches of the trees are like forsaken skeletons, I can't raise my eyes to look outside. I cover the windows with fine curtains as high as a man's head, and I feel an endless melancholy, a desire to flee the country, to know I am alive among living beings, not ghosts and the silence of a great cemetery. Verdi, with a character of iron, would perhaps have enjoyed the country even in winter and have succeeded in finding pleasure and occupations suited to the season; but in his kindness he took pity on my loneliness; after much hesitation over the choice of a place, we pitched our tents facing the sea and the mountain, and now I am furnishing the fifth and certainly the last apartment of my life.

I find I have started to write a long yarn. You must be charitable in forgiving these childish details, out of your affection for Verdi . . . and even a little for me.

GIUSEPPINA

To Léon Escudier   *Genoa, June 11, 1867* (F)

A few months later "Don Carlos" was put on in London, and it was extremely successful. Sir Michele Costa (1808-1884), a Neapolitan by birth, achieved great eminence in England as a conductor. The Belgian instrument makers, Charles Sax and his son, Adolphe, enjoyed a great reputation in Paris. Adolphe invented new wind instruments, among them the saxophone.

Dear Léon: So the London production is a success? If it is, what will they say at the Opéra, seeing that at London a work is staged in forty days while they take four months!! However, you are not telling me anything new when you say that Costa is a great conductor and that the brass is better than Sax's. Any instruments are better than Sax's! Nor am I surprised at the encore of some numbers. That may appear strange at Paris, but I can imagine the effect the Trio is capable of producing when sung by three performers who have rhythm. But rhythm is a dead letter for the performers at the Opéra. Two things will always be wanting at the Opéra—rhythm and enthusiasm. They do many things well, but they will never exhibit the fire that transports and carries one away, or at any rate not until they teach singing better at the Conservatoire and find a conductor like Costa or Mariani. But it is also a little the fault of you French, putting stumbling blocks in the way of your artists with your *bon goût, comme il faut,* etc. You should leave the arts in complete liberty and tolerate defects in matters of inspiration. If you terrify the man of genius with your wretched measured criticism, he will never let himself go, and you will rob him of his naturalness and enthusiasm. But if you are content as things are, and if the Opéra likes losing several hundred thousand francs and eight or ten months' time in producing an opera, then go on doing it—I don't mind. I am affectionately yours.

To Vincenzo Luccardi   *Busseto, July 23, 1867* (A)

Dear Luccardi: A terrible blow has fallen upon us!

Poor Signor Antonio is dead!! He died in our arms and he recognized us almost up to the last minute!

You know what sort of person he was; what he was to me, and I to him. You can imagine how great is my grief!!

I haven't the courage to go on. Farewell, farewell.

To Paolo Marenghi   *August 15, 1867* (A)

Why did you use the machine, when I expressly forbade it to be touched before my return? I'd like to know whether my orders are going to be followed or not. You'll never learn either to *command* or *obey!* It's time this disorder stopped, and I certainly intend that it shall.

You were wrong, and Guerino was wrong to let anyone have the keys to the workshop—I had entrusted them to him.

I'm leaving for Paris. Send your letters there: *Monsieur Verdi, poste restante, Paris,* and that's all.

To Paolo Marenghi   *Turin, August 16, 1867* (A)

When I told you to balance the accounts, if you had said a word to Spagna, he would have told you what the bill for the wood was. But the trouble is that each person only pulls his own rope, there is no cooperation and so the place is badly managed.

I am leaving tomorrow for Paris and I repeat my orders just to see whether I can succeed for once in being understood and obeyed.

1. Aside from your inspector's duties, you are to supervise the horses and the coachman, whom I do not trust much with orders. He is to exercise the horses every other day, without taking them to Busseto.

2. Tell Guerino that he shouldn't have given anyone the key to the machine, and tell him to clean it now and keep it locked until I give him further orders.

3. Repeat to the gardener what I have already told him. The garden is to be kept closed. No one is to go in, and no one from the house is to go out excepting the coachman, for a short time to exercise the horses. If anyone goes out he must stay out for good.

Remember, I am not joking. From now on I intend to be master in my own house.

To Paolo Marenghi   *Paris, September 4, 1867* (A)

Allow me to say now, between ourselves, that it would be better for you not to write such empty letters. A week is a long time. You say, for example, that the expenses amount to 518.06 lire, and that you need 276 lire. But in Heaven's name

[253]

explain how and what the expenses were incurred for, and why you ask for 276 lire.

Then you don't say a single word about my house and the servants! Are they all dead then? And how is the coachman? What is he doing? And has my old coachman, Carlo, really died in Piacenza? Yes, and now that we're on the subject, what's happening with the cholera at home? It seems to me that these are all important things, and that I can reasonably expect to be told about them. I'm leaving Paris very soon. Write me immediately, just as soon as you get this letter, and give me an answer to everything I've asked you about.

To Vincenzo Torelli   *Genoa, December 23, 1867* (A)

Thank you for your picture and that of your Achille. But both of you have written words on them which would make me blush if the sun and country air had not already tanned my skin to leather. However, I send you my thanks, and if I don't send you my picture, that's for the simple reason that I have none.

I highly approve Achille's refusing the pension. If there is anything in life to be cherished, it is the bread earned with the sweat of one's own brow. He's young, let him work. If his health is not particularly good, he should work carefully, but he should work. He should imitate nobody, particularly none of the great. Now and only now (may the scholars forgive me for saying this) he can dispense with studying them. Let him lay his hand on his heart and study *that,* and if he really has the stuff in him to be an artist, his heart will tell him all. He mustn't be puffed up by praise nor intimidated by blame. If criticism, even the most honest criticism, confronts him, let him go his way calmly. Criticism performs its office. It judges and must judge according to existing rules and forms. But the artist must look into the future, perceive new worlds amid the chaos; and if he spies a tiny light far, far ahead on his new path, the enveloping darkness must not frighten him. He must stride ahead, and if he sometimes stumbles and falls, he must stand up again and go on. Some of the heads of schools have had their falls too, and it was good that they did. . . . But what the devil am I prating about here? . . . I am saying things your Achille knows better than I. Excuse me, credit it to my wish and hope that some day he will be one of the glories of Italy. Farewell! A happy New Year to all of you; Peppina, too, echoes this with her whole heart. Farewell!

To Opprandino Arrivabene   Genoa, December 29, 1867 (C)

My poor Black is very sick; he hardly moves about any longer, and will not live very long. I've ordered another Black, who is being made in Bologna, for in case I should get the idea of composing another "Don Carlos," I couldn't do it without a collaborator of that species.

To Léon Escudier   St. Agata, Busseto, May 8, 1868 (F)

"La grande boutique" was the derisive nickname of the Paris Opéra.

Dear Léon: I really have cause to be annoyed. You have not even written to me about the bad performance of "Don Carlos" at Bordeaux, Brussels, and Darmstadt! Poor "Don Carlos"! We don't do things quite so badly in Italy. When they are done with enthusiasm one gets vigorous and spirited

[255]

performances such as you gentlemen of the Opéra never even dream of.

I have read your article, which is really excellent, only you put it a little too strongly. Let things run their own course. Truth will out. That French singers are the best in the world —granted; all the same they must learn to use their voices. But that they perform music well at the Opéra—ha, ha, ha, ha!

I say nothing of Mazzoleni. It is a phenomenon that often recurs at the Opéra. He must have been spoilt by over-training. Oh, *la grande boutique!*

I rejoice to hear you are in good health again. Write to me soon and believe me, yours affectionately.

May, 1868 (G)

In his Conversazioni Verdiani, *Monaldi quotes the following letter to an Italian minister, who had written to Rossini that no Italian opera had been composed in forty years (roughly since Rossini had written "Guglielmo Tell").*

Your Excellency: I have received the diploma naming me a Commander of the Italian Crown.

This Order was established to honor men who have done some service to Italy under arms or in literature, science, and art.

Yet although (as you yourself said and believed) you are *not* at home in music, a letter addressed by Your Excellency to Rossini expresses the opinion that no opera has been written in Italy for the last forty years.

Why, then, is this decoration sent to me? Surely there must have been some mistake in the address. I return it.

Your Excellency's respectful servant

To Ricordi   *St. Agata, November 17, 1868* (A)

Rossini died at Passy, near Paris, on November 13, 1868. From 1823 to 1836 he had lived in Paris; from then until 1853 in Italy, particularly in and around Bologna; and 1853 in Paris again. The Mass as it was suggested by Verdi—he had chosen to compose the Libera, *the end of the composition, himself—was never completed. The difficulties made by Mariani, the conductor of operas at Bologna, when he had not been invited to write a part of the Mass himself, seem to have contributed to his break with Verdi.*

My dear Ricordi: In order to honor the memory of Rossini, I would like to get the most prominent Italian composers (above all Mercadante, even if only with a few measures) to compose a Requiem Mass, to be performed on the anniversary of his death.

I wish that not only the composers, but all the performing artists as well would give their services, and also contribute to the current expenses.

I wish no outside hand, none strange to music, however powerful it may be, to come to our assistance. Otherwise I should withdraw at once from the committee.

The Mass should be performed in San Petronio in the city of Bologna, which was Rossini's real musical home.

This Mass should be neither an object of curiosity nor of commercial speculation. It should be sealed and deposited in the archives of the Liceo Musicale of the city immediately after the performance, and it should never be removed. An exception might be made for anniversaries of the great man, should later generations wish to celebrate them.

If I were in the good graces of the Holy Father, I should

[257]

beg him to allow, this once, that the music be sung by women's voices as well as men's. Since I am not, it will be advisable to find a more suitable person to arrange it.

It would be well to appoint a committee of intelligent men to arrange matters for the performance, and particularly to choose the composers, distribute the pieces, and supervise the general form of the work.

This composition will necessarily lack unity from the musical point of view, no matter how good its separate parts may be. But in spite of this, it will still be a valid testimonial of how highly we honor the memory of this man, whose loss the whole world laments.

To Léon Escudier　　　*St. Agata, December 2, 1868* (A)

Dear Léon Escudier: If, after having accustomed me for so many years to receiving news both about you and about interesting things, especially in the field of art, in Paris—if after all this, if you wanted to break off our correspondence, which may have become burdensome for you, if you wanted to break off even our business relations, you were quite within your rights in doing so. But that you should do it at the moment when Rossini disappeared from the world, surprised and grieved me deeply. While everybody talked and talked and wrote and wrote about his death, you couldn't find a little piece of paper to write me: "Rossini is dead"? No, I can't believe you acted this way without some very strong reason, that you were merely seizing upon some pitiful little breach of etiquette. Well, if you have such a reason, tell me what it is, frankly and openly. Your answer will show me how to guide myself in the future. Meanwhile, farewell, and believe me, I am yours sincerely.

To Tito Ricordo   *Milan, December 15, 1868* (A)

I am coming to Milan myself to direct such rehearsals as I think necessary for "La Forza del Destino"; and I am changing the last finale and various other numbers here and there in the course of the opera.

I want to have nothing to do with the management of La Scala, I don't want my name put on the bill board and I shall not stay for the first performance, which, however, cannot be given without my permission. [. . . .]

You will retain the rights to the new numbers, excepting that you must give a copy of them to the management of the St. Petersburg Theatre, if they ask for them.

In compensation for all this you will give me:

1. Author's rights according to the law, and as was done with "Don Carlos."
2. A payment of fifteen thousand lire.

If these proposals suit you, fine; if not, no ceremony: write me a word and the matter is closed.

Meanwhile, farewell, and believe me, I am affectionately yours.

To Opprandino Arrivabene   *Genoa, March 1, 1869* (C)

Dear Arrivabene: I returned here from Milan last night at midnight, dead-tired.

I need fifteen days continuous sleep to feel myself again. By this time you've heard about "La Forza del Destino." It was a good performance and a success. La Stolz and Tiberini were superb. The others, good.

To Senator Piroli   *Genoa, March 1, 1869* (A)

I got back last night at midnight from Milan. "Forza del Destino," as you know by this time, was a success. Excellent performance. Stolz and Tiberini superb; the others good. Orchestra and chorus divine. What fire and enthusiasm they had! Too bad, too bad that the government pitilessly refuses to help this art and this theatre which still has so many virtues. You will ask: why can't it support itself without government aid? No, it is impossible. La Scala has never been so well attended and so active as it is this year. In spite of this, if the management doesn't succeed in giving 15 performances of the "Forza" with over 5000 lire nightly receipts, they are lost. I don't think they can possibly achieve that many, and then they will have to close the theatre with a deficit before the season is over. What a shame, what a shame!

To Signor Filippi   *March 4, 1869* (A)

Dear Signor Filippi: I can take no offense at the article in *La Perseveranza* on "La Forza del Destino," and there is no reason why I should. If you felt obliged to add a little criticism to a great deal of praise, it was absolutely your right to do so and I approve of it. And in any case, you know I never complain about hostile articles, just as I never pay thanks for friendly ones (which is perhaps wrong). I set great store on my independence in everything, and I have the fullest respect for that of other people. I am particularly thankful to you for your attitude of reserve during my stay in Milan; for since you had to write about my opera, it was wise not to let yourself be influenced by even a handshake or a visit paid or received. And as far as your article is concerned, since you ask me about it, I want to assure you herewith that it didn t and couldn't displease me.

I know nothing about what happened between you and Ricordi, but it may be that Giulio who, if I am not mistaken, prefers Leonora's *cantabile* to a lot of other compositions, lost his temper somewhat when he saw you call it an imitation of Schubert. If that's what it is, then I'm as surprised as Giulio, for, musical ignoramus that I am, I couldn't tell you how many years it has been since I've heard Schubert's "Ave Maria"; so it would have been hard for me to copy it. Please don't think that when I speak of *my extreme musical ignorance* I'm merely indulging in a little *blague*. It's the truth, pure and simple. In my home there is almost no music, I've never gone to a music library, or to a publisher to look at a piece of music. I keep up with a few of the best operas of our time, not by studying them but only by hearing them now and then in the theatre. In all this I have a purpose that you will understand. So I repeat to you: of all past or present composers, I am the least erudite. Let's understand each other—I tell you again that this is no *blague* with me: I'm talking about *erudition,* not about musical *knowledge.* I should be lying if I denied that in my youth I studied long and hard. That is why my hand is strong enough to shape the sounds as I want them, and sure enough for me generally to succeed in making the effect I have in mind. And when I write something that doesn't conform to the rules, I do it because in that case the strict rule doesn't give me what I need, and because I don't really believe all the rules that have been taught up to now are good. The schoolbooks of counterpoint must be revised.

[261]

What a lot of words! And what's worse, so many useless ones! Forgive me, and accept the assurance of my high regard.

To Léon Escudier   *Genoa, August 1, 1869* (A)

Piave had a stroke in 1867. He lived on for eight years in great distress unable to work. Verdi suggested that an album of pieces by famous composers be compiled and sold for Piave's benefit.

Dear Léon Escudier: [. . . .] I'm sorry to have to bother you about something else. The album for poor Piave is waiting now only for the three Romanzas by Auber, Thomas, and Ricci, which you said were in your hands. I have Mercadante's, Cagnoni's is done, and so is mine. We are only waiting for yours, so please send them immediately either to me or to Ricordi.

Forgive all this annoyance, I assure you it is as painful for me to inflict it on you, as it is for you to suffer it. Forgive me again and believe me sincerely yours.

To Antonio Gallo   *Genoa, August 17, 1869* (A)

The addressee was a theater manager at Venice in the fifties, and a long-time admirer of Verdi's.

[. . . .] It's curious, and at the same time discouraging! While everybody shouts *reform* and *progress,* the public is generally indifferent, and as for the singers, they can sing only arias, romanzas, canzonettas effectively. I know that dramatic scenes are popular now too, but indirectly, as a frame for the rest. They've got it the wrong way around. The frame has turned into the picture! And in spite of the praises you all have sung to me about the performance, I am firmly convinced that while the solos and the numbers for several solo voices came out wonderfully, the opera, please understand me, the *opera,* the *musical drama* was only imperfectly presented. What do you think about it, Master Toni?

Well, joy be with them! It really doesn't matter much to me, but the Art of the Future will really have to think about it. This way, we aren't getting anywhere. Either the composers must take a step backward, or all the rest a step forward.

To Angelo Mariani   *Genoa, August 19, 1869* (A)

Pesaro was the birthplace of Rossini (he was therefore called "The Swan of Pesaro"), and a great funeral service was held there on the composer's death.

Sleep on undisturbed; I have already answered that I can't go to Pesaro.

I go back to your letter of yesterday because there are two sentences in it which I don't understand very well: "What will the commission in Milan do?" and further on: "If I can be of any service to you, tell me what to do." Do you mean that we mustn't ask you for the chorus you have at Pesaro? The first thing you should have understood long ago is that my own person has disappeared in this business, and that I am now nothing but a pen to write a bit of music as well as possible, and a hand to give my little offering so that this *patriotic celebration* may come about.—Finally, I must tell you that in this affair no one should ask, and no one should be asked for anything, because it is a matter of duty which every artist must and should fulfill.

I have never been able to find out whether the project of the Mass for Rossini has had the fortune to win your approval or not. When it is a question, not of personal interest, but of an art and of the fame and honor of one's own land, a good deed has need of no one's approval. If there is any one who doesn't recognize the fact, so much the worse for him! A man, a great artist who put his stamp on a whole epoch, dies; some individual invites the artists who are his contemporaries to honor that man, and in honoring him, to honor our art. A work is composed especially for this occasion and performed in the principal church of the city which was his musical home, and in order that this composition may not be a breeding-ground for miserable vanities and intrigues, it is sealed, after the celebration, in the archives of a celebrated conservatory.

The history of music will one day have to record that "at that time, the whole world of Italian Art united to commemorate the death of a great man, with a performance in the church of St. Petronio in Bologna of a Requiem Mass, which was composed by several masters expressly for this occasion, and the original of which is preserved under seal in the Liceo Musicale of Bologna." The thing becomes an historical fact, not a musical circus. What difference does it make then, whether the composition be lacking in unity, or whether one part or another be more or less beautiful? What does it matter if neither the vanity of such and such a composer, nor the pride of a singer gets anything out of it? Individuals have nothing to do with this: it is enough for the day to arrive, for the solemnity to take place, in short for the *historical fact*, you understand, the *historical fact* to exist.

If we admit this, then it is the duty of all of us to do whatever we can to achieve our goal, without expecting either humble requests beforehand, or praise and thanks afterwards.

If this ceremony takes place, we will undeniably have performed a good patriotic and artistic work. If not, we shall have proved once more that we only take pains when there is a reward for our own interests and vanity involved, when articles and biographies burn incense before us and pay us shameless praise, when our names are bawled out in the theatre and dragged through the streets like a mountebank's in the public square. But when our own personalities are to disappear behind an idea, a noble, generous deed, then we withdraw under the mantle of our egotistical indifference, which is the scourge and ruin of our country.

To the Mayor of Busseto   *St. Agata, October 10, 1869* (A)

Dear Mr. Mayor: It is my desire to devote the pension of 600 lire a year which I shall receive, according to a Royal Decree of the 23rd of June, 1869, as Knight of the Order of Savoy for Civilian Merit, to the common weal. While reserving the right to make later such permanent arrangements as may prove best on the ground of experience, I have decided for the time being to donate the above-named sum of 600 lire for two prizes of 300 lire apiece to be awarded at the end of the next school year, 1869-70. The first to that needy young man who shall have shown the greatest gifts and industry in the final examinations of his last school year, according to the present school regulations. The second to that needy scholar of the girls' school in Busseto, who has passed her final examinations in the same manner.

I shall have these 600 lire paid over in good time into the Town Treasury of Busseto. The details of this endowment I leave entirely to the regulations which Your Honor will set up in common with the local school commission. I am your devoted servant.

To Giulio Ricordi   *St. Agata, October 13, 1869* (A)

Dear Giulio Ricordi: Just as I was against advancing the date of performance of the Requiem Mass for Rossini before, so I am opposed to having it postponed now. The ceremony has no *raison d'être* except on the anniversary of his death. Otherwise it becomes just one of the usual concerts. Furthermore, if it can't be given now, it will be even harder to do in December. Orchestra and chorus in December?

Under the present circumstances, the commission has, in my opinion, only one course to take: announce publicly that the pains taken to obtain the necessary material for a performance of this Mass were in vain, and at the same time return the compositions to each of the composers with many thanks for the interest they have taken in the project. The expenses the commission has incurred up to now should be, as is quite natural, charged to me. Send me the bill and let's forget the whole business.

To Giulio Ricordi   *St. Agata, October 27, 1869* (A)

Dear Giulio: It would be well for the commission to publish the reasons why the Mass for Rossini is not to be performed in Bologna, in order to avoid useless gossip in case the Mass should be performed later somewhere else.

I am still of the same opinion. If the Mass does not take place:

1. In Bologna,
2. On the anniversary of his death, then it has no meaning at all, and it is just one of the usual concerts. This was, and still is my opinion, but it should carry no particular weight

[266]

because, after all, I am neither more nor less than one of several composers, who has contributed his piece of music. So the commission has the full right to do and arrange everything as it thinks best.

This said, allow me to make a few remarks, half in confidence.—If the Mass is given in Milan for example, will we find sufficient forces who are capable of an imposing performance?

The average opera chorus lacks the necessary musical skill (I am not speaking of style, which depends on the conductor). A fugue is not as easy to perform as the *Rataplan* in "La Forza del Destino." In Bologna, thanks to the *cappella* of the city itself and of the neighboring cities, it was easier to find the necessary material, and Mariani could have been of great assistance in this. But he has failed in his duties both as a friend and as an artist.—And in Milan, who would conduct the chorus and orchestra? It cannot and should no longer be Mariani,—and all this is quite aside from the other difficulties which I won't mention for the sake of brevity, but which would make the performance extremely difficult. We, and I most of all, have made a *fiasco* at Bologna, a fiasco of which no one need be ashamed, but don't let us risk making another at Milan.

To Camille Du Locle Genoa, December 7, 1869 (A)

My dear Du Locle: Thank you for "Froufrou." I read the play in one sitting. If, as the *Revue* says, the whole thing were as distinguished and original as the first three acts are, it would be extremely fine; but the last two acts descend to the commonplace, though they are effective, extraordinarily so. Good as "Froufrou" is, I would, if I had to work for Paris, prefer to Meilhac's and Halévy's *cuisine* (as you call it), another, a more refined, more piquant one: that of Sardou, with Du Locle to write the verse! But *hélas!* it's neither the hard work of writing an opera, nor the taste of the Parisian public that holds me back, but the certainty that I can never succeed in having my music done in Paris the way I want it. How curious that a composer must always find all his plans crossed and his ideas misunderstood! In your opera houses (this is not meant to be an epigram) there are too many connoisseurs! Everyone wants to pass judgment according to the light of his own wisdom, according to his own taste, and worst of all, according to a *system,* without taking any account of the character and individuality of the composer. Everyone wants to express an opinion, give voice to a doubt, and if a composer lives long enough in this atmosphere of doubt, he cannot help being shaken in his convictions, and then he begins to correct and alter his work, or rather to spoil it. And so instead of a work in one piece, the final result is a *mosaic,* and however fine, it remains a *mosaic.*—You may reply that a lot of master-pieces have come out of your Grand Opéra this way. Well, they may be masterpieces; but allow me to say that they would be much more perfect if this piecemeal work and these corrections were not obvious at every turn. Most certainly no one will deny the genius of Rossini. Well, in spite of his genius, "William Tell" betrays this fatal atmosphere of the Paris Grand Opéra, sometimes, if not as frequently as with other composers, you have the feeling that there is too much here, too little there, that the work does not flow with the freedom and assurance of say, the "Barber." I have no intention of belittling what you have achieved. All I mean is that it's quite impossible for me to crawl under the Caudine yoke of your

French theatres again. I know perfectly well that success is impossible for me if I can't write as my heart dictates, free of any outside influence whatsoever, without having to keep in mind that I'm writing for Paris and not for the inhabitants of, say the moon. Furthermore the singers would have to sing as I wish, not as they wish, and the chorus, which, to be sure, is extremely capable, would have to show the same good will. In short, everybody would have to follow me. A single will would have to rule throughout: my own. That may seem rather tyrannical to you, and perhaps it is. But if the work is an organic whole, it is built on a single idea and everything must contribute to the achievement of this unity. You may perhaps say that nothing stands in the way of all that in Paris. No! In Italy it can be done, or at least I can always do it; but in France: no. For example, if I come into the foyer of an Italian theatre with a new work, no one ventures to utter an opinion, to pass judgment, before understanding everything thoroughly. And no one would even dare to make inappropriate requests. There is respect for the work and for the composer, and decisions are left to the public. In the foyer of the Opéra on the other hand, everybody starts to whisper after the first four chords: *Oh, ce n'est pas bon . . . c'est commun, ce n'est pas de bon goût. . . . Ça n'ira pas à Paris.* What do such pitiable words as *commun . . . de bon goût . . . Paris* mean, if you're dealing with a real work of art, which should belong to the whole world!

The conclusion from all this is that I'm no composer for Paris. I don't know whether it's for lack of talent or not, but in any case my ideas of art are too different from those held in your country.

I believe in *inspiration;* you people believe in construction.

I don't object to your *criterion,* for the sake of argument, but I desire the *enthusiasm* that you lack, in feeling and in judging. I strive for *art,* in whatever form it may appear, but never for the *amusement, artifice* or *system* which you prefer. Am I wrong? Am I right? However it may be, I have reason enough to say that my ideas are completely different from yours, and still more: my backbone isn't pliable enough for me to give way and deny my convictions, which are profound and deeply rooted in me. And I should feel very badly, my dear Du Locle, if I wrote an opera for you which you might have to withdraw after a dozen performances, as Perrin did with "Don Carlos." If I were twenty years younger, I should say to you: "Perhaps later the character of your theatres will take a turn which will bring it nearer to my views." But time is rushing past, and for the present it's impossible for us to understand each other, unless something completely unforeseen should happen, which I can't imagine. If you come here (as you wrote my wife you might), we will talk about this much more in detail. If you don't come, I shall probably go to Paris for a while at the end of February. If you come to Genoa, we unfortunately can't offer you the *ravioli* again, for we haven't our Genoese cook anymore. But in any case, we won't let you die of hunger, and you'll be sure to find two friends who are fond of you and to whom your presence will be a real treat. Many greetings from us both to your charming Maria and a kiss for little Claire.

To Giulio Ricordi   *Genoa, December 27, 1869* (A)

Dear Giulio: I am making every effort to convince myself that it would be right to have the Mass for Rossini performed, but I haven't succeeded. The same cursed question keeps popping up in my mind: "Why should it be performed?" For the sake of the justified self-esteem of the composers? . . . But what need have they of it, they, who are famous for so many other works? To make an important musical work known to the public? But let me ask *sotto voce:* can this Mass stand comparison with the other famous Requiem Masses, which themselves are perhaps not such masterworks as the world pretends to believe? If it could, then I too would be reconciled to the idea of its being performed.—But not in the church of St. Antonio, nor in the Conservatory Hall. You will never achieve performances of solemn grandeur in those places. I hate their shrill acoustics which never permit either a real *piano* or a full *forte.* Everything sounds hollow and noisy. For those halls there should be six first violins, six second violins, six violas, six 'celli, four double basses, and wind instruments without trumpets or trombones. So if the work is of grand proportions, this material is too scant. If the material is adapted to the work, the effect it will be *gross,* not great. But if you still want to present the Mass think of something else . . . think of some excuse . . . a benefit . . . and give it . . . at . . . La Scala!!—*"Rash men!"* cries the shade of the composer of the "Stabat Mater" and the "Petite Messe"!!— Yes, sir, as rash as you like, but there's no help for it. Either you must fight or not get into the battle in the first place. In other words (this also *sotto voce*) can our Mass stand comparison with Rossini's two works? I'm not speaking of their religious character, not of the contrapuntal science of the fugues. There can be two opinions about that, and I am something of a skeptic, but I do believe in the musical value of those two works, and especially in the solo numbers, the disposal and arrangement of which is so great as to place Rossini perhaps even above the ancient Italian composers.

Conclusion: can the new Mass stand up against those of Mozart, Cherubini, etc. . . . with the "Stabat," the "Petite Messe"? . . . Yes? . . . Then give it. No? . . . Then *pax vobis.*

To Carlino del Signore   *Genoa, 1870* (A)

Dear Carlino del Signore: I have nothing but the highest praise for the pains you are taking for your friend, but you will understand, my dear Carlino, that it would be embarrassing for me to answer Mariani's letter. What could I say? Reproach him? Accuse him? . . . He can always reply: "I have done nothing that was wrong." I am not accusing Mariani of doing anything that was wrong; I accuse him of having done nothing at all. No one has cast any aspersions upon him, and anyhow when deeds speak, words make no impression on me. He quotes my letter from Pesaro to justify his strange and unaccustomed silence. But this very letter said nothing other than: "Whoever is a real artist should assist in the realization of the project, etc. . . ." and it implied, "It will also be a test of our friendship." If there was anything in the project which displeased him, he should have refused the assignment which was given him by the commission of Milan. But once having accepted it, he was doubly bound to do something. What did he do? Nothing! . . . All right, I accept the deed, but I cannot accept the idea that he has acted as an artist and a friend should.

Mariani asks to speak with me. Very well, but I wish you to be present at the interview.

Good-bye, my dear Carlino, excuse this too lengthy chatter.

To Camille Du Locle　　　　　*St. Agata, June 2, 1870* (A)

*The "Egyptian affair" refers to "Aida." Its antecedent history
(cf. second letter following) was this: After twice refusing,
Verdi decided to write the opera for the gala opening of the
Suez Canal, as the Khedive wished; following an outline of
the plot presented to him by Du Locle. The outline and the
idea originated with the French Egyptologist, Mariette, who
had received the title of Bey from the Khedive for his services.
Du Locle and Verdi worked out the plan in French prose at St.
Agata. The Italian author Ghislanzoni, a physician, double-
bass player, operatic baritone, journalist, and novelist, was to
put it into Italian verse. But Verdi actually ordered each scene
according to his own specifications, even setting the metres
himself. The letters containing these specifications occupy
fifty printed pages in the Italian edition. The most important
are included here. Ghislanzoni (1824-1893) had already
helped with the revision of "Don Carlos" and "La Forza."
The publisher first learned the plan for "Aida" in the letter
of June 25.*

Dear Du Locle: Here I am with the Egyptian affair. Above
all you must give me time to compose the opera, because we're
dealing with a work of vast proportions (just as if it were
for the *Grande Boutique*), and because the Italian poet must
first think of the ideas which the characters are to express,
and then shape the poem from them. If we assume then that
all this works out in time for me, my stipulations are as
follows:

1.　I have the libretto written at my expense.

2.　I send, also at my expense, some one to Cairo to prepare the opera and conduct it.

3. I send you a copy of the score and transfer therewith to you the exclusive rights to the libretto and the composition, but only for Egypt. I retain the rights to the libretto and music for all other parts of the world.

As compensation I receive the sum of fifteen thousand francs, payable in Paris at the Rothschild Bank, as soon as I turn over the score.

Here is a letter for you, as dry and sober as a cheque but this is a business matter, and you, my dear Du Locle, will excuse me if I don't digress any further now. Forgive me, and be assured of my devotion.

To Camille Du Locle   *St. Agata, June 18, 1870* (F)

Dear Du Locle: I am impatient to see you—first, for the pleasure of seeing you, secondly because I think that in a very short time we shall agree on those modifications which, it seems to me, it would be well to make in "Aida." I have already considered them, and shall submit my ideas to you.

I asked Muzio if he would be disposed to return to Cairo in case we made a contract. Now that I know that he is negotiating with Bagier, I would not for all the world have him turn down an engagement at Paris, which would be much more advantageous for him.

To Giulio Ricordi   *St. Agata, June 25, 1870* (A)

Dear Giulio: Are you at the waters of S. Pellegrino? If you aren't, can you postpone going there for a few days to come here with Ghislanzoni? This is what it is all about:

Last year I was invited to write an opera in a far distant country. I answered no. When I was in Paris, Du Locle was commissioned to speak to me about it again and to offer me a good sum of money. Still I answered no. A month later he sent me a printed outline of a plot, telling me it was written by a powerful personage (which I don't believe), that it seemed good to him, and that I should read it. I found it excellent, and I answered that I would put it to music on such and such conditions. Three days after the telegram he answered: "Accepted." Then Du Locle immediately came here, and together we worked out the conditions for the contract, studied the outline of the plot, and made the modifications we thought necessary. Du Locle left with the conditions for the contract and with the modifications, to submit them to the powerful and unknown author. I studied the outline further, and I made, and still am making, more changes. Now we must think about the libretto, or rather about having the verses done, because all we need now are the verses. Could Ghislanzoni do this work for me, and does he want to? It is not original work, explain this to him carefully. It is only a question of writing the verses, which, you understand (that is, I tell this to you), will be paid very generously. Answer me immediately, and be prepared to come here with Ghislanzoni as soon as M. Rogier, whom I'm expecting any day, leaves St. Agata. I shall wire you.

In the meanwhile study the outline I am sending you, with Ghislanzoni. Don't lose it, because only two of them exist: this one, and the other which is in the hands of the author.

Don't say anything because the contract has not yet been signed. Anyhow, there's no use talking about it now. . . . We'll talk about it here.

To Cesare De Sanctis   *Genoa, August 10, 1870* (B)

*This letter, like everything Verdi writes on political condi-
tions, has an almost prophetic character.*

I'm very grieved over the French defeats. I've lived too
long in France not to understand how insupportable the
French have made themselves with their insolence, their
pride, and their boasting. But anyone who thinks seriously
and who feels himself a real Italian must rise above these
pinpricks of *amour propre* and must remember that Prussia
once declared that "the seas of Venice and Trieste belong to
Germany!" Prussia victorious means: a permanently constituted German Empire; Austria destroyed and relegated to
a corner of Europe; the Adriatic Sea as far as the Adige River
in the possession of the Empire. Just think what would become of the rest of Italy! This is what we shall have to fear
later and what frightens me now. And we bewilder ourselves
meanwhile by shouting death to one and hurrah to the other
without even knowing why.

In spite of the fact that the situation is very grave, I still
hope. I place my hope in the valor of the French soldier,
although I fear the strategic knowledge of the German.

Farewell. Write me at St. Agata.

(PEPPINA'S POSTSCRIPT)

My dear Cesarino,   (B)

I am sorry not to see you at St. Agata, and I am even
more grieved for the reason that makes it necessary for you to
stay near your family. I shan't talk about the war, but tell you
only that I no longer believe in progress if it is manifested in
machines for the destruction of humanity. The thought of all

those dead, all that slaughter, and so much desolation, over-
comes me! Poor mothers, poor wives, poor families and poor
Italy, if things keep on at this pace! Best wishes to your
Teresa, a kiss to your children, and a handshake to you from
your affectionate friend,

GIUSEPPINA

To Camille Du Locle   *St. Agata, August 25, 1870* (A)

*Verdi was deeply perturbed at the French defeats, forgetting
his old grudge against France. His rage at Prussia was repeatedly expressed. Thus, the letter of September 8, which
is a parody of Wilhelm I's victory communiqués.*

Dear Du Locle: In these very sad hours we are now living
through, I really wouldn't have dared to speak to you about
the contract for Cairo. But you asked me for it, and here it is
with my signature, but with two reservations, two articles,
which you will think fair, and which you will have approved
by Signor Mariette:

I accept the present agreement with the following modifications:

 1. The payments shall be made, etc., etc.

 2. If because of some unforeseen eventuality which has
nothing to do with me, that is, which is *not my fault,* the
opera should not be given at the Cairo theatre during
January, 1871, I shall have the right to perform it elsewhere six months later.

You will have the kindness, I hope, to request the fifty
thousand francs for me, for which I send you the receipt.
From this amount take two thousand francs, and donate them
where you think they will do the most good to succour your

poor, brave, wounded soldiers. With the remaining forty-eight thousand, buy me Italian bonds. Keep the papers with you and give them to me the first time we meet again.

To Antonio Ghislanzoni   St. Agata, August 22, 1870 (A)

Cabaletta (properly cavatinetta): the short, usually fast closing section of an aria or duet.

Signor Ghislanzoni: I received the finale yesterday, the duet today. It's good except for the *recitative* which, in my opinion (forgive me), could have been put in even fewer words. But I repeat, it can very well remain as it is.

This isn't the time to write to Mariette, but I've already thought of something for the consecrational scene. If it doesn't seem appropriate to you, we can look further. But in the meantime it seems to me that we might make a rather effective musical scene of this. The piece would be composed of a *litany,* intoned by the priestesses, to which the priests respond; a sacred dance with slow, sad music; a short *recitative,* powerful and solemn, like a Biblical psalm; and a prayer of two stanzas, spoken by the priest and repeated by everyone. I would like it to have a serene grandeur, particularly the first stanza, so that it may differ as far as possible from the other choruses in the finale of the Introduction and the finale of the second act, in both of which there seems to be a whiff of the *Marseillaise.*

I think the *litanies* should be composed (for the thousandth time, forgive my boldness) of short stanzas, each with one long line and one five-syllable line, or (and perhaps this would be better so as to be able to say everything) two eight-syllable lines. The five-syllable line would be the *Ora pro nobis.* Thus there would be short strophes of three verses

[278]

apiece, six in all, and that would be more than enough to do a piece with.

Be reassured, I have no aversion to *cabalettas,* but I must always have a situation and justification for them. In the duet of "A Masked Ball" there was a magnificent justification. After that whole scene, if I say so myself, an outburst of love was inevitable.

To Antonio Ghislanzoni   *St. Agata, September 8, 1870* (A)

Signor Ghislanzoni: Since you left I have worked very little, I have only done the march which is very long and full of detail. The entrance of the King with his court, Amneris, and priests: the chorus of the people, of the women; then a priests' chorus (to be added); the entrance of the army in full war-equipment; dancing girls who are to carry holy vessels, treasure, etc.; Egyptian girls who dance and sing; and finally, Radames with the whole raft of impedimenta—and all this constitutes one piece, the march.

But you must help me, and arrange it so that the chorus sings something in praise of Egypt and the King, and also of Radames. So the first eight verses will have to be changed a little; the second eight, those of the women, are all right; and there must be eight more for the priests: "We have triumphed with the help of divine providence. The enemy has surrendered. May God continue his assistance." (See the telegrams of King Wilhelm!) I can make this clearer if I sketch the scene:

PEOPLE: Glory to Egypt, to Isis.
   And to the Pharaoh. . . .
   Light. . . .
   He will rule the world.

[279]

Glory to the Warrior. . . .

. . .

Twine the myrtle and the laurel
On the brow. . . .

WOMEN: With hymns, etc. (as it stands)

You take care of the sense and the rhyme.

I think the ten-syllable lines you sent me will work out very well. If the other stanzas succeed as well it will be really excellent.

In the *recitative* that now follows there is a place where the situation demands an additional musical phrase. After the words: "Hear me, oh king; hear thou too, oh youth, a wise counsel," have the eleven-syllable lines stop, and add four lyric lines of seven or eight syllables. These verses must be solemn and sententious; they are sung by the priest. At the close it would be good to have the first stanza of the people's chorus repeated: "Glory," etc.; a four-line stanza; priests . . . ; a four-line stanza; all the others; another four-line stanza. Finale. Amen [. . . .]

To Antonio Ghislanzoni *October 8, 1870* (A)

Dear Ghislanzoni: Let me say this once and for all: I am never criticizing your verses, which are always good, I am only expressing my opinion about the stage effect. The duet between Radames and Aida, in my opinion, has turned out much less happily than that between the father and daughter. Perhaps that is due to the situation, perhaps to the form, which is more commonplace than that of the preceding duet. Certainly that string of vocal passages, all of eight lines, spoken by one and repeated by the other, are not calculated to keep the dialogue moving. And then the parts between these vocal passages are also rather cold.

At the beginning of the duet I rather prefer the first verses to the *recitative,* which is too dry. [. . . .]

Then the verses:

> "Amneris's anger would be terrible.
> With my father I should have to die."

are not suited to the stage, that is, they give the singer no opportunity for acting; the audience's attention is not held, and the situation is not effective. There ought to be more development, and approximately the following ideas should be expressed:

AIDA: "And do you not fear the anger of Amneris? Do you not know that her vengeance would smite me like a thunderbolt, would smite my father, and fall upon us all?

RADAMES: I shall protect you.

AIDA: In vain! You could not! But if you love me, there remains to us one way of escape.

RADAMES: What way?

AIDA: To flee.

You may say: "But those are trifles, my verses say the same thing." Very true: trifles, if you like. But phrases like "would smite me, would smite my father, and fall upon us all. . . . In vain. . . . You could not. . . ." and such, if they are only well delivered always hold the attention of the audience and sometimes produce a great effect.

The eight verses of Aida, "We flee," and the first four of Radames are good. But in the four which have been added, I don't much like the idea of the bride. Wouldn't it be better to say, as in the sketch: "Here, where I was born, where I lived, where I became the saviour of my country?" You have left out Aida's outburst:

> "And my gods shall be your gods,
> Home is where one loves."

That must be said either in the verses you have already done or, if you would rather, as *recitative*.

Then the transition which follows must be given more significance:

AIDA: Go! You do not love me.

RADAMES: I not love you! Never have men on earth, never have the gods in heaven loved more passionately.

(Whether these or other words, does not matter; but the phrase must have a turn that grips you! Theatre . . . theatre!)

AIDA: Go, go! At the altar your Amneris waits for you.

RADAMES: No—never!

AIDA: Never—you say? Then fall . . . (etc. to the end of the duet.)

To Antonio Ghislanzoni   *Monday* (A)

Dear Ghislanzoni: In reading over the scenario of Aida, I find the fourth act duet between Amneris and Radames has been cut and changed according to your suggestions.

I am sending it to you, not to use as a model (I have already told you to work out this scene as seems best to you) but in order that you may take over any good turn of phrase, any appropriate outburst of feeling you may like. I repeat now for the twentieth time that *the only thing I'm looking for is success*. And that is why I take the liberty of suggesting anything that seems to me necessary to achieve that goal. So have patience. Here is the duet:

SCENE 2

(If we begin with a *recitative* here, it would be hard to find a place where we could change to song. I think we might begin immediately with the lyric verses, whatever metre you please, and then keep the same metre right up to the end. But quite according to the poet's inclination.)

AMNERIS: Soon the priests will be assembled to judge you. The accusation weighs heavy upon you, heavy will be your punishment. But if you recant your crime before your judges, I will try to move the heart of the King and obtain your pardon.

RADAMES: No! The judges will never hear a word from me in self-justification. You, O Queen, know that I am guiltless; although my lips spoke too carelessly, my heart is pure. And yet it is true that I betrayed my country. Remorse gnaws my soul, and my blasted hopes make me hate my life; I wish for only one thing now—and that is death!

(If the following words seem too violent, they can be toned down. But the speeches of Amneris must be passionate, fiery!)

AMNERIS: Death! But I wish you to live, do you hear? Oh, you do not know how great my love for you is. You know nothing of my days of fear and anguish, my endless nights. For you I would renounce the throne, the King, my fatherland.

RADAMES: Mad with love for her, I too denied my duty, the gods, the King, my country.

[283]

AMNERIS: (angered) Do not speak to me of her!

RADAMES: What? And you want me to live? You, who were witness of my shame, you, who were the cause of my misfortune, and perhaps of her death?

AMNERIS: Her death? No! She is alive!

RADAMES: What did you say? She is alive?

AMNERIS: That night, only her father was caught, and killed in the fighting. But she fled; we have not yet been able to find her.

RADAMES: (aside) Oh gods, let her reach her country safely, and may my love banish the memory of my misfortune! (Much feeling here, there must be a place for a beautiful vocal passage at this point!)

AMNERIS: But if I save you, swear to me that you will never see her again.

(There is no danger of being reminded of "Norma" here, if only the verse form is different.)

RADAMES: Do not ask that!

AMNERIS: Renounce Aida!

RADAMES: I cannot.

AMNERIS: Once again: renounce Aida—or you shall die.

RADAMES: Then I will die.

AMNERIS: Oh rash one! You do not know that I can love boundlessly—but that I can hate no less terribly. Ah, be off! Away! Let justice take its course! May your death appease the anger of the gods!

(Not until here and in the following should the metre be changed. Do a stanza of four or six lines for a *cabaletta*.)

RADAMES: Pour all your wrath upon my head! Death will be sweet if I die for her.

To Antonio Ghislanzoni   *Saturday* (A)

Dear Ghislanzoni: Amneris's outburst is marvelous. Now this piece is finished too. I shall not go to Genoa until the opera is completely finished. We still lack the last piece, which has to be written in score; the fourth act; and then the whole opera has to be orchestrated from beginning to end. Work for a month at least! So have patience and arrange it so that you can come to St. Agata and you won't be rushed, for we must get the whole libretto in order.

Here we are at the last scene [. . . .] Aida is already there too and she must appear as soon as possible.

After Aida's beautiful lines there is nothing more we can have Radames say. I should first do eight seven-syllable lines for Radames with this content: "You must die! So innocent, and so beautiful, so young! And I cannot save you. . . . Oh, agony! My fatal love was your undoing," etc. etc.

At the end I should like to avoid the conventional death struggle, and not have words like these: "My senses fail me. I go on before you. Wait for me! She is dead! And I still live!" etc., etc. I would like something sweet, ethereal, a quite short duet, a *farewell to life*. Aida should then sink quietly into Radames' arms. Meanwhile Amneris, kneeling on the stone of the vault, should sing a *Requiescat in pace,* etc.

I shall put down the last scene to make myself clearer.

LAST SCENE

The stone closes my grave forevermore. I shall never again see the light of day. Never again Aida.

Aida, where are you? May you live happily. May you never learn of my terrible fate! A sigh . . . Here?

A shade! A ghost! No, this is a living being!
Heaven! Aida!

(These naturally are only words, as I have jotted them down.
It is for you to make beautiful verses out of them. The same
holds for the following:)

AIDA: It is I!

RADAMES: You here? Tell me—how?

AIDA: My heart knew your sentence.

      For three days I have waited here.

      And now, far from human eyes

      I will die with you. (One more verse.)

RADAMES: Die, you, so guiltless? Die?

(Eight beautiful seven-syllable lines.)

AIDA: See there the angel of death (and so forth as in the
text of the finished opera.—Editor's note).

Chant and dance of the priests and priestesses in the interior of the temple.

AIDA: What mournful chants!

RADAMES: It is the triumph of the priests.

AIDA: It is the hymn for our death.

RADAMES: Even my strong arms cannot heave you aside, oh
fatal stone.

AIDA: In vain! Our fate is sealed. No hope smiles to us
any more. We must die!

RADAMES: It is true, it is true!

TOGETHER: Oh life, farewell, farewell to earthly love.

      Farewell, pain and joy.

      Already I see the dawn of eternity.

      Inseparable is our bond in Heaven!

(Four beautiful twelve-syllable lines! But the accent must fall on the fourth and eighth syllables in order to make them suited for singing!)

Aida expires in Radames's arms. Amneris, in deep mourning, comes from the interior of the temple. She kneels on the stone that seals the vault.

AMNERIS: Rest in peace
       Thou beloved soul.

When you have arranged this scene for me and sent it to me, come two days later yourself to St. Agata. In the meantime, I shall have sketched the music. [. . . .]

To Antonio Ghislanzoni (A)

Dear Ghislanzoni: I received your verses. They're beautiful, but they don't seem right for me at all. Since you sent them so late, I had already composed the piece, in order to lose no time, to the terrible verses that you received from me.

Come quickly, immediately, at once! Then we will arrange everything. Don't be afraid of the last scene! Only, it doesn't stir one deeply yet. It is cold steel!

To Cesare De Sanctis   *St. Agata, September 2, 1870* (B)

So, in spite of her *blague* and her defects, may God help France and let her keep her original standing among the nations of Europe. I repeat, in spite of her defects and her errors, she is a nation with a heart; and she is still worthy because of her philanthropy, her progress, her civilization, in short, for every reason she is still worthy to remain what she was, the head and the heart of Europe.

To Opprandino Arrivabene

St. Agata, September 13, 1870 (A)

Verdi wished that Italy had come to the aid of France, in gratitude for the help given by Napoleon III in 1859.

Dear Arrivabene: Thank you for your very nice letter, and I'm glad to hear that you're well. I am depressed by the bad turn of the war. I lament France's misfortunes and I'm afraid a terrible future is in store for us: both the land and the people of the North terrify me. Personally, I should have liked our government to follow a more generous policy and pay a debt of gratitude. I know people will say: Yes, but what about the European war? . . . But the European war is unavoidable, and if France were saved we should be safe too.

I'm writing, as you know. I wish I didn't have to, but I can't help it.

I shall probably go to Parma and it will be a pleasure for me to admire your brother's pictures.

To Clarina Maffei   *St. Agata, September 30, 1870* (A)

The disaster of France fills my heart, as well as yours, with despair. Yes, the *blague,* the impertinence, the presumption of the French was and is (in spite of all their misfortunes) unbearable. But after all France gave the modern world its freedom and civilization. And if it falls, let us not deceive ourselves, all our liberties will fall, and then falls our civilization too. Let our litterateurs and our politicians praise the knowledge and science and even (God forgive them) the art of these victors. But if they would only look a little below the surface, they would see that the old blood of the Goths

OIL PAINTING BY EUGEN FELIX *Courtesy Musical Courier*

GIUSEPPE VERDI, 1872

still flows in their veins, that they are monstrously proud, hard, intolerant, rapacious beyond measure and scornful of everything that is not German. A people of intellect without heart—a strong people but they have no grace.—And that King who is always talking about God and Divine Providence, with whose help he is destroying the best part of Europe! He thinks he is predestined to reform the morals and punish the vices of the modern world!!! What a fine messenger of God he is!

Old Attila (another emissary of God!) halted before the majesty of the capital of the old world. But this one here is about to bombard the capital of the modern world! And now that Bismarck is trying to make us believe Paris will be spared, I am more afraid than ever that it will be at least partly laid in ruins. Why? . . . I cannot imagine. Perhaps so that there may no longer be any such beautiful capital, since they themselves will never succeed in building its equal. Poor Paris! And last April I saw it still so gay, so beautiful, so shining!

What now? . . . I should have preferred to have our government follow a more generous policy, and pay a debt of gratitude. A hundred thousand of our men might have saved France. Anyhow I would rather have signed a peace after being defeated along with France, than to have been a passive spectator. That we are doing this will expose us to contempt some day. We shall not escape the European war and it will engulf us. It will not come tomorrow, but it is coming. An excuse is easily found . . . perhaps Rome . . . the Mediterranean . . . and then what about the Adriatic, which they have already proclaimed a German sea? . . .

The business in Rome is a great event, but it leaves me cold, perhaps because I feel that it might lead to internal as

[289]

well as external disaster; because I can't reconcile the idea of Parliament with the College of Cardinals, a free press with the Inquisition, civil law with the Syllabus; and because I am frightened at the way our government just goes ahead any old way, hoping that time will take care of everything. If tomorrow we should have a shrewd, adroit Pope, a really crafty fellow, such as Rome has often had, he would ruin us. A *Pope* and a *King of Italy*—I can't bear to see the two together, even in this letter.

The paper is giving out. Forgive this tirade! It is a release for me. I am very pessimistic. Even so I haven't told you half my qualms and fears. Farewell!

To Cesare De Sanctis   *Genoa, January 1, 1871* (B)

Saverio Mercadante, operatic composer and director of the Naples Conservatory, had died in December 1870. The professors at the Conservatory instructed Florimo to offer the post of Director to Verdi. Among the famous teachers of the Conservatory were: Alessandro Scarlatti (1659-1725, one of the most distinguished composers of his time); his pupil, Francesco Durante (1684-1755); Leonardo Leo (1694-1744). N. A. Zingarelli (1752-1837) is mentioned as one of the teachers who showed little understanding for the new trends of his day. Saverio Mercadante (1795-1870) was a pupil of his.

You too talk to me about your Conservatory? But how do you expect me to accept the position? How could I succeed, with my ideas, which certainly are not yours? You, who one day were so great and so progressive, and are now so "stationary"? Please note that when I use the word "stationary," I don't mean to be depreciative. Who knows? Perhaps you

[290]

are right and I wrong: but it's certain that I can't admit what is now acknowledged; and perhaps I would upset the whole structure which, so well founded by Scarlatti, Durante, Leo, etc., etc., has now been allowed to go almost to total ruin.

Is this possible with the retrogressive spirit which prevails? Didn't you see, two years ago when I proposed to adopt the normal diapason of Paris, how much opposition was put up by the whole orchestra and by the two principal conductors? And, strangely enough, in order to come to an agreement, a half-measure was offered me, and it was the most utter absurdity. We didn't understand each other then, and we would not understand each other now. If, in such a clear and obvious matter, there was so much objection, what would there not be concerning much more important things! At every moment I would hear some one say to me: "But Mercadante, but Zingarelli!"

Would you like me to answer: "Zingarelli, Mercadante, are two great names, two great masters, but they haven't done anything so far as the exigencies of the times are concerned; and in addition, they allowed those profound and austere studies which have been the glorious foundation of the school of Durante, Leo, etc., etc., to go to ruin."

It is impossible. Therefore I shall remain in my fields at St. Agata.

To Francesco Florimo   *Genoa, January 4, 1871* (A)

This letter closes with the famous sentence: "Torniamo all' antico: sara un progresso." On the basis of this letter a commission was appointed to reform musical instruction at all the Italian conservatories. Verdi unwillingly accepted the presidency of the commission.

Dear Florimo: If anything could flatter my vanity, it is the invitation to become Director of the Conservatory in Naples, as sent to me through you from the teachers of the Conservatory and other musicians of your city. It is very painful for me not to be able to answer this demonstration of confidence as I should like to. But with pressure of business, my habits, my love of independence, it would be impossible for me to undertake so weighty an office. You may say: "And what about art?" Of course; but I have done my best for art, and if I am to be able to go on doing something from time to time, I must be free of all other obligations. Otherwise you can imagine how very proud I should be to occupy the place held by such fathers of tradition as Alessandro Scarlatti, Durante, and Leo. It would be an honor for me to instruct the students in the weighty, vigorous, and lucid teachings of those fathers. I should have been able to stand, so to speak, with one foot in the past and the other in the present and future (for I am not afraid of the "Music of the Future"). And I should have said to the young pupils: "Practise the fugue constantly and persistently until you are weary of it and your hands are supple and strong enough to bend the music to your will. Thus you will learn assurance in composition, proper part-writing, unforced modulation. Study Palestrina and some few of his contemporaries. Then skip everybody up to Marcello, and pay particular attention to the *recitatives*. Attend but few performances of contemporary opera, and don't be seduced by the profusion of harmonic and instrumental beauties, nor by the chord of the diminished seventh, that easy subterfuge for all of us who can't write four measures without half a dozen sevenths."

When they have gone thus far and have achieved a broad

literary background I would say finally to these young students: "Now lay your hands on your heart and go ahead and write. If you have the stuff of artists in you, you will be composers. In any case, you will not swell the legion of modern imitators and neurotics who seek and seek, but never really find, although they may do some good things." In singing I would have modern declamation taught along with time-honored studies. But to apply these few deceptively simple principles, it would be necessary to supervise the instruction so closely that twelve months a year would be almost too little. I have a house, business, property, and all, here—tell me yourself: how could I do it? So, my dear Florimo, will you express to your colleagues and the other musicians in your beautiful Naples my deep regrets that I cannot accept an offer which does me such honor? I hope you may be able to find a man who is, above all, learned and a strict teacher. Liberties and mistakes in counterpoint can be condoned and are even sometimes quite good . . . in the theater. But not in the conservatory. Let us turn back to the old masters: progress will be the result.

A warm farewell! I remain devotedly yours.

To His Excellency Draneth Bey, Cairo [*Written in French*]
Genoa, January 5, 1871 (A)

Your Excellency: It is quite true, I did instruct M. Muzio to go to Cairo to conduct the rehearsals of "Aida," and I was on the point of signing an agreement to do the same opera at the Scala in February, with Mme. Fricci, Tiberini, etc. I did not then know that Mariette Bey was shut up in Paris, and with him the settings, costumes, etc., for "Aida." The moment this news came to my knowledge, I hastened to inform the management of the Scala in order to suspend all preparations for the new opera.

At present I am in Genoa, and I have not got with me the contract with Mariette Bey, but the contract (as I remember perfectly well) simply says that I was to deliver the score of "Aida" in good time for performance at Cairo during January 1871, and if through unforeseen circumstances, beyond my control, *the opera should not be presented in Cairo during the month of January 1871, I would have the right to present it elsewhere six months later.* This is why I wrote to Cairo the letter Your Excellency knows of, in which I said that, the opera being finished, I had made arrangements to send it to Cairo in December, 1870, so that the first performance might take place during January of 1871.

Now, owing to the position that the disastrous events which are ruining France and Europe have put us in, Your Excellency can assure His Highness the Khedive that I would never have exercised my rights (even if I had any) at a moment like this, and although with great regret, I shall give up my desire to put on my opera in Cairo and at the Scala this season.

I must however bring to Your Excellency's notice that the management of the Scala has not given up the intention of performing "Aida" in the coming Carnival season, 1871-72, and with this end in view it has even engaged several artists whom I suggested. Consequently I would ask Your Excellency to let me know what arrangements you plan to make for the performance of "Aida," so that I on my part can look after its future and my own interests. I shall need, Your Excellency, to know when I must deliver the score, and when it will be given in Cairo. Awaiting the favor of your reply,

I have the honor to be Your Excellency's devoted servant.
P.S. I believe it may be well to remind Your Excellency that
the performance of "Aida" requires two prima donnas of
first-rate capacity—one a soprano, the other a mezzo-soprano;
a dramatic tenor; a baritone; two basses, etc.

To Maestro Nicola De Giosa   Genoa, January 5, 1871 (A)

*Originally, Nicola de Giosa was to have conducted the
première of "Aida" in Cairo. Finally, after Verdi had unsuc-
cessfully suggested Mariani, Giovanni Bottesini undertook
the task.*

I am in receipt of your esteemed letter of December 22,
and before answering it in detail I would like to say that
there cannot be any *misunderstanding* between us, because
I have never had the good fortune to entertain relations with
you except in the question of pitch in Naples two years ago;
and because it is difficult to have misunderstandings with me
as I stick to my own business. On that subject I always say
frankly what I think, precisely to avoid misunderstandings.
To return to the question of the pitch, it is true, we did not
agree then, and I see that we still do not. I wanted to establish a standard pitch, and make its use as universal as possible. You proposed a compromise that was a remedy worse
than the evil. I wanted only one pitch in the musical world;
you wanted to add another to the too many already in existence.

It is quite true that I have commissioned Muzio to go to
Cairo and stage "Aida" (in accordance with a clause of my
contract) and I do not see how you can find his going preju-
dicial to you. Let me say to you, Signor Maestro, that you
see this as a purely personal matter, and I see it purely as an

artistic matter. Let me make myself clear: You know better than I do that operas nowadays are written with scenic and musical intentions, so many and various that it is almost impossible to interpret them; and I do not think anyone can take offense if the composer, for the first production of a work, sends someone who has carefully studied the work under the direction of the composer himself. I must say that if I were to produce an opera by a colleague for the first time I would not feel in the least humiliated but would be the first to inquire what his intentions were, no matter whether I asked the composer himself or someone else.

Possibly you will not be of my opinion this time either; but in my case it is not merely an opinion, it is a profound conviction born of twenty-eight years' experience.

To Minister Correnti   *Genoa, February 1, 1871* (A)

Your Excellency: I do not know how to begin this letter, so great is my regret at being unable to accept the invitation extended by Your Excellency to preside over a Committee for the reform of musical study. You must allow me, Mr. Minister, to confine myself for the present to the Naples Conservatory, on which the attention of everybody is now concentrated, and which is to be the principal object of the reorganization of studies. I am firmly convinced that the reform can be carried out only by the maestro who is chosen as Director. If he is a real musician and enthusiastic about his mission, it will be unnecessary, and perhaps even awkward, for a Commission to establish standards of instruction. If he is not, all the studies and all the Commission's work will be useless. To confirm my statement, let me add that there were no fixed standards of instruction in the old Conservatories of Naples directed by Durante and Leo. They themselves laid out the path to be followed. Those paths diverged at some points, but both were good. Nor were there fixed standards later under Fenaroli, whose *partimenti* are now universally adopted. The same was true of the *Liceo Musicale* of Bologna at the time of Padre Martini, a name revered by all Italians and foreigners alike, among the latter being Gluck and Mozart. The Conservatory of Paris, on the other hand, has excellent rules; but in spite of that it has produced good results only when the Director was a man of great capacity: Cherubini.

Being convinced, as I had the honor of telling you above, that reforms can only be accomplished by the Director, I must ask to be excused, Your Excellency, for my inability to accept the honor of presiding over the Commission appointed to reform our courses of musical study. I hope Your Excellency will not attach great weight to my opinion. I may be mistaken, and I hope, if it is for the good of art, that I am greatly mistaken.

To Maestro Alberto Mazzucato
Genoa, February 4, 1871 (A)

It will be remembered that Verdi was to contribute the "Libera" for the intended Requiem Mass for Rossini. When this came to the knowledge of Mazzucato, a professor at the Milan Conservatory, he wrote Verdi an enthusiastic letter, the reply to which follows. This praise strengthened Verdi's determination to write the whole Mass, and the Requiem was the result.

If one could still decently blush at my age, I would blush at the praise you give my work; I will not deny that praise from a composer and critic of your standing carries great weight and it flatters my self-esteem not a little. And such is the ambition of a composer that your words almost inspired in me a desire to write the complete Mass some day—the more so since, with some further elaboration, I would find the *Requiem* and *Dies Irae* already complete, their recapitulation already having been written in the *Libera.* So consider and regret the deplorable consequences your praise might have! But have no fear, it is a temptation that will pass, like so many others. I don't like useless things. There are so many Masses for the dead already!!! It is useless to add another.

To Dr. Angelo Carrara *Genoa, February 7, 1871* (A)

Your wish to ignore all the things that have been said against me in Busseto for the past twenty years is a highly laudable one. Not to go too far back, ask your cousin Leopoldo, who may be willing to amuse you with an account of the kindnesses lavished on me by him and others in connection with the Società Operaia before, around and after October 9, 1870, a time when the philharmonic part of the society were pleased to offer me the tribute of some concerts.

In Busseto (as you yourself will agree) there are ignorant people; all right, so there are everywhere. There are malicious people; their equivalent may be found anywhere. Fortunately I am even-tempered enough to laugh at them and to be above their spite. But no one who has a sense of dignity, and calls himself a friend of mine, can possibly advise me to accept ostentatious demonstrations of respect from a town where the scurrilous slander of the few would not have been so long-lived unless they had been fed by the approval of the many. I have heard the same refrain for the past twenty years; they may repeat it for twenty years more, and then begin all over again. I can live quite happily without bothering about them. But I do think it would be only decent of them to stop talking about me at all, either kindly or spitefully.

Let me add in conclusion what you already know, that I have never seen the use of a theater in Busseto. And I do not believe now that the establishment of a Philharmonic-Dramatic Society would be lasting or even feasible. Being convinced of this, I cannot lend my name to a society in whose practicability I do not believe. I might at most be a contributing member, but never honorary president.

To Giuseppe Piroli   *Genoa, February 20, 1871* (A)

Dear Piroli: In view of the musical conditions and tendencies of our day, the guiding principles which should be adopted by a commission for the reorganization of musical instruction are, in my opinion, as follows. These are quite general ideas which I have often told you, both in conversation and in writing, and which I mentioned in my letter to Faccio.

I shall speak only about composition and singing, because it seems to me that there is little to reform in the instrumental classes, which have always produced excellent results.

For young composers I should wish a long and thorough course of counterpoint in all its ramifications. Study of old music, both sacred and profane. But it must be kept in mind that not all old music is beautiful either, and therefore it is necessary to choose.

No study of the moderns! Many people will think this strange. But today, when I hear and see so many works put

[299]

together the way a bad tailor puts clothes together on a standard model, I cannot budge in my opinion. I know, of course,
that many modern works could be cited which are as good as
the old, but what of that?

When a young man has gone through a severe course of
training, when he has achieved his own style, then, if he sees
fit, he can study these works, and he will no longer be in
danger of turning into a mere imitator. It may be objected:
"But who will teach him instrumentation? Who will teach
him the theoretical aspects of composition?"—His own head
and heart, if he has any.

For singers, I should want a wide knowledge of music,
exercises in voice production, long courses in *solfège* as in
the past, exercises for clear enunciation both in speaking and
singing. Then, without having any finishing master teach
him embellishments or style, let the young man, who by now
is solidly grounded in music and has a practiced, subtle voice,
sing with his own feelings as his only guide. The result will
not be singing according to any specific school, but according
to inspiration. The artist will be an individuality; he will be
himself; or better yet, he will be the character he has to portray in the opera.

I need not add that these musical studies should be combined with a broad literary education.

There you have my ideas. Can they be approved by a commission? Yes? Then I am at the minister's disposal. No? . . .
Then it's better for me to go back to St. Agata.

To Opprandino Arrivabene   *Genoa, April 8, 1871* (C)

What do you think of things in France? Could anything
be worse?

Much worse than the year '93! Then it was a question of acquiring and consolidating a liberty which they had not yet had; and they hadn't suffered so many disasters, nor had they an enemy in the country! Some day the pages of history that record these infamies will seem incredible.

To Giulio Ricordi   *Genoa, April 11, 1871* (A)

Verdi is here referring to the Report of the Commission for the Reform of the Conservatories. The make-up of the orchestra as demanded by Verdi started with fourteen first violins.

. . . . I have read your article on the orchestra, I am returning it, and believe that I should reply.

1. As to the aims and success of our masters in matters of instrumentation, as you list them there;

2. As to conductors' inspiration . . . and to "creative activity in every performance." . . . That is a principle which inevitably leads to the baroque and untrue. It is precisely the path that led music to the baroque and untrue at the end of the last century and in the first years of this, when singers made bold to "create" (as the French still say) their parts, and in consequence made a complete hash and contradiction of sense out of them. No: I want only one single creator, and I shall be quite satisfied if they perform simply and exactly what he has written. The trouble is that they do not confine themselves to what he has written. I often read in the papers about effects that the composer never could have thought of; but for my part, I have never found such a thing. I understand everything you say about Mariani; we are all agreed on his merit. But it is not a question of a single person, were he ever so eminent, it is a question of art itself. I deny that either singers or conductors can "create," or work

creatively—this, as I have always said, is a conception that leads to the abyss. . . . Shall I give you an example? You spoke to me recently in praise of an effect that Mariani achieved in the Overture to "La Forza del Destino" by having the brass enter fortissimo on *G*. Now then, I disapprove of this effect. These brasses, intended to be *mezza voce*, could not express anything but the Friar's song. Mariani's fortissimo completely changes the character of the passage, and turns it into a warlike fanfare. It has nothing to do with the subject of the drama, in which all warlike matters are mere episodes. And there we are again on the path to the baroque and untrue;

3. As to the make-up and disposition of the orchestra, which is very bad nearly everywhere. You cite the orchestra of the *Opéra Comique* as a model. But why ten first violins and eight seconds?

We in Florence have suggested in our Proposals an orchestra for the big theaters of San Carlo and La Scala. As I was the chief perpetrator, I should like to keep to my arrangement. This work of the Commission will be published within a reasonable time; I think your article would be appropriate afterward, not before, and with many changes commenting on or criticising this work of ours. But do as you see fit. I say all this just for the sake of saying it, and because you asked me to.

To Mme. Du Locle   *May, 1871* (F)

The great French opera composer, Auber, died during the uprising of the Commune in Paris (May 1871). Ambroise Thomas, the composer of "Mignon," became his successor as director of the Conservatoire. The following letter is from Peppina.

At what a moment your poor Auber departed this life! In what a state did he leave that Paris which he so dearly loved! It appears that Thomas will be his successor, and that is right. I hope to see your Camille in a few days, and you may imagine with what delight I shall press his hand after all that has happened! A kiss for your children, and another for you, my dear Madame Du Locle, from your friend,

GIUSEPPINA VERDI

To Vincenzo Luccardi　　　　　*St. Agata, June 9, 1871* (G)

[. . . .] Events in France are painful and astounding. Principles pushed to extremes lead only to disorder. France— or rather, Paris—pushed both good and evil to extremes, and these are the consequences. The same thing will happen to us, if we don't learn how to control ourselves. You have an ex- ample under your own eyes. The intransigeance of your priests over the dogma of *infallibility* is causing a schism in Germany. Your priests are certainly priests, but they aren't Christians. The Papal Court couldn't find a word of pity for those poor martyrs of Paris, and that is really scandalous.

Peppina sends her greetings, and I embrace you heartily.

To Giulio Ricordi　　　　　*St. Agata, July 10, 1871* (A)

You know the libretto of "Aida," and you know that Am- neris requires an artist who has dramatic character and can dominate the stage. How can anyone expect this quality from a near-beginner? The voice alone, however beautiful (and that, by the way, is hard to judge in a room or empty theater), is not enough for the role. So-called vocal perfection concerns me little; I like to have roles sung as I wish, but I am unable to provide the voice, the soul, that certain something which should be called the spark—it is usually described by the Italian phrase "to have the Devil on your back."

I wrote to you yesterday what I thought of Waldmann and I repeat it today. Though finding an Amneris will not be easy, we are talking of it in Genoa. But that is not enough; and so far you have not told me whether the terms I have indicated in my various letters are acceptable.

Remember this, my dear Giulio, that if I come to Milan it is not for the vain pleasure of giving an opera of mine: but to secure a truly artistic performance. To achieve that, we must have the means. So please answer me categorically whether, beside the troupe of singers,

1. The conductor is decided upon.
2. The choral conductors are engaged, as I directed.
3. The orchestra has been constituted according to my directions.
4. The kettle-drum and brass-drum are being exchanged for much bigger instruments than you had two years ago.
5. The standard-pitch is being retained.
6. The orchestra has accepted this standard-pitch, in order to avoid the flatting that I have heard on other occasions.
7. The instruments will be arranged this time as I indicated in a sort of sketch which I made last winter in Genoa.

That arrangement of the orchestra is much more important than is usually assumed, for the color mixtures of the instruments, for the sonority, for the effect. Such small improve-

OIL PAINTING 1840   *Courtesy Musical Courier*

VERDI'S SECOND WIFE,
THE SINGER GIUSEPPINA STREPPONI

ments should pave the way for us to other innovations that will certainly come some day. Among these, particularly the disappearance of the spectators' boxes from the stage—the curtain must come up to the footlights. Then: the invisible orchestra. The idea is not mine, but Wagner's; and it is excellent. It is impossible today to tolerate horrible tailcoats and white ties against Egyptian, Assyrian, and Druid costumes; to set the orchestra, part of an imaginary world, so to speak, in the middle of the floor, right in the crowd as it claps or hisses. Add to all this the objectionableness of having harps, double basses, and the windmill arms of the conductor himself jutting into the air.

Answer me flatly yes or no; because if I cannot be promised what I require, it is useless to continue negotiations.

To Draneth Bey   *Genoa, August 2, 1871* (A)

Your Excellency: Though various passages in the role of Amneris may lie too high for Grossi, I stand by what Signor Ricordi has told you by word of mouth: entrust the part of Amneris to this artist, and do not gamble on an inexperienced one; it would be very hard to find an adequate one.

As I wrote to you, the libretto is in Paris, and in the hands of Mariette Bey at the moment.

Last year I took the liberty of giving two orders concerning "Aida," since there was no time to write and wait for an answer from Cairo.

1. I instructed Signor Ricordi to get all the scores, the choral and instrumental parts, of "Aida" copied out for Cairo.

2. I ordered from Pelitti six straight trumpets of the

ancient Egyptian type; they are no longer in use, and so had to be specially made.

If you think it proper that I should be responsible for these orders, I will lay out the money, and Your Excellency can repay me when we come to the matter of payment for the score. Otherwise you can address Ricordi and Pelitti direct, and settle accounts with them.

To Opprandino Arrivabene   *September 2, 1871* (A)

. . . . In music one must not be exclusively a melodist. Music includes more than melody, more than harmony. Namely, music! That will puzzle you. I shall try an explanation: Beethoven was no melodist; Palestrina was no melodist. I mean, of course: melodists in our sense. . . .

To the Mayor of Milan   *St. Agata, October 13, 1871* (A)

Dear Mr. Mayor: A few days ago I went to Milan to see whether the projected rearrangement of the orchestra was going to work out properly. Unfortunately we, the members of the commission, the machinist of the theater and I found one very serious drawback. The double-basses make a kind of a hedge that interferes at various points with the spectators' view of the stage. This is due to the way the old parquet is built. But it would be deplorable, and I should be particularly sorry, if we were forced to put the double-basses back where they were before. It would spoil my plan to group the orchestra more closely so as to produce a fuller sonority and avoid weak, wavering performances of the music, and we should have gone to a lot of trouble without achieving any decisive result.

But there is a possible remedy for the situation. When I examined the parquet I found, as did all the others, that the floor is in a very bad condition, so bad that mere repairs here and there will not serve their purpose much longer, and the whole thing will have to be reconstructed. Since this will soon become an imperative necessity, and the expense is inevitable, would it not be possible, my dear Signor Mayor, to begin the work at once, lowering the floor at the same time so that if we take the height of the floor at the entrance as zero, it would be about 50 centimeters lower by the time it reaches the stage?

This would naturally put the orchestra on a lower level, and the difficulty with the double-basses would no longer exist in the plan I have indicated.

The stage would be higher, and with the sloping parquet, *common to all theaters,* the spectators would have a better view of the action.

In spite of your many grave responsibilities, will you not endeavor, my dear Mr. Mayor, to steal a moment to consider this plan of mine? If it can be put into execution, you will be conferring a great benefit on art and a great service upon the man who has the honor to sign himself your devoted servant.

To Giulio Ricordi   *Turin, November 12, 1871* (A)

So here I have arrived in Turin, with my good bundle of music in my hand. Too bad! If I had a piano and a metronome here I would send you the third act this evening. As I wrote you, I have substituted a chorus and a romanza for Aida for another chorus, which was worked out in four-voiced imitation in the style of Palestrina. With that I might almost have hoped to earn applause from the pedants; I might have hoped (but what will Faccio say?) to be given a position as teacher of counterpoint in some lyceum. . . . But then my conscience pricked me for working à la Palestrina, for the harmonies, for the Egyptian music! . . .

Well, that seems to be my fate! I shall never get far enough in music to be a savant—I shall be a muddler forever!

To Filippo Filippi   *Genoa, December 8, 1871* (A)

The first performance of "Aida" took place on December 24, 1871, at Cairo. The Egyptian government had invited the critics Filippi, of Milan, and Ernest Reyer, of Paris, to attend. When Verdi heard of this, he wrote the present highly characteristic letter.

What I am about to say to you will seem strange, very strange. Forgive me if I cannot conceal all that moves me.

You in Cairo?—That is about as effective publicity as I can imagine for "Aida"!—But it seems to me as if art taken this way were no longer art but a profession, a pleasure-trip, a hunting party, something to be chased around after, something one wants to endow if not with success, at least with notoriety at any cost. My feeling about it is nausea, humiliation! I always remember with joy the time when I first presented my operas to the public. I was almost without a single friend, without anyone to talk about me, without preparations, without any influence whatsoever, ready to trade blows, and overjoyed if I succeeded in creating a favorable impression. And now—what an apparatus for an opera? Journalists, soloists, chorus, conductors, players and so on; all of them must contribute their stone to the edifice of publicity, to build up a framework of wretched little superfluities, which add nothing to the merit of an opera, but rather dim its real worth. That is deplorable, deeply deplorable!

To Clarina Maffei   *December 11, 1871* (A)

I wrote that letter (of which Giulio Ricordi has a copy) to Filippi under the most mournful impression. In another letter, which I got today, Filippi tries to defend publicity in certain cases. Not I: it is always a degrading thing and never of any use. At this moment, I am so out of sorts, so much provoked with this theatrical clap-trap, that I would be capable of the most drastic resolves. Oh, the years have not quite turned my blood to ice yet! I cannot smother my feelings, gay or sad. . . . Poor wretch that I am! Never, never an hour's peace!

To Giulio Ricordi   [*Probably 1872*] (G)

Nicolini always cuts his part!!!. . . . Aldighieri several times the duet in the third act!! Even the second finale was cut down one evening!!! Aside from the fact that the romanza was transposed downward, some measures in it were changed.

A mediocre Aida! A soprano singing Amneris! And on top of all that, a conductor who dares to change the tempi!!! . . . . I hardly think we need to have conductors and singers discover new effects; and for my part I vow that no one has ever, ever, ever even succeeded in bringing out all the effects that I intended. . . . No one!! Never, never. . . . Neither singers nor conductors!!

. . . . But now it is the style to applaud conductors too, and I deplore it not only in the interest of the few whom I admire, but still more because I see that the bad habits of one theater spread to others, without ever stopping. Once we had to bear the tyranny of the prima donnas; now comes that of the conductors as well!

Well? And you talk to me about composing, about art and so on!!! . . . . Is that art?

I close with the request that you tell the house of Ricordi that I cannot tolerate the above-mentioned state of affairs, that the house of Ricordi may, if it pleases, withdraw my three last scores from circulation (and I should be very glad of it) but that I will not tolerate any changes being made. Whatever may happen, I repeat: I cannot tolerate it. . . .

To Giulio Ricordi [*A few days later*] (G)

After an interval of twenty-five years at La Scala I have been whistled off after the first act of "La Forza del Destino." After "Aida," endless chatter about how I am no longer the Verdi of "Un Ballo in Maschera" (The very "Masked Ball" that was first whistled off at La Scala); how the only compensation (according to Arcais) is the fourth act; how I don't know how to write for singers; how the few bearable things are all in the second and fourth act (nothing in the third); and how on top of all that I am an imitator of Wagner!!! A fine outcome after thirty-five years to wind up as an imitator!!!

This much is sure, that such chatter will not sway me a hair's breadth from my goal, any more than it ever has done; I have always known what I wanted. Now that I am where I

[310]

stand, whether high or low, I can say: If this is so, do what you please. If I want to make music, I can do it in my own room, without having to listen to the opinion of scholars and blockheads.

I cannot take your statement that "the complete salvation of the theater and of art is in your hands," for anything but a joke. No, no. Make no doubt of it, there will always be composers; and I too would repeat the toast proposed by Boito to Faccio at the performance of his first work: ". . . . And perhaps the man is already born who will smash the altar." Amen!

To Opprandino Arrivabene   Milan, February 9, 1872 (C)

At the Milan première of "Aida," Stolz took the title rôle, and Waldmann was the Amneris.

Dear Arrivabene: Last night "Aida," very good. Performance of ensemble and parts excellent; *mise-en-scène* the same. Stolz and Pandolfini very good. Waldmann good. Pacelli, beautiful voice and nothing else. The others good and the orchestra and chorus also very good. As for the music, Piroli will speak to you about it. The public received it favorably. I don't want to play up modesty with you and certainly this isn't the worst of my musical creations. Time will give it the place it deserves. In a word, it seems to me a success that will pack the theatre. If this doesn't prove to be so, I'll write you. Meanwhile, good-bye in haste.

To Giulio Ricordi   Genoa, March 31, 1872 (A)

Dear Giulio: So this evening will be the last for "Aida." I can breathe: It won't be talked about any more, or at least nothing but a few, final words. Maybe some new insults accusing me of Wagnerism, and then *Requiescat in pace!*

And now will you be good enough to tell me what sacrifices this opera of mine has cost the management? Don't be surprised at the question; I am bound to suppose there must have been sacrifices, seeing that none of the gentlemen, after all my work and thousands of lire in expenses, have given me so much as a "Thank you, Dog."

Or should I by chance be thanking them for having accepted and performed poor old "Aida," which brought in 165,000 lire of profit in twenty performances, not counting the season tickets and the galleries? Ah, Shakespeare, Shakespeare! The great searcher of the human heart! But I shall never learn.

To Cesare De Sanctis   *St. Agata, April 20, 1872* (B)

I have just read a few words in the *Omnibus* which displease me. I don't want to *excuse* myself for being anyone's disciple. I am what I am. Every one has a right to think me what he wishes.

And you are, I repeat, very pompous with your Italian music. No, no, there is no Italian music, nor German music, nor Turkish: but there is MUSIC. Don't tire me with all these definitions: it is useless. I write as I please and as I feel. I don't believe in the past nor in the present; I detest all schools, because all lead to conventionalism. I don't idolize any individual, but I love beautiful music when it is really beautiful, whoever wrote it.

"Progress of Art" is another senseless phrase. It is obvious. If the author is a man of genius, he will add to the progress of art without seeking to nor desiring to.

[312]

So tell Torelli to say all he wants to, but that I shan't defend myself, nor do I want the jokes I make in private to be exposed to the public.

Farewell in haste.

To Giuseppe Verdi   *Reggio, May 7, 1872* (1)

On the second of this month, attracted by the sensation which your opera, "Aida", was making I went to Parma. Half an hour before the performance began I was already in my seat, No. 120. I admired the scenery, listened with great pleasure to the excellent singers, and took pains to let nothing escape me. After the performance was over, I asked myself whether I was satisfied. The answer was in the negative. I returned to Reggio and on the way back in the railroad carriage, I listened to the verdicts of my fellow travelers. Nearly all of them agreed that "Aida" was a work of the highest rank.

Thereupon I conceived a desire to hear it again, and so on the fourth I returned to Parma. I made the most desperate efforts to obtain a reserved seat, and there was such a crowd that I had to spend five lire to see the performance in comfort.

I came to the following conclusion: the opera contains absolutely nothing thrilling or electrifying, and if it were not for the magnificent scenery, the audience would not sit through it to the end. It will fill the theater a few more times and then gather dust in the archives. Now, my dear Signor Verdi, you can imagine my regret at having spent 32 lire for these two performances. Add to this the aggravating circumstance that I am dependent on my family, and you will understand that this money preys on my mind like a terrible spectre. Therefore I address myself frankly and openly to you, so that you may send me this sum. Here is the account:

Railroad: one way	2.60 lire
Railroad: return trip	3.30 "
Theater	8.00 "
Disgustingly bad dinner at the station	2.00 "
	15.90 lire
Multiplied by 2	x 2 "
	31.80 lire

In the hope that you will extricate me from this dilemma, I am yours sincerely,

BERTANI

My address: Bertani, Prospero; Via San Domenico, No. 5

Verdi's reply [*Addressed to Ricordi*]   *May, 1872* (1)

. . . . As you may readily imagine, in order to save this scion of his family from the spectres that pursue him, I shall gladly pay the little bill he sends me. Be so kind, therefore, as to have one of your agents send the sum of 27 lire, 80 centesimi to this Signor Prospero Bertani, Via San Domenico, No. 5. True, that isn't the whole sum he demands, but for me to pay for his dinner too would be wearing the joke a bit thin. He could perfectly well have eaten at home. Naturally, he must send you a receipt, as well as a written declaration that he promises never to hear another one of my new operas, so that he won't expose himself again to the danger of being pursued by spectres, and that he may spare me further travel expenses! [. . . .]

May 15, 1872 (J)

I, the undersigned, certify herewith that I have received the sum of 27.80 lire from Maestro Giuseppe Verdi, as reimbursement of my expenses for a trip to Parma to hear the opera, "Aida." The Maestro felt it was fair that this sum should be restored to me, since I did not find his opera to my taste. At the same time, it is agreed that I shall undertake no trip to hear any of the Maestro's new operas in the future, unless he takes all the expenses upon himself, whatever my opinion of his work may be.

In confirmation whereof I have affixed my signature,

BERTANI PROSPERO

To Dr. Cesare Vigna   *May 9, 1872* (A)

All his life long Verdi's faith remained independent of the church. This letter is from Giuseppina.

Verdi thinks too highly of you not to believe what you say, and in spite of the fact that you are a doctor, he counts you among the believers in spiritual things. But between us, he himself is the strangest phenomenon in the world. He is an artist, not a doctor. Everyone agrees in saying that the divine gift of genius has fallen to his lot. He is a jewel among good men, he understands and feels himself the most delicate and exalted sentiments, and yet this *rascal* dares to be, not an outright atheist, but certainly a man of little faith. And this with a calm obstinacy that is enough to make you want to trounce him. I rave at him about the marvels of sky, earth, and sea, etc., etc. It's wasted breath. He laughs in my face, and freezes me in the midst of my incoherent oratory and my quite god-

[315]

like enthusiasm by saying "You're all crazy." And unfortunately he says it perfectly honestly.

GIUSEPPINA VERDI

To Cesare De Sanctis   *Busseto, July 17, 1872* (B)

In 1872, Cesare De Sanctis' business declined. He thought that a loan of 25,000 lire could save him, and Verdi lent him the sum. But already in the following year, De Sanctis saw that it was not sufficient. The poor man became blind, and was barely able to support himself and his family as an exchange broker. He dared confide his sorrow only to Giuseppina, and was able to continue payments only in maccaroni, for which Verdi showed a great predilection. In the course of years, he paid off 5,000 lire in this manner, and mortgaged two houses he still owned to make up for the rest. From that time on, Giuseppina kept up the correspondence with the old "kinsman." Cesare De Sanctis died in 1881. Verdi then let the mortgage lapse in favor of Giuseppe, his godson.

My dear Cesarino: The tempest which threatened to ruin your and your family's future has now subsided. Of course, I'm very happy about it. Let peace return to your home and tranquility to your heart! Redouble both your activities and your prudence in your commercial operations so as to heal up your wounds. Live so that your name may shine honored and pure always and everywhere. This is the best heritage that you can leave your children. It is the light that will guide them, with their heads high in the future that awaits them. And since you bless—and you are right to bless the name of Verdi —let us bless it together. It is the name of a man rare for every virtue, whom I shall venerate and bless to the last of

[316]

my days. Be always worthy of such a friend! That's the best wish I can make for you!

GIUSEPPINA

To Opprandino Arrivabene   *Aug. 29, 1872* (A)

I have tried to raise some of our theaters to a high place and to give tolerable performances there. At the four theaters where I directed performances and dictated the execution, theaters that had failure after failure for years, so that they were regularly unable to pay the last quarter-year, people suddenly began to flock into the house and the receipts were tremendous. You will object: what business of yours are the receipts? But they are my business, because they prove that the show was interesting and thus they show us how to go about things in the future. You know that at Milan and Parma I was there in person. In Padua I was not, but I sent the chorus from Parma, the same scene-painter, the same mechanic, properties, and wardrobe exactly as in Parma. I sent them Faccio, who had conducted the work in Parma. We discussed everything necessary in daily letters back and forth; and the opera went well. Attendance receipts were large.

The impresario came all the way over to see me yesterday to thank me, which he certainly was not obliged to do.

It is the same way now with the "Forza del Destino" at Brescia. I stayed here, but I supervised everything . . . the same troupe as in Milan, the same chorus and so on, and again Faccio. And so after the eighth performance all the expenses were paid and all the rest now is pure profit. Here too there are full houses and everybody is happy. Perhaps you will say again: others can do that too. . . . No and again no—they

[317]

don't know how. If they did, they would not put on such dreadful spectacles!

Now I shall deal with Naples, which is a trifle more difficult. At Naples, as at Rome, perhaps because they have had their Palestrina, Scarlatti, and Pergolese, they think they know more than anyone else.

And yet they have lost their bearings, and nowadays they know very little indeed. They are rather like the French: *Nous, nous, nous.* . . .

But do forgive this gabble which must be very dull for you. Yet I wish our theaters might get into the swim a bit. And it could be done. . . .

To Clarina Maffei   *August-September 1872* (A)

This letter is from Giuseppina.

It is certain that religious convictions (I don't mean priestly narrow mindedness) and the broad principles of evangelic charity elevate the soul to the realms of calm and serenity where we may find the strength to follow the right road, the indulgence to forgive the erring, and the charity to guide them back to the right.

According to your means you do a great deal of charity work, which is not mere material but moral benevolence as well; for good counsel, a kind word in time, may do much good; of such is true charity. Now and then you find people who are grateful, and who demonstrate their gratitude. You are blessed indeed! Enjoy that pleasure; savor it, it is one of the most exquisite that man can taste on earth.

Verdi is busy with his grotto and his garden. He is in fine health and splendid spirits. A happy man he is—and may God make him happy for many long years to come. There are virtuous natures that need to believe in God; others, equally perfect, are happy not believing in anything, and simply keeping strictly to all the precepts of an austere morality. Manzoni and Verdi: those two men make me think—to me they are a real subject for meditation. But my imperfection and my ignorance keep me from solving the knotty problem. Remember me to God and to Manzoni. I wish I might be in your shoes to talk of God with him!

GIUSEPPINA VERDI

Naples, December 15, 1872 (A)

*To the President of the Committee of the Accademia
Filarmonica-Dramatica of Ferrara*

Here is my contribution for the victims of the flood in Ferrara, although I do not belong to the Province of Ferrara and am one of those who has suffered the greatest damage from the inundation of the Po.

To Clarina Maffei *Naples, December 29, 1872* (A)

Good morning and a Happy New Year, that is to say, here's to your health and a peaceful life. Peace is the best thing in this world, and the one I want most at the moment. What imp ever put it into my head to get myself embroiled in the theater again? And after I had enjoyed the happy life of a peasant for so many years! Now that I am at the ball I must dance, and I can assure you the dancing is good. I knew about the turmoil at this theater; but neither I nor anyone else could have imagined it would be so bad as this. It is impossible to describe the ignorance, the inertia, the apathy, the disorder, the complete indifference of everybody to everything. It is unbelievable. It almost makes me laugh when I think calmly

[319]

of all the trouble I go to, all the harassment I suffer, of my obstinacy in feeling I must do so absolutely, at any cost. I feel as if everyone were watching me, laughing and saying: Is the fellow mad?

Oh, my vanity has been well punished; for I confess I really had a moment of vanity. Let me explain. When the government withdrew the subsidies from the theaters, I said, well, let's show the government that it is wrong and we can get along without its help. Then I came to Milan for "La Forza del Destino." People had many reservations about the music, but the production and the performance of the chorus were thought impressive. This was what I wanted. I then made the trip for "Aida." The usual story about the music (meanwhile "La Forza del Destino" had become good) but again the setting and the performance were a success. A brilliant audience, and very good receipts. I went to Parma and the results were excellent once more: again a brilliant audience and very good returns. I watched over Padua from afar, and through Faccio's efforts again there were returns and success. I came to Naples with the hope of succeeding as well, but here, plop! the earth slips from under my feet and I don't know what to catch hold of.

It serves me right.

My coming has been well punished. Now I am thoroughly disillusioned, and if I hadn't been unlucky enough to give my word to Giulio [Ricordi] like a fool, on some other contracts, I would have rushed to dig in my fields even in the middle of the night and forget all about music and theaters.

Otherwise, though infuriated, I am in good health.

To Tito Ricordi   *Naples, January 2, 1873* (A)

[. . . .] But as far as fame is concerned and the certain justice of history that you speak of at the end of your letter— for Heaven's sake let's not even talk about it! You see how the press has treated me this whole year, during which I have been at such pains, and have undergone such expense and labor. . . . Stupid censure and even stupider praise. . . . Never an exalted or artistic thought. . . . Not a soul who discussed my aims; nothing but incoherent, silly stuff; and on the basis of all this a vague animosity toward me, as if I had committed a crime in writing "Aida" and taking care that it was well performed. And not a soul cared to point out the important fact of an unrivaled performance and production. None gave me so much as an "I thank you, dog." And just remember how we, the mayor, the theater directors, and I, parted!

So let us talk no more about this "Aida," which may have earned me a pretty sum of money, but also endless irritation and the most staggering artistic disillusionments. If only I had never written it, or at least never published it! If it had only stayed in my portfolio after the first performances, I could have had it performed when and where I pleased, and it would never have become food for the malice of the curious, the carping of the masses, the critics and schoolmasters, who know nothing about music except its grammar, and that badly. Something would have been lost to speculation, but much won for art.

To Clarina Maffei   *April 9, 1873* (A)

. . . . The success of "Aida," you should know, was honest, decisive, and not poisoned by "ifs" and "buts," and the awful phrases of "Wagnerism," "music of the future," "endless melody," and such. The audience surrendered to its feelings and it applauded. That was all. It applauded and even let itself be swept away by an enthusiasm that I cannot approve: but after all—it expressed its feelings without reservation or restraint. And do you know why? Because there are no critics playing the apostle, no crowd of composers who know nothing of music except what they can glean from a Schumann, Mendelssohn, or Wagner: no aristocratic dilettantism, which glows with enthusiasm about things it doesn't understand, because that is the smart thing to do. The result of all that is the meanderings and the uncertainty of the young men. Shall I be more explicit? Imagine today, for example, a young man of the temper of Bellini: not very certain of himself, shaky because of his scanty training, guided by his instinct alone, unsettled by the Filippis, the Wagnerites, and the rest; he would finally lose confidence in himself, and he would be lost. Amen, amen. . . .

To Opprandino Arrivabene   St. Agata, April 16, 1873 (C)

I've written a quartet in my leisure moments in Naples. I had it performed one evening in my house, without attaching the least importance to it and without inviting anyone in particular. Only the seven or eight persons who usually come to visit me were present. I don't know whether the quartet is beautiful or ugly, but I do know that it's a quartet!

To Clarina Maffei   *1873* (J)

The poet Alessandro Manzoni, one of the great figures of the time, was close to death. Verdi greatly admired him. The "Requiem" was immediately dedicated to his memory.

I am deeply moved by what you say of Manzoni. The description you gave me moved me to tears. Yes, to tears—for hardened as I am to the ugliness of this world, I have a little heart left, and I still weep. Don't tell anyone . . . but I sometimes weep! . . . .

To Giulio Ricordi   *St. Agata, May 23, 1873* (A)

Dear Giulio: I am profoundly grieved at the death of our Great One. But I shall not come to Milan tomorrow: I could not bear to attend his funeral. However I shall come soon, to visit the grave, alone, unseen, and perhaps (after more reflection and after I have taken stock of my strength)—to propose a way to honor his memory.

Keep this a secret and don't say a word about my coming. It is so painful for me to hear the papers talk about me and attribute things to me that I never say or do.

To Clarina Maffei   *May 29, 1873* (A)

. . . . I was not at the funeral, but there were probably few people more saddened this morning, more deeply moved than I, though I was far away. Now it is all over. And with him ends the purest, holiest, highest of our glories. I have read many papers. Not one speaks fittingly of him. Words and words, but none of them profoundly felt. There is no want of gibes. Even at him! . . . . Oh, what a rotten lot we are! . . . .

To Clarina Maffei   *June 2, 1873* (A)

. . . . I am in Milan, but please tell nobody, nobody! Where is our saint buried? I shall visit you tomorrow, after ten. Please don't even tell Giulio. I shall go to see him tomorrow, then to you. Farewell! . . . .

To the Mayor of Milan   *June 9, 1873* (A)

I deserve absolutely no thanks (neither from you nor from the city authorities) for my offer to write a Requiem Mass for the anniversary of our Manzoni. It was simply an impulse, or better, a heart-felt need that impelled me to honor, to the best of my powers, a man whom I valued so much as a writer, and honored as a man and as a model of virtue and patriotism. When the work on the music is far enough along I shall not fail to inform you what elements are necessary to make the performance worthy of our fatherland and of a man whose loss we all lament.

To Giuseppe Cencetti   *July, 1873* (I)

My dear Cencetti: I know the theater in Rome is being reorganized, and I wish the reformers were really convinced that the requirements of modern opera are very different from those of an earlier day, and that to achieve success, you have to have a good ensemble. Consequently the direction should be entrusted to only two men who must be capable and energetic. One should be entrusted with all musical matters: singers, orchestra, chorus, etc., and the other with scenic matters: costumes, properties, scenery, production, etc. These two men should decide everything and assume full responsibility. Only then can there be any hope of good performances and successful ones.

I wish that you, whom I have known for so many years, would be entrusted with the direction of the scene, because I am convinced that you would do everything to produce the works according to our intentions.

To Cesare De Sanctis   *Paris, August 26, 1873* (B)

I've been in Paris with Peppina almost two months, and we haven't yet decided what day we shall leave. Your letter, which in truth is very difficult to answer, was forwarded to me here. In the meantime, make every attempt to complete the payments on your property. Then, as far as I am concerned . . . do what any honest man should! Try, however, not to forget the time limits that you yourself have set yourself.

I should be very glad to recommend you to the publishers, Ricordi, but besides it not being so easy to succeed, I don't know what good you can derive from being employed by that concern. I hear on all sides that the Ricordis are very sharp in money matters. You have the proof of that in Naples in the person of Clausetti; if he didn't have the piano business, I'm not sure that what he earns at the Ricordis would suffice him.

I would advise you, however, not to leave Naples, and to look in your own town for something worth while. Besides the difficulty of succeeding elsewhere, for you, for your wife, and such a large family to leave relatives, friends, habits and move to another city doesn't seem to me a wise course. Trees to be transplanted to foreign lands must be young!

Listen to me, Cesarino, look around you and stay where you have grown up and where you are esteemed. If, however, you'd like me to look into the matter, I will, though with little hope of success.

Paris, September 5, 1873 (A)

To the President of the Teatro Communale, Triest

It was for artistic reasons that I thought it necessary to

be present for the production of "Aida" at two or three large theaters, which I did in Milan, Naples, and Parma. In this latter city I went also because I am a native of the province, and consequently almost a fellow-citizen. Now "Aida" is launched, and I have left it to its fate, only hoping that it will be performed with feeling and intelligence, and, above all, according to my intentions.

I thank the Theatrical Management of Triest for its courteous invitation to attend the opening performance; but, aside from the fact that my presence would not be of any advantage to the performance of the score, I do not care to go to theaters purely and simply to put myself on display as a curiosity. I must therefore offer my excuses for being unable to accede to your request.

To Maria Waldmann   *October 23, 1873* (A)

Dearest Maria: Since it was about music, my wife has handed me your letter, which I will answer directly; and so, dear and kind Maria, here I am at your disposal.

Certainly I would be delighted if you could take part in the Funeral Mass for Manzoni's anniversary—May 22, 1874. You would gain neither reputation nor money by it. But since it is something which will make history,—not because of the merit of the music, of course, but because of the man it is dedicated to—it would, I think, be a fine thing if history could some day record: "On May 22 there was a high Mass at . . . for the anniversary of Manzoni's death performed by Messrs. . . . etc." So see if you can arrange to be free at that time, and write to Ricordi, telling him what's what. I will write to him tomorrow, so that the two letters will get there together. I think we shall merely have to postpone the Florence season.

To Tito Ricordi   *Genoa, March 1, 1874* (A)

Dear Tito: Just read this little piece in the Naples *Pungolo*. How is it possible that "Aida" could be performed repeatedly in such fashion without the House of Ricordi showing the slightest interest in the whole matter? And is your representative allowing this to go on?

I hereby formally demand, on the strength of my contract, that a claim for damages be made to the Naples management; and they must be claimed in the name of the author. The proprietor, having received the fees, has suffered no infringement. It is art that has been brought into contempt, and this I feel it my duty to uphold . . .

No concessions, no settlements here! I will conclude by repeating that I am still stunned to think the House of Ricordi's representative could have allowed such an outrage. Hastily yours.

To Tito Ricordi   *Genoa, March 11, 1874* (A)

Musella was the impresario at the San Carlo in Naples.

Dear Tito: I cannot understand, I simply cannot understand this whole business in Naples!

What is this? Can the contract with Musella have been drawn up with such negligence that he had, in a way, the right to do what he has done?

And on top of all that you have accepted an explanation from Musella?

But what about me? What then am I supposed to do? A workman, a day laborer, who turns his wares over to the publishing house, which the house then exploits at its good pleasure! But that is not what I want. I said not long ago that if I had wanted to be a businessman, after "La Traviata" nobody could have stopped me from writing a new opera every year and making myself a fortune three times as great as the one I have! But I had other artistic aims (as proved by the pains I have taken with my recent operas) and I should have achieved something too, had I not come up against obstacles, or at least indifference, with everything and everybody!

I wish to distinguish between Tito Ricordi and Ricordi, the publisher, and so I ask Tito Ricordi to tell me frankly how things stand. If the managers of the publishing house have not looked after my interests I still do not want to subject Tito Ricordi to the embarrassment of a lawsuit. But let me say again that the publishing house has treated me quite without any consideration whatever. Farewell! Farewell!

To Cesare De Sanctis　　　　　*Milan, May 6, 1874* (B)

I hear that "Aida" went well in Berlin, and very well in Vienna. This is what I consider a piece of good luck, because I can imagine the interpretation they gave that inspired music. The Germans know a great deal about science, art, literature, everything, but they don't feel Verdi's music, and until now they haven't known how to perform it. It seems that "Il Trovatore" enjoys great popularity in Germany, and is performed with tempi and accents completely contrary to the composer's intention.

To Opprandino Arrivabene　　　*St. Agata, July 21, 1874* (C)

Tell me, frankly, you who are somewhat of a journalist, can all the criticisms of these gentlemen be taken seriously?

Do you think that all—or almost all of them—know what they're talking about? Do you think that all—or almost all of them—penetrate to the essence of a composition and understand the intentions of the composer? Never, and again, never! But it's useless to talk about it. Art, true art, the art that creates, is not the unintelligible art that the critics preach to us, who don't even understand one another. I should like them to define two words which they always have on their lips, *melody* and *harmony*. Do you know what they mean? . . . I certainly don't.

To Clarina Maffei   *Genoa, March 11, 1875* (A)

"I Lituani," music by Faccio, book by Boito, played at La Scala at the time.

[. . . .] I was glad to hear about *I Lituani*—so much the better for everybody! He himself is the only person to be sorry for, because if he isn't stout-breasted, he'll see . . .

Are you really serious about my *conscientious obligation to write?* No, no, you're joking. You know as well as I do that the *accounts are balanced.* Which is to say that I have always conscientiously fulfilled every obligation I've undertaken; and the public has welcomed everything with equal *conscientiousness,* with vigorous hissing or applause, etc.

To Vincenzo Luccardi   *Vienna, June 12, 1875* (A)

The "Requiem" was such a sensational success in Italy that Verdi agreed to conduct it on a tour which took the work to Paris (April, 1875), London, and Vienna. Only Verdi and the soloists traveled, the chorus and orchestra being supplied in the cities themselves. Verdi was particularly pleased with Vienna; in fact he considered the Vienna Hofoper "the best

[329]

theater in the world." The soloists were Mme. Stolz and Mme. Waldmann (for whom he had written the parts), the tenor, Masini, and the bass, Medini.

Since you wish it, I may tell you that the success of the "Requiem" was very great. A performance such as you will never hear again! Orchestra and chorus wonderful! The duet for the two women's voices, *Offertory* and *Agnus Dei* were called for again!

To Opprandino Arrivabene   St. Agata, July 17, 1875 (A)

I cannot tell you how we are to escape from this musical ferment. One person wants to be a melodist like Bellini, another a harmonist like Meyerbeer. I want to be neither the one nor the other, and if I had my say, a young man beginning to compose would never think about being a melodist, harmonist, realist, idealist, musician of the future or whatever other pedantic formulas the Devil may have invented. Melody and harmony should be simply the means in the hand of the artist to make music; and if ever the day comes when people no longer talk about melody and harmony, about German and Italian schools, about the past and the future of music, then the kingdom of art will probably begin. Another evil of our times is that all the young men's works are the offspring of fear. No one writes as his heart dictates. Instead, when young men set out to write they have but one thought: to be sure not to offend the public, and to get into the critics' good graces.

You shall tell me that I owe my success to the union of both schools. I have never had anything of the sort in my mind. All this is an old story, which is gone through by others after a certain period.

[330]

To Opprandino Arrivabene
St. Agata, December 25, 1875 (C)

"That town" is Busseto, against whose small-town spirit Verdi was in constant rebellion.

[. . . .] You know that I'm a kind of pariah in that town. I've committed so many sins against them! They've never forgiven me because I didn't write an opera expressly for the opening of their theatre, because at that time I donated 10,000 lire (which they, however, accepted), and because I didn't get Patti, Fraschini, Graziani, etc., to come and sing. . . . That's history! How the deuce could I take those artists by the scruff of the neck and make them sing in Busseto! You'll understand from this that I'm not at all concerned with the going-on at Busseto and when they shout I let them shout, when they sing, play, dance, I let them sing, and dance as they please, and if they do something good and useful, I send my contribution and good night!

To Clarina Maffei   *Genoa, January 30, 1876* (A)

"Il Suicidio" and "Color del Tempo" were Italian plays of the time. Filippi and Arcais were critics.

[. . . .] Yesterday I went to see "Il Suicidio." A beautiful production. It has blood, nerves, and temperament. From the newspaper accounts I had thought it was quite different. But when can you ever believe . . . Oh, fanatical friends! oh, stupid enemies! oh, *posans*. Monday I'm going to see Torelli's "Color del Tempo." For quite a while now, everybody has been lambasting poor Torelli; but I shouldn't be surprised if he were quite right. When a young artist, under thirty, allows himself two or three successes, he may be sure that the public will quickly get tired of him, and take every opportunity to show its disdain. If the artist has the strength to stand up against this current of opinion and keep straight ahead on his own way, he will be safe by the time he is forty. Then the public no longer disdains him; it merely puts on its grand manners, but still keeps a gun cocked, waiting to let him have a good volley any time. He may have genius, talent, as much skill as you like; it's no use: it's a battle which only ends with life itself (fine consolation for an artist!). But he will not fall if he is armed with a heavy shield of indifference and conviction. If he is *afraid,* beware! Fear is the ruin of our artists. Everything that is being done now is born of fear. No one thinks of following his own inspiration any more, they're only concerned with not jarring the nerves of the Filippis, the Arcais, and all the rest of them.

I beg your pardon . . . what the devil am I saying?!

To Opprandino Arrivabene   Genoa, February 5, 1876 (A)

The best thing would be a repertory theater, but I don't believe it is feasible.

In Germany the orchestras and choruses are more alert and conscientious. They play well and exactly, although I have heard pitiful performances in Berlin. The orchestra is coarse and sounds coarse. The choruses not good, the production without character or taste. The singers . . . oh! the singers are bad, absolutely bad. . . . This year I heard la Meslinger (I don't know if I'm writing that right), who passes for the Malibran of Germany. Ye Gods! A wretched, worn-out voice; baroque, uncouth singing; inappropriate acting. Three or four of our featured prima donnas are infinitely her superiors in voice and style of singing, and at least her equals in acting.

In Vienna (at present the leading German theater) matters are better so far as chorus and orchestra go—they are most excellent. I went to various performances, and found the chorus very good, the production mediocre, and the singers less than mediocre. But the show usually costs little. The audience (which is made to sit in the dark during the performance) sleeps or is bored, applauds a little each time an act is over, and goes home at the end of the performance, not displeased, and not enthusiastic. That may very well be the right thing for these northern natures; but just put on a performance like that in one of our theaters, and see what a symphony the audience will give you!

Our audiences are much too excitable and would never be satisfied with a prima donna who only cost 18,000 to 20,000 florins a year, as in Germany. Here they want prima donnas who go to Cairo, Petersburg, Lisbon, London, etc., for 25,000 to 30,000 francs a month; and how is it to be paid for? Take an example: this year at La Scala there is a troupe of singers whose superiors cannot be found. A prima donna who has a beautiful voice, sings well, is lively, young, handsome, and one of our own, besides. . . . A tenor—perhaps unique, certainly one of the very best . . . a baritone who has but one rival: Pandolfini. . . . A bass who has no rivals. And still the theater is having slim pickings. Last year they liked Mariani very well; this year they began saying that she was really a little tired (which is quite untrue, by the way); and now they are saying that she sings well but doesn't draw, and so on. . . . If she were to come again next year they would say: "Oh, always the same person. . . ."

[333]

I remember having met in a certain villa at Milan an old impresario from the days when there were singers like Lalande, Rubini, Tamburini, and Lablache at La Scala. He said that after the storm of enthusiasm at the beginning, the audiences finally went so far as to whistle Rubini off the stage, and stay away from the theater to such an extent that one evening the company sold just six tickets! Incredible!

And now I ask you whether, with our public, it would be possible to establish a permanent company engaged for at least three years at a time. And do you know what a company, like the one playing at La Scala now, would cost for the year? Mariani might deign to sing for a season at La Scala for 45,000 to 50,000 francs. But if she were offered a year's contract, naturally she would ask 15,000 francs a month, since she can earn 25,000 to 30,000 in other countries. And it would be the same with the tenor, and so on.

Good Lord, what a long letter! I have much, much else to tell you, but from what I have said you will understand the rest.

To Opprandino Arrivabene   *March 15, 1876* (A)

Completely agreed as to the orchestra and the permanent chorus, paid by the government and the cities for the Italian theaters. Since late in 1861, I suggested to Cavour that the three leading Italian theaters (those of the capital, Milan, and Naples) should have choruses and orchestras maintained by the government. Free evening singing courses for all in return for a promise to put themselves at the disposal of the theaters in these cities.

Three conservatories in the three above-named cities, with reciprocal obligations between theaters and conservatory.

The program would have been feasible if Cavour had lived; with other ministers it is impossible.

To Opprandino Arrivabene   *Busseto, June 14, 1876* (A)

The funeral services for Cavour were celebrated Tuesday with all the pomp that could be expected of this little country town. The clergy officiated free of charge, and that's saying a good deal.

I attended the funeral ceremony in full mourning, but a deeper mourning harrowed my heart.

Between ourselves, I could not hold back my tears, and cried like a little boy.

Poor Cavour. . . . And poor us!

To Maria Waldmann   *St. Agata, July 10, 1876* (A)

The contralto, Maria Waldmann, an Austrian by birth, was about to marry; she became Duchessa Galeazzo-Massari

Dearest Maria: You must have been in Venice for several days now, calm and happy and busied only with rehearsals for this season's opera which for you will be the last. . . . *The last!* A sad word: it embraces a whole world of memories and a whole life of excitements, sometimes happy, sometimes sad, but dear to anyone with the blood of an artist. However, you are fortunate, you will find rich compensations in your change of fortune. It is different for others, to whom that word *last* means: It is all over!!

But why do I go on repeating distressing things to you, my dear Maria? I said almost the same things to you that last evening in Paris! I was sorry then, and here I am beginning all over again! Please forgive me. And if I have no cheerful news about myself, please tell me that you have much, you who are young, beautiful, and at the summit of your happiness. So write me, not only to tell me the news about "Aida" and the Requiem, but to talk to me about yourself.

We live here quietly and if not merrily, well enough. Peppina joins me in affectionate greetings to you and your sister.

To Clarina Maffei   *St. Agata, October 20, 1876* (A)

. . . . It may be a good thing to copy reality; but to invent reality is much, much better.

Those three words: "to invent reality," may look like a contradiction, but ask Papa! [Shakespeare.] Falstaff he may have found as he was; but he can hardly have found a villain as villainous as Iago, and never, never such angels as Cordelia, Imogene, Desdemona, etc., etc. And yet they are so very real!

It's a fine thing to imitate reality, but it is photography, not painting.

To Léon Escudier   *January, 1877* (A)

Dear Léon: [. . .] The thing I had hoped for then was a revival of the Théâtre-Italien; for this I have made and am ready to make any sacrifice. But I no longer have the hope I once had. I know you are having some successes just now (I don't mean "Aida," which you have degraded to the position of a try-out piece for all your beginners—something that you, *you above all,* should never have done). In spite of this I believe, as I always have, that individual successes are advantageous only to the individual, never to art. And I as an

VILLA VERDI, SANT' AGATA, NEAR BUSSETO

Italian, an Italian maestro, had hoped for a revival of our theater. You may have other partial successes, and you may have your good evenings; but in view of the friendly terms we have been on I know you will forgive my saying that you can not resurrect the Théâtre-Italien, and in the long run you will simply swallow up your fortune.

To Opprandino Arrivabene   Genoa, March 21, 1877 (C)

Arturo Toscanini has often performed Verdi's quartet in an adaptation for string orchestra.

The quartet is going rather well, it's true, even outside Italy; as a matter of fact, a few days ago I was asked for permission to perform it in London, doubling each part by twenty. Performed by eighty players, it ought to be good, above all because there are melodic phrases that require a full, thick tone rather than the thin one of a solo violin. I was almost tempted to answer, "I'll come myself." But instead, I'm going to Cologne for the Festivals of May 20, 21, and 22. On the first day Haydn's "Creation" is to be given; on the second, the "Requiem," which I shall direct myself; and the Ninth Symphony of Beethoven. On the third day, I don't know what. You yourself will tell me candidly the news about "Mefistofele"! It's hard to say now whether Boito will ever endow Italy with any masterpieces. He has great talent, he aspires to be original, but he succeeds only in being strange. He lacks spontaneity and he lacks the real incentive: much musical quality. With such tendencies one may succeed more or less with so strange and theatrical a subject as "Mefistofele," with "Nero" it's more difficult! I've read your articles in the *Sentinella*. They make sense, are honest and what I expected from you. However, I hardly know anything more about politics; for the time being I close my eyes so as not to see. You too, must be closing both your eyes and ears, reading all the foolishness I've written you in these four pages.

To Opprandino Arrivabene   *Cologne, May 22, 1877* (C)

Dear Arrivabene: I said I was going to write you before leaving Italy, and I write you only now, after having been here for eight days. But now I can tell you many things. I can tell you in the first place that I am half-dead from hard work, not only on account of the rehearsals, but because of continuous comings and goings, of invitations, visits, dinners, suppers, etc., etc. I refused as many as I could, but I couldn't refuse to go to a concert given by a Choral Society, where I heard various choruses by their greatest masters. They were splendidly performed. The Quartet Society invited me to hear my quartet, also marvelously performed. I heard rounds, lieder, etc. . . . Finally, last night the "Messa," with 300 choral singers and 200 orchestra players. A most excellent performance by the chorus, but not by the four soloists. A very good success. The ladies of the chorus, trained amateurs of Cologne and of the near-by cities who sing *gratis,* presented me with a baton of ivory inlaid with silver, to conduct with. The ladies of the city gave me a magnificent crown of silver and gold: on each leaf is engraved the name of one of the ladies. Also the members of the Festival presented me with a magnificent Album, containing all the views of the Rhine, all magnificent pictures by one of their best painters; a true work of art. Tomorrow there will be seven bands at the

Garden to say "goodbye" in music. In short, a fine reception from all and in all respects. I shall take a short trip to Holland and then I shall go to Paris for a few days to rest. Best wishes from Peppina. Farewell with all my heart.

To Giulio Ricordi   *St. Agata, October 6, 1877* (A)

I am reading the letter you wrote to Corticelli and am answering it myself. I don't understand: was Patti engaged to give "Aida"? If so, you can imagine how happy I should be. If not, then not.

So, a great success! It couldn't help being so! You heard her ten years ago and cry now: "What a change!" You are wrong! Patti was then what she is now—a perfectly organized being, the perfect union of actress and singer, a born artist in every sense of the word.

When I first heard her—in London (she was eighteen)—I was dumbfounded not only by her marvelous vocal execution, but by certain dramatic traits in which she revealed a great actress. I remember the chaste modesty with which she lies on the soldier's bed in "La Sonnambula," when she leaves the libertine's room dishonored in "Don Giovanni"; I remember her by-play in Don Bartolo's aria in the "Barber," and better than anything else, the *recitative* before the Quartet in "Rigoletto," when her father shows her her lover in the tavern and says: "And do you still love him? . . ."—and she answers: "I love him." Nothing can express the sublime effect of these words as she spoke them. All this and more she was able to say and do—more than ten years ago. But many would not admit it then and you acted just like your public. You wanted her to have your stamp of approval first, as if the audiences all over Europe who were going crazy over her didn't know a thing. But "after all we are the Milanese . . . the first theater of the world,"—don't you think all that bears a strong resemblance to the detestable *chez nous* of the French? And—the first theater in the world?! I know five or six such first theaters; often they are the very ones to have poor music. And between ourselves, come, admit it, six years ago, what a mediocre orchestra, what a pitiful chorus you had! What terrible machinery, what horrible lighting equipment, what impossible scenery! Stage direction was a thing unknown . . . so much the better! Today things have improved a little, but not much; as a matter of fact, very little!

When you see Patti give her warm greetings from me and my wife! I am not sending her the usual congratulations, because it really seems to me that for Patti that would be the most superfluous thing in the world: She knows, and knows very well, that I didn't wait for her success in Milan but from the first time I saw her in London, almost as a child, I declared her a marvel of acting and singing—an exception in the world of art.

So greet her for me . . . and nothing more.

To Opprandino Arrivabene   Genoa, December 27, 1877 (c)

Nothing new here, except that there were three performances by Patti, who was received with indescribable enthusiasm. She deserves it, for she is an artist by nature, so perfect that perhaps there has never been her equal. Oh! Oh! Malibran? Very great, but not always great. Sublime at times, but sometimes in bad taste! The style of her singing was not very pure, the tone production not always correct, the voice shrill in the high notes. In spite of all that, a very great artist, marvelous. But Patti is more perfect. A marvelous voice, a very pure style of singing, a stupendous artist with a charm and naturalness which no one else has!

To Opprandino Arrivabene   *Genoa, February 8, 1878* (C)

Monaldi wrote a biography of Verdi. Fétis (François Joseph, 1784-1871) is otherwise considered one of the most praiseworthy of musicologists.

Dear Arrivabene: I too, have read, or at least have glanced through Monaldi's little book. It is full of inaccuracies! It is obvious that this sort of writing can be only a mass of errors, even when it is inspired by the protagonists, for *amour propre* always gets in the way, along with at least enough vanity to prevent the unveiling of evil and to enlarge upon the good. There are so few candid men, men of lofty spirit. Thus these writings copy what others have said on the same subject before them, and what they don't know, they invent. That's the way the Grea-a-at Fétis wrote, who was a very eminent personage to all musicians, but who in reality was a mediocre theoretician, a very bad historian, and a composer of an innocence to be found only in the Garden of Eden. I detest this charlatan, not because he has spoken so badly of me, but because one day he made me run to the Egyptian Museum in Florence (Do you remember, we went together?) to examine an ancient flute on which he pretends in his Musical History to have found the system of ancient Egyptian music: a system similar to ours, apart from the tonality of the instrument! The son-of-a-dog! That flute is nothing but a whistle with four holes like the ones our shepherds have. And that's the way history is written! And the idiots believe it!

To Clarina Maffei   *Genoa, February 12, 1878* (A)

The Syllabus referred to here was a summary of errors, par-
ticularly in the field of politics, promulgated by the Papal
Encyclical of 1864.

[. . . .] But everybody is dying now! Everybody! This
time it is the Pope! Poor Pope! To be sure I am not for the
Pope of the *Syllabus,* but I am for the Pope of the amnesty,
and of the *Benedite, Gran Dio, l'Italia.* . . . If it were not
for him, who knows where we would be now!

They accused him of retreating, of lacking courage, of
not daring to draw the sword, like Julius II. It was a good
thing he didn't! Supposing he had been able to chase the
Austrians out of Italy in '48, what would we have now? A
government of priests! Probably anarchy and dismember-
ment! . . . It's better as it is. Everything he did, both good
and evil, helped our country, and at bottom he was a good
soul, and a good *Italian*—much better than a lot of others
who are full of patriotic exclamations, but . . . So may the
poor Pope rest in peace!

To Cavaliere Cavagnari (Mayor of Parma)
Parma, February 25, 1878 (A)

I am truly sorry that I cannot consent to what you ask in
your very kind letter.

I have given no further attention to the quartet I wrote,
for mere amusement, when I was in Naples some years ago.
It was performed at my house for a few people who were in
the habit of dropping in every evening. This is to tell you
that I never have attached any importance to this piece, and

at least for the moment I do not care to have it brought forward in any way.

Please accept my apologies, and believe me, faithfully yours.

To Signor Bettoli   *Parma, February 27, 1878* (A)

I did, it is true, write a quartet at Naples, which was privately performed at my house. It is also true that I have had requests for the quartet from some societies, first among them the so-called Milan Quartet Society. I refused because I did not want to give any weight to the piece, and because I believed then, as I still do (perhaps mistakenly), that the quartet is an exotic growth in Italy. I do not mean to say that this species of composition may not eventually strike root and be useful here, but I should like to see our societies, Lyceums, and conservatories adding vocal quartets to the string quartets, and performing Palestrina, his contemporaries, and Marcello.

I told Signor Cavagnari, who was kind enough to ask for this quartet, that for the present I had no intention of making it known publicly. To you I can only repeat the same thing, begging you to accept my apologies and to believe me faithfully yours.

To Giulio Ricordi   *April 20, 1878* (A)

We are all working, without meaning to, for the downfall of our theater. Perhaps I myself, perhaps you and the others are at it too. And if I wanted to say something that sounds foolish, I should say that the Italian Quartet Societies were the first cause; and a more recent cause was the success of the performances (not the works) given by the Scala orchestra in Paris. I've said it—don't stone me! To give all the reasons would take up too much time. But why in the name of all that's holy must we do German art if we are living in Italy? Twelve or fifteen years ago I was elected president of a concert society, I don't remember whether in Milan or elsewhere. I refused, and I asked: "Why not form a society for vocal music? That's alive in Italy—the rest is an art for Germans." Perhaps that sounded as foolish then as it does now; but a society for vocal music, which would let us hear Palestrina, the best of his contemporaries, Marcello and such people, would have preserved for us our love of song, as it is expressed in opera. Now everything is supposed to be based on orchestration, on harmony. The alpha and omega is Beethoven's Ninth Symphony, marvelous in the first three movements, very badly set in the last. No one will ever approach the sublimity of the first movement, but it will be an easy task to write as badly for voices as is done in the last movement. And supported by the authority of Beethoven they will all shout: "That's the way to do it. . . ."

Never mind! Let them go on as they have begun. It may even be better so; but a "better" that undoubtedly means the end of opera. Art belongs to all nations—nobody believes that more firmly than I. But it is practised by individuals; and since the Germans have other artistic methods than we have, their art is basically different from ours. We cannot compose like the Germans, or at least we ought not to; nor they like us. Let the Germans assimilate our artistic substance, as Haydn and Mozart did in their time; yet they remained predominantly symphonic musicians. And it is perfectly proper for Rossini to have taken over certain formal elements from Mozart; he is still a melodist for all that. But if we let fashion, love of innovation, and an alleged scientific spirit tempt us to surrender the native quality of our own art, the free natural certainty of our work and perception, our bright golden light, then we are simply being stupid and senseless.

To Maria Waldmann   *St. Agata, May 22, 1878* (B)

Prince Montenuovo was a son of the Empress Marie Louise (widow of Napoleon I, and later Regent of Parma) by her morganatic marriage with Count Neipperg (German: Neuberg=Montenuovo). The Prince later became Emperor Franz Joseph's Obersthofmeister, and as such, supreme head of the Austrian Imperial Theatres, including the Vienna Opera, a position which he held as late as the time of Gustav Mahler. An embittered opponent of the heir to the Austrian throne, Archduke Franz Ferdinand, it was he who had to make the arrangements for the Archduke's funeral in 1914, which were so strange that they roused the indignation of the Austrian aristocracy.

[. . . .] Just guess whom I saw here yesterday! Right here in St. Agata! I give you a hundred guesses. . . . Prince Montenuovo of Vienna. Do you remember him? As you know, he is Maria Luigia's son and has relatives here in Parma, the Counts Sanvitali, whom he came to visit, and he drove all the way down here. We talked a lot about you, and the time of the Requiem and "Aida" and Vienna, and so on . . . and it gave me the greatest pleasure to think back to all those things.

To Opprandino Arrivabene   *St. Agata, May 26, 1878* (c)

I shan't talk about music, because I no longer remember any. I know only that I've never understood what music of the past and music of the future mean, just as I've never understood in literature the terms classical and romantic poetry, since Dante, Ariosto, etc., are classical.

To Opprandino Arrivabene

St. Agata, October 14, 1878 (c)

I know little about Gounod's success. But we mustn't delude ourselves. We must consider men as they are. Gounod is a great musician, a great talent, who composes excellent chamber and instrumental music in a manner all his own. But he isn't an artist of dramatic fibre. "Faust" itself, though successful, has become small in his hands. "Romeo and Juliet" and this "Poliuto" will be the same. In a word, he always does the intimate piece well; but his treatment of situations is weak and his characterization is bad. The same can be said of many, many others. Don't think me malevolent; I'm giving my sincere opinion to a friend with whom I don't want to be hypocritical.

To Achille Torelli   *St. Agata, November 7, 1878* (A)

Dear Torelli: Thank you for the pretty little book with so many beautiful and distinguished poems by you. I wish I were a writer, a poet, a . . . something or other, some great bigwig so I could spout one of those grave, imposing verdicts, one of the kind that stupefy the . . . , that is, the greater part of the human race, into open-mouthed wonder.

[346]

But I'm only a peasant, a rough diamond who has never been able to pronounce an opinion worth two cents. Now and then I've found poetry that I liked, pictures that moved me deeply, like Morelli's Savior, which bears consolation and comfort amid such suffering (the look of the eyes saddens and exalts me); and sometimes I have even found a piece of music which interested me, but I have never been able to say anything other than: "I like that." And so I say of your poems: "I like them." Nevertheless I can't forgive you for having abandoned the theater for so long. That was a serious offense and the Duchess of Bovino did a good deed when she contrived to force you to return to the theater, for which you, Signor Achille, have a unique gift. Was it inertia? Was it irritation at the public, or the newspapers?

"The true bard is a hero . . ." Those are your words. As for the newspapers, does anybody force you to read them? And as to the public, when your conscience tells you that you have written something good, never mind if it is abused (sometimes it's a good sign). The day of justice will come, and it is a great pleasure for the artist, a supreme pleasure, to be able to say: "Imbeciles, you were wrong!"

To Clarina Maffei   *Genoa, February 21, 1879* (A)

The composer who came from abroad was Ambroise Thomas.

Thank you for the little book of Professor Rizzi's poems. I shall read it, and write to you about it when I am through. And thank you too for the newspaper cuttings; they are papers I had seen, because somebody—I don't know who— sent them to me straight from Milan. Among them was one paper that said some very unkind things about intrigues and camarillas and the like. I don't know and don't care to know whether there is any truth in it; but I do know that all this fuss, this noise about one opera, the praises and flattery, all make me think of the old times (of course old people always praise their own day) when we stood up to the public without publicity, almost without knowing a soul; and if we were applauded, we simply said thank you, or not even that. If they hissed us—all right, see you again some time! I don't know if it was agreeable, but it was certainly more dignified.

Corticelli showed me one paper that really made me laugh. They proposed putting up a tablet in the Scala, with the inscription: "In 1879 A.D. a composer came here from abroad; he was welcomed with great celebrations and a banquet attended by the Prefect and the mayor. In 1872 a certain Verdi came and brought out his own 'Aida.' He was not offered so much as a glass of water."

Well, well, I thought—a glass of water! I came closer to getting a thrashing. Don't take that literally; I simply mean to say that I tussled with everybody over "Aida," and everybody glared at me as if I were a wild animal. I hasten to say that it was my fault, and mine alone. For to tell the truth I am not very gracious in the theater . . . or anywhere else. I have the misfortune never to understand what others understand so well. And because I don't understand, I never succeed in coming out with any of the pretty talk, the phrases that throw everybody into ecstasies. No, for example I shall never be able to say to a singer: "Oh, such talent, such expression! It couldn't be done better! What a divine voice! What a baritone! Not in fifty years has there been such a phenomenon! And what a chorus! What an orchestra! . . . .

This is the first theater of the world." . . . . There's where I get stuck. Time and again I have heard them say in Milan (especially at the time I produced "La Forza") and one person repeated it after another: La Scala is the first theater in the world. In Naples: San Carlo is the first theater in the world. In Venice, they used to say: La Fenice is the first theater in the world. In Petersburg: the first theater in the world. In Vienna: the first theater in the world (and that I would say too). And in Paris: the Opéra is the first theater in two or three worlds . . .

And then I stand there with my head going round, eyes and mouth agape, and say that I, the crown witness, don't know what it's all about. I will only say that I should prefer one second-rate theater to so many firsts. . . .

But enough of these jokes. I should laugh at them much more if I had not happened to become an artist.

To Opprandino Arrivabene   *March 20, 1879* (A)

All of us, composers, critics, listeners, have done our best to repudiate our national character in music. Now we have attained our goal. One step further and we shall be Germanized in this too, as in most other fields. It warms the cockles of one's heart to see how chamber music and orchestral societies are being founded everywhere, more and more chamber music and orchestral societies, orchestral and chamber music—to educate the public to "high" art, as Filippi calls it. Sometimes I have a very evil thought and I say privately to myself: if instead we Italians were to together a chorus to perform Palestrina, his contemporaries, Marcello and others—wouldn't that be "high" art too?

[349]

And it would be an art for Italians. The other isn't . . . but quiet, or someone might hear me.

To the Scala Orchestral Society

Genoa, April 4, 1879 (A)

Verdi was asked to be an honorary president of the Scala Orchestral Society, which gave concerts under Faccio, and made guest appearances in Paris.

Gentlemen: I am extremely sorry that I cannot accept the honorable title which you so kindly offer me. As you say, I am by nature averse to such posts, the more so in the present chaos of ideas, into which tendencies and studies, contrary to our nature, have plunged Italian music. This chaos, which may very well bring forth a new world (though not our world), but more likely simple nothingness, is something in which I wish to have no part. I therefore sincerely hope that this orchestral branch of our art may flourish, but at the same time it is my fervent wish that the other branch may be equally cultivated, in order some day to restore to Italy that art which was *ours,* and which had its own character, distinct from *this.*

It is quite right to educate the public, as the savants say, to high art, but it seems to me that the art of Palestrina and Marcello is also a high art . . . and it is our *own.*

By these words I do not mean to pronounce a judgment (Heaven forfend!), nor even to express an opinion. My only purpose is in some measure to justify my decision.

I beg you, gentlemen, to accept my apologies; and wishing the new institution a splendid success, believe me, with highest regard, faithfully yours.

[350]

To Giulio Ricordi   *St. Agata, August 26, 1879* (A)

According to the "Gazzetta Musicale," the house organ of the House of Ricordi, Rossini was supposed to have said Verdi would never succeed in writing a comic opera.

Dear Giulio: I have read in your *Gazzetta* Dupré's words about our first meeting, and the verdict of Jupiter Rossini (as Meyerbeer called him). But wait a bit! For twenty years I have been looking for an *opera buffa* libretto, and now that I may be said to have found one, you with your article put into the public's head a mad desire to hiss the opera off the stage before it is even written, thus ruining both my interests and yours.

But never fear. If by chance, by misfortune, by some disaster, despite the Great Verdict my evil genius should tempt me to write the *opera buffa,* never fear, I repeat . . . I will ruin another publisher. Good-bye, and believe me yours.

To Giulio Ricordi   *End of August, 1879* (A)

"Chocolate scheme"; the familiar name for "Otello" among Verdi's intimates.

It seemed to me that, in your paper, that extract from Dupré's book could have no purpose except to say to me: "Maestro, take care that you never write any *opere buffe!*" And so I thought it my duty to say to you, "I will ruin another publisher." Well, if you want to ruin yourself on my writing this *opera buffa,* so much the worse for you.

A visit from you with a friend (who would be Boito, of course) will always be welcome. But on this subject you will allow me to speak very plainly. A visit from him would commit me too far. You know how the chocolate scheme came into being. You had dinner with me and Faccio. There was talk about "Otello," about Boito. Next day Faccio brought Boito. Three days later Boito brought the outline for "Otello." I read it, and thought it was good. I said, go ahead with the verse; it will always do for you, for me, for somebody, etc., etc. . . .

If you come now with Boito, I shall have to read the libretto. Either I think it is good in every way, and you leave it with me; then I am committed to some extent. Or I still like it, but suggest some changes, that Boito accepts, and I am still further committed. Or I don't like it, and then it would be too unkind for me to give my opinion right to his face.

No, no. You have already gone too far, and we must stop before there is any gossip or unpleasantness.

To Opprandino Arrivabene

St. Agata, September 3, 1879 (C)

Dear Arrivabene: Don't misjudge me. I've been busy, distracted by a small trip to the neighboring towns. I've been to Milan, as you probably know, for a concert for the flood-victims.

I've been to Genoa for the Exposition. I returned here in the midst of a suffocating heat, with hardly enough energy to breathe. I've wasted time and done nothing worth while.

No, I've done one worth-while thing. I've helped out at a concert which produced 37,000 lire for the poor. I am not speaking of the artistic success and of the performance which, although outstandingly good, had only a secondary impor-

OIL PAINTING BY BODINI   *Courtesy Arturo Toscanini*

GIUSEPPE VERDI, 1885

tance in the circumstances. The first and only aim was the 37,000 lire! And that gave me immense pleasure.

What the Devil are you doing at Orvieto? I hope you went there just for diversion, and that you're keeping your health for the second half-century we still have to live.

Farewell. Write me, and believe me always, yours affectionately.

To Emanuele Muzio   *St. Agata, October 7, 1879* (A)

"Aida" was performed at the Théâtre des Italiens in Paris in 1876. Verdi conducted the first two performances himself; Muzio started with the third performance. Cast: Mme. Stolz and Mme. Waldmann; young Édouard de Reszke was the king. At this time there was a reconciliation with Escudier. He died in 1880, and the Théâtre Italien in Paris disappeared the same year. The Grand Opéra vainly tried for a long time to secure "Aida." In 1880, Verdi finally yielded, and came to Paris again to supervise the performance (with the libretto in French). It was almost a bigger success even than it had been at the Théâtre-Italien. Honors were heaped upon Verdi, who was made a Grand Officier *of the Legion of Honor.*

Dear Em: As the matters stood, even I realized that I could not withhold "Aida." But between ourselves, I am not very happy about it. Either I don't go to Paris, and the opera will be performed dully, without zest, without any effectiveness whatsoever; or I shall go, and consume myself, body and soul.

Escudier is his very own, everlasting self. This last contract for "Aida" is a wretched performance. If only Heugel had managed to acquire the rights to "Aida," I should be rid of Escudier forever. The man makes it even harder for me to go to Paris. After thirty years' association between publisher and maestro, it is hard to break off. Everyone who is calling him a rascal now would scream at me if I changed publishers. That's the way of the world.

The Italian papers disapprove of my giving way on "Aida." Only yesterday the *Corriere della Sera* said that after the rudenesses I had had to put up with I had refused to let "Aida" go on. Goodness knows what they will say when they find out that I did give in. The best part is that I really agree with them ten times over. Capponi has written to me about "Aida" at Paris. If he can think of anything, let him put a few words in *Fanfulla* and *Perseveranza* to say that for such and such reasons I couldn't help doing as I did, etc., etc.

Don't print this letter. You can show it to anyone you like, but not print it, because in that case it would look as if I wanted to beg favors from the Opéra gentry.

What a to-do! What a bore! What a nuisance! There isn't any peace even at Sant' Agata!

To Domenico Morelli   *Genoa, January 6, 1880* (A)

Dear Morelli: Thanks, a thousand thanks for the two photographs. I have kept other photographs, engravings, etc., of your last masterpiece, but this that you send gives me a fuller idea of it. That picture of the Temptation [of St. Anthony] must be beautiful indeed! What do you say? I have heard and read so much about it that I can't wait to see it myself.

And what a wonderful sketch that is of King Lear! It's as tragic as the subject. How tremendous the expression of that figure must be—old Kent, I take it.

Why not do a scene from "Otello" as a pendant to the sketch?

For instance, when Otello smothers Desdemona; or, better yet (it would be less hackneyed), when Otello falls in a trance, distracted with jealousy, and Iago looks at him with a fiendish smile, saying: "Work on, my medicine, work . . ."

What a figure Iago is!

Well? What about it?

Write to me; work, which is still better; and clasp my hand. I embrace you with the most unbounded admiration.

To Domenico Morelli   Genoa, February 7, 1880 (A)

The scene with the kneeling brothers occurs in the "Forza del Destino."

Dear Morelli: Good, excellent, splendid, miraculous! Iago with the mask of a gentleman!

You've hit it. I know it; I'm sure of it. I seem to see that priest, that is, that Iago with the face of an honest man. Quickly then! Dash off a few brush strokes, and send me the scrawled picture. Go on, go on—speed! However the inspiration takes you! Just as it comes. Don't do it for painters; do it for a musician.

Don't put on modesty and tell me you are scared, because it's no use; I won't believe you. When anybody has done what Domenico Morelli has, he doesn't raise his voice or talk like the common run of people; he looks inside, and tells himself: I am I, and always I.

So dash off that scrawl!

The scene of the kneeling brothers—the Virgin of the Angels, etc.—is a fine one, but it's a scene for opera. The Iago

[355]

is Shakespeare, it's humanity—that is, a part of humanity, the brute.

To Opprandino Arrivabene   *March 25, 1881* (A)

The first performance of the revised "Simone Boccanegra" took place at La Scala on March 24, 1881, with a cast including Maurel, Tamagno, and Édouard de Rezké.

Even before last night's performance I would have told you, if I had had time to write, that the cracked legs of old "Boccanegra" seemed to me to have been well repaired. The outcome of the evening confirms my opinion. An excellent performance on everyone's part; simply stupendous on the part of the leading man [Maurel]. A splendid success.

To the Minister of Education   *April, 1880* (A)

On April 11, 1880, Verdi had been awarded the Grand Cross of the Order of the Italian Crown.

Your Excellency: What I have done is little indeed to deserve the high honor His Majesty the King has deigned to bestow on me; I am profoundly grateful. But if my merits in the art I profess are slight, love of the Fatherland has always been strong within me, and I have ardently hoped to do it what honor my abilities would permit.

Your Excellency will have the kindness to offer my thanks and my deep obeisance to His Majesty the King; I have the honor to be your Excellency's devoted servant.

To Opprandino Arrivabene   *Genoa, April 2, 1881* (A)

Dear Arrivabene: From what they write, apparently "Boccanegra" on the fourth night got certainly as much, if not more, applause as on the other nights. What pleases me most

is that the theater was even more crowded than for the second
and third performances.

In case you are interested, I can tell you that "Boccanegra"
will be able to make the tour of the theaters like its many
sisters, despite the subject, which is sad enough.

It is sad because it has to be sad, but it holds the interest.
In the second act the effect seems to slacken somewhat; but in
a different theater, supposing the first finale were less successful, I should not be at all surprised if this second act were to
be as successful as the rest. That's the way of the world—that
is, of the theater. We shall see, and meanwhile we shall hope.

To Opprandino Arrivabene   *May 27, 1881* (A)

*France had occupied Tunis, which the Italians regarded as a
semi-Italian city.*

Dear Arrivabene: Are you crazy?!! Give "Boccanegra"
at Paris?!! Do you really think I should like to go to that
country just now? Never! Not for all the money in the world!
That was a pretty blow for us! Of course it's true that it
was our own fault, all our fault! There never has been, there
isn't now, and there never will be such a —— government
(supply the epithet yourself) as this one. . . . I'm not talking about the Reds, the Whites, or the Blacks. . . . Neither
the form nor the color makes any difference to me. I look at
history and read about great deeds, great crimes, and great
virtues in all kinds of governments; monarchies, theocracies,
and democracies! . . . I repeat, it makes no difference to
me. But what I do demand is that those in charge of public
affairs be citizens of outstanding ability and unquestioned
honesty. I am in despair when I see such an extremely able,
wise, brave, honest man as Sella, ridiculed, libeled, and in-

sulted. I repeat: I despair of my own country. I have a sad presentiment of our future! The leftists will destroy Italy!

And it will be the French who will give us the *coup de grâce*. The French have never loved us, and since 1870 they hate us. It will be easy for them to find some pretext! . . . And then who will defend us? The Cairolis? The Garibaldians?

We have offended every other country. They will just laugh and let things take their course.

Don't let's talk about it any more. You see that I'm not in a very pleasant mood, and I don't feel like talking about anything else. . . .

To Domenico Morelli   *St. Agata, September 24, 1881* (A)

Dear Morelli: "What do you say to it?" are the last words of your letter. I say that if my name were Domenico Morelli, and I wanted to do a scene from "Otello"—in particular, the scene where Otello faints—I wouldn't rack my head about the stage directions: "Before the castle." In the libretto Boito has written for me, this scene plays inside, and I am very pleased with it. Inside or outside, it makes no difference. Besides, you don't have to be so particular, because in Shakespeare's day the *mise-en-scène* was a matter of . . . God's will!

Nothing could be better than to have Iago clothed in black, just as his soul is black. But I don't understand why you want to dress Otello in a Venetian costume. I know perfectly well that the general who was in the service of the Serene Republic under the name of Otello, was simply a Venetian by the name of Giacomo Moro. But if Master William wanted him to be a real Moor, that was his affair. You can't very well have Otello in a Turkish costume, but why not in Ethiopian clothes, without the usual turban?

The type of Iago's build is a more serious question. You would like him to be small, with (as you say) rather under-developed limbs, and, if I understood you rightly, one of those crafty, malicious, *pointed* faces. And if that's the way you see him, do him that way. But if I were an actor and wanted to play Iago, I would rather have a long thin face, thin lips, small eyes close to the nose, as monkeys have, a high receding forehead, with the back of the head well de-veloped. His manner would be absent-minded, *nonchalant,* indifferent about everything, sceptical, bantering, and he would say both good and evil things lightly, as if he were thinking about something completely different from what he is saying, so that if anyone were to reprove him and say: "What you're saying, or what you're doing is monstrous," he could perfectly well answer: "Really? . . . I didn't see it that way. . . . let's say no more of it then! . . ." A fellow like that might deceive everybody, even his own wife, up to a certain point. But a malicious looking little fellow makes everybody suspicious and deceives no one! —— *Amen.* You can laugh if you like, just as I am laughing at all this prattle! . . . But whether Iago turns out short or tall, and Otello Turkish or Venetian, do as you see fit, and it will be right. Only don't think it over too long. Go on, go ahead . . . fast!

To Opprandino Arrivabene   *St. Agata, 1881* (J)

For about two weeks now we've been definitely at St. Agata. I say definitely, because I had been here off and on, during the winter, to take a look at the work I was having done out in the fields and in the house. If you could see the house now (when are you coming to see it?), you would never recognize it!

You probably think I'm a bit daft, but I'm not really, as much as I seem. First of all, these undertakings were a diversion for me; and then I put some money into them, which gave a good many poor workers bread and butter. For you must know, you inhabitants of the city, that the misery among the poor is great, very great, much too great—and if nothing is done about it, either from above or below, some time or other a catastrophe will result. . . . Look! If I were the government, I wouldn't bother so much about parties, about the Whites, the Reds, or the Blacks. I'd bother about the daily bread that people must have to eat. [. . . .] But don't let's talk politics—I know nothing about politics, and I can't stand them, at least not the kind we have had up to now. . . .

To Giulio Ricordi   *November 20, 1880* (A)

This letter refers to the revision of "Simone Boccanegra" for La Scala which Boito helped prepare.

The score as it stands is impossible. It is too sad, too desolate. There is no need to touch anything in the first act or the last, and nothing except a few notes here and there in the third. But the whole second act has got to be done over, and given some relief, variety, more animation. Musically speaking, we could keep the women's *cavatina,* the duet with the tenor, and the other duet between father and daughter, in spite of the *cabalettas!* (Open, earth, and swallow us!) Anyway, I have no such horror of *cabalettas,* and if a young man were born tomorrow who could write any as good as, for instance, *Meco tu vieni a misera,* or *Ah perchè non posso odiarti,* I would go to hear him with all my heart, and let the harmonic fancies and the refinements of our learned orchestration go. Ah, progress, science, realism! Alas, alack! Be a realist as much as you please, but . . . Shakespeare was a realist, only he did not know it. He was a realist by inspiration; we are realists by design, by calculation. And so, after all, system for system, the *cabalettas* are still better. The joke of it is that in the fury of progress art is turning around and going backward. Art without spontaneity, naturalness, and simplicity is no art.

Getting back to the second act, who could do it over? I have said in general that the act needed something to lend variety and a little life to the excessive gloom of the drama. How? For instance, a hunting scene? It would not suit the stage. A festival? Too commonplace. A battle with African corsairs? Not very entertaining. Preparations for war with Pisa or Venice?

In that connection I remember two magnificent letters of Petrarch's, one to Doge Boccanegra, the other to the Doge of Venice, telling them they were about to start a fratricidal struggle, that both were sons of the same mother, Italy, etc., etc. This idea of an Italian fatherland at that time was quite sublime! All this is political, not dramatic; but a skilful man could certainly turn it into drama. For instance, Boccanegra, struck by this thought, means to follow the poet's advice. He convokes the senate or a privy council, and expounds the letter and its idea. Universal indignation, harangues, quarrels, even accusations of treason against the *Doge,* etc., etc. The argument is interrupted by the abduction of Amelia. . . .

I'm simply talking. Anyway, if you find a way to adjust and smooth out the difficulties I have told you of, I am ready to do over the act. Think it over and let me know.

To Opprandino Arrivabene

Genoa, December 23, 1881 (J)

Last night I arrived from St. Agata, where I had been for two days. You are probably saying: what the Devil has he had to do in the country now? But you know (or perhaps I never wrote to you) that I am building; that I had a dairy farm built last year and am building two even bigger ones this year, and that about two hundred laborers are working on it; they have been busy at it up to now. I had to give them orders so that they could continue work as soon as the frost allows.

The work isn't necessary to me. Such buildings will not increase the income from my property by a penny. But the men earn a little something and that means there is no emigration from my village.

To Opprandino Arrivabene   *Genoa, March 17, 1882* (A)

In the matter of musical opinions we must be broad-minded, and for my part I am very tolerant indeed. I am willing to admit the melodists, the harmonists, the bores—those who want to be boring at all costs, as it is smart—I appreciate the past, the present, and I would appreciate the future too, if I knew anything about it and liked it. In a word, melody, harmony, coloratura, declamation, instrumentation, local color (a word so frequently used, which in most cases serves no purpose but to hide the absence of thought): all these are only means. Make good music with these means, and I will accept everything, and every genre. In the "Barber," for example, the phrase, *Signor, giudizio per carità*, is neither melody nor harmony: It is simply good, truthful declamation, and it is music. . . . Amen.

To Opprandino Arrivabene　　　　　*June 5, 1882* (A)

Berlioz was a poor, sick man who raged at everyone, was bitter and malicious. He was greatly and subtly gifted. He had a real feeling for instrumentation, anticipated Wagner in many instrumental effects. (The Wagnerites won't admit it, but it is true.) He had no moderation. He lacked the calm and what I may call the balance that produces complete works of art. He always went to extremes, even when he was doing admirable things.

His present successes in Paris are in good part justified and deserved; but reaction is even more largely responsible. When he was alive they treated him so miserably! Now he is dead: Hosanna!

To Baron Hoffmann　　　　*St. Agata, October 31, 1882* (A)

This letter is addressed to the superintendent-general of the Imperial Court Theatre in Vienna.

Greatly honored by your esteemed letter, I hasten to confirm what Signor Ricordi has written you. It is true, I am working on the new version of "Don Carlos," shortening and condensing it into four acts. It is a disagreeable and rather lengthy undertaking, but it will not be long before it is finished, and then you can have it performed whenever you think it opportune and convenient.

I would be greatly obliged to you for the telegram you promised to send me after the first performance of "Simone Boccanegra."

[363]

To Giuseppe Piroli   *Genoa, February 2, 1883* (A)

I admire the Minister's wish to reform our musical schools, but I do not believe it possible to carry it out to a successful conclusion. Nowadays there are no students or teachers to be found who have not been infected with Germanism, and it would hardly be possible to pick a commission free of this sickness; the disease, like any other, must run its course. And at present neither commissions nor programs nor regulations will cure it. (Remember the regulations that were drawn up in Florence during the Correnti ministry.)

The remedy for the ailment might be

1. A new man, an artist of genius, young and uninfluenced by schools;

2. Theaters in a flourishing condition.

Our music differs from German music. Their symphonies can live in halls; their chamber music can live in the home. Our music, I say, resides principally in the theater. Now the theaters can no longer exist without governmental subsidy.

It is a fact not to be denied: they all are being forced to close, and it is exceptional when one still clings precariously to life. La Scala, yes, even La Scala may perhaps close next year.

With these convictions of mine, it is impossible for me to be part of a commission that, in my opinion, could offer no help to art.

Please offer my warmest apologies to the Minister; I shall write him two days hence so that you may have time to inform him. Tell him that I am truly sorry to reply in this fashion to such a gracious and flattering invitation.

To Giulio Ricordi   *February 14, 1883* (A)

Sad sad sad.

Wagner is dead!

When I read the news yesterday, I may truly say that I was completely crushed. Let us not discuss it. It is a great personality that has disappeared. A name which leaves a mighty imprint upon the history of art.

To Giulio Ricordi   *Genoa, March 24, 1883* (A)

Dear Giulio: This morning I read in *Fanfulla:* "Maurel also tells us that Verdi is preparing some tremendous surprises for the musical world and some great lessons for the young musicians of the future, in his Iago, etc."

God preserve me!

It never has been and never will be my intention to give lessons to anyone. Without regard to schools, I admire everything that pleases me, I do as I feel, and I let everybody do as he pleases.

For the rest, I have not yet written any of this "Iago," or rather "Otello," and I don't know what I shall do later.
P.S. Please put together a little article on those lines; or publish my actual words in some big paper, as soon as possible.

To Clarina Maffei   *St. Agata, October 11, 1883* (A)

One of the best friends of the Countess Maffei had died.

Dear Clarina: I heard about everything, I admired your courage, and now that the first nervous excitement is past, I can well understand your heavy heart. There are no words to lend comfort in such misfortune. Nor will I exhort you with that one stupid word, "courage," a word that has always angered me when it was uttered in my direction. That is not what you need! You will find comfort only in your strength of soul and steadfast spirit. [. . . .]

I wish you good health in your mountains; lay in a good store of it to bring back with you to Milan.

Ah, health, health! I haven't given it a thought for many years, but I don't know how it's going to turn out in the future.

Now the years are really beginning to pile up and it seems . . . it seems to me that life is a very stupid and, what is worse, a useless thing. What do we do? And what shall we do? Taking it all in all, there is one single, humiliating, tragic answer:

NOTHING!

Farewell, my dear Clarina. Let us shun sad things and ward them off as far as possible, and keep our affection as long as we may. . . .

To Giuseppina Negroni-Prati

St. Agata, November 11, 1883 (A)

Dear Signora Peppina: I was by no means pleased to have my friends remember that a short time ago at 9.30 in the evening I became a round seventy years old. Seventy is a fine number, there's no denying that. And I hope too that the wish you expressed on the seventieth birthday of poor Hayez, who went on working and lived another twenty-one years, may come true for me as well. But what use would it really be? And besides . . . work? . . . What for? For whom? I shall stop. Otherwise I would end up by saying much too melancholy things, which might possibly destroy the rather wry sense of humor that you still have. You speak of the training of young people in the past. What a difference! you exclaim. True, only too true. But we must admit that in those days a great, lofty, noble idea was capable of dominating the world. Today everything has been done. What use now are memories, gratitude to the unfortunate dead of that time, and an admiring new generation such as used to be expected? And then, my dear Signora Peppina—you know the world and you know that gratitude is a burden to most people. It is terrible to have to say so—but it is true.

Enough, enough, enough! We can't change the world.

To Maria Waldmann   *St. Agata, November 18, 1883* (B)

Better late than never! says a proverb, which is very convenient for all the lazybones who never succeed in doing anything they have to do, on time. Now I too, who am always saying to other people, "Let's not waste time!"—I have delayed a century in answering your good wishes for my ——th year. I leave a blank for the number, because it's so big I'm ashamed of it.

But please don't think I dislike being reminded of my birth certificate by my friends. And you gave me the greatest pleasure, my dear Maria, with your few kind words, which really meant: "To your health on your seventieth birthday!!" This time I said the number, and I hope you will be able to repeat your words for ten or twelve years to come. If for more years than that, so much the better! But beware, not for any fewer. . . .

To Giulio Ricordi   *Genoa, December 13, 1883* (A)

This letter refers to the revised version of "Don Carlos" in four acts. The first performance of this version took place on January 10, 1884.

Dear Giulio: "Maestro Verdi is coming to Milan to attend the rehearsals of 'Don Carlos' and naturally, we hope, to be present at the first performance, etc, etc." These words in the *Corriere* put me under an obligation to the public, which accordingly might demand that I come and, in the name of all that's holy, perform the usual *pirouettes* and show my beautiful snout! I wrote you a penciled note yesterday from Fiorenzuola to have this *réclame* denied before I come to Milan. I repeat the same thing today.

It is impossible to produce the opera as you say either on the 2nd or on the 3rd or any time. It is impossible to fix a date. Don't tell me that the singers have been studying and know the opera. I don't believe it for a minute. Two things they certainly don't know: how to *enunciate clearly* and *keep in tempo,* two things that are more essential in "Don Carlos" than in any of my other operas.

Faccio can begin, or can continue the rehearsals. I recommend and demand that he insist above all on *enunciation* and *keeping in tempo.* You may think this is pedantry! But it can't be helped: that is the way the opera is written, and if you expect any success, that is the way it will have to be performed.

Just as soon as I see the above report contradicted I shall come to Milan; and let me repeat: *I shall attend only some of the rehearsals, principally those of the new numbers.*

VERDI'S STUDY AT SANT' AGATA

Nothing else, nothing else! Absolutely *nothing else!!!* A hearty farewell.

To Giulio Ricordi   *Genoa, December 26, 1883* (A)

The publisher was also a composer under the pseudonym of Burgmein.

You know, as I do, that there are people who have good eyesight, and are fond of bold, strong, pure colors. Others, who have a touch of cataract, prefer pale, muddy shades. They are in fashion, and I don't object to following the fashion (after all, we must move with the times). But I would like to see it coupled with a little judgment and common sense. In other words, neither "music of the past" nor "music of the future." It is true that I said, "Let us turn back to the old masters," but I meant the old masters who are the groundwork, fundamental, solid. I meant the old masters who have been pushed aside by modern excesses, to whom we must inevitably return sooner or later. For the present, let the flood overflow. In time the dams will form of themselves.

Peppina thanks you for the "Piano Pieces" by Burgmein that you sent. And I thank you for the four Spanish songs, which are pretty and characteristic. My compliments; keep well, and enjoy the holidays.

To Opprandino Arrivabene   Genoa, February 12, 1884 (C)

Giovannini's opera didn't go so badly. Whether it is good or not is another question! Good operas have always been rare at all times; now they are almost impossible. . . . Why? you'll ask. Because we write too much music! Because we try too hard! Because we search in the dark and neglect the sun!

Because we've exaggerated contours! Because we make our work big, not great! And from the big, the little and the baroque are born. . . . And there we are!

To Opprandino Arrivabene   *Genoa, March 18, 1884* (A)

Your good wishes were among the very first to arrive, and they are doubly dear to me because, since they come from you, I know they spring from loyal and sincere feelings. I thank you with all my heart and my wife joins her thanks to mine.

Sometimes the proverb that the wolf may lose his hide but not his malice is right. You are lucky that you still have the leisure and the will to write verses. Verses which, as friends have told you, have turned out very well and are well adapted, excellently adapted, to be put to music. But not by me, for I have lost both hide and malice. Besides, I never could write music for one party or another, for the Whites, Reds or Blacks. Once I barely escaped! In '48 I was in danger of writing a hymn on Pius IX!!! Only a miracle saved me.

You mention poor Sella! That, I believe, is a real misfortune. *He had real brains and character.* In 1861 the three of us sat together on the same bench in the Chamber in the Palazzo Carignano: Sella, Piroli, and I. . . . Sella was the youngest, and he was the first to be taken from us!

To Franco Faccio   *Genoa, March 27, 1884* (A)

Dear Faccio: A few words to thank you for your kindness toward the person I recommended to you; a few more about something that concerns me personally.

Pungolo reports from the Naples *Piccolo* the following:

[370]

"Apropos of Iago, Boito says that he undertook the subject almost against his will; but that when he finished, he was sorry he could not have composed the music for it himself . . ." It must be admitted that these words, spoken at a banquet, are not very important; but unfortunately they may lead to interpretations. It might, for instance, be said that I had forced his hand in picking the subject. So far there is little harm done; and anyway you know how things actually were. The worst of it is that Boito, being sorry he could not compose the music himself, naturally leads one to suppose he had no hope of my writing the music as he would have wished it done. I entirely admit this; I admit it altogether; and for that reason I'm addressing you, as Boito's oldest and most steadfast friend, to get you to tell him by word of mouth, not in writing, when he returns to Milan, that I will return the manuscript untouched—without a shadow of resentment, with no grudge of any kind. Furthermore, the libretto being my property, I offer it to him as a gift in case he means to write the music. If he accepts, I shall be delighted, hoping thus to help and further the art we all love.

You must forgive the trouble I am putting you to; but it is a matter to be confidentially handled, and there is no one more suitable than you.

To Arrigo Boito   *Genoa, April 26, 1884* (A)

Since you do not accept, the letter I wrote to Faccio is without meaning or purpose.

I read hastily, and never believe all I see in the papers. If something strikes me, I stop, consider, and try to get at the root of things so that I can see clearly. The question fired at you point-blank that way at the Naples banquet was at least . . . odd, and certainly concealed intentions that the words did not express. Possibly you could not have answered otherwise than as you did, I agree; but it is also true that the total effect of the conversation might give rise to the interpretations I referred to in my letter to Faccio.

It is useless now to discuss the matter at length, however, since you absolutely decline to accept the offer I made—without, believe me, a trace of ironical intent.

You say: "Either I shall finish 'Nerone,' or I shall not finish it." I will repeat your words on my own account, so far as "Otello" is concerned. There has been too much talk about it; too much time has elapsed. I have too many years on my back, and too many *years of service* behind me! Too many for the public not to tell me all too plainly that they have had enough.

The consequence is that all this has dashed some cold water on "Otello," and stiffened the hand that had begun to sketch a few measures.

What next? I don't know. Meanwhile, I am delighted with our discussion, though it might have been better right after you came back from Naples. I shake your hand affectionately, and give you Peppina's best.

To Opprandino Arrivabene   *June 10, 1884* (A)

I have heard the composer, Puccini, well spoken of. I have seen a letter too reporting all kinds of good things about him. He follows the new tendencies, which is only natural, but he keeps strictly to melody, and that is neither new nor old. But it seems that he is predominantly a symphonist: no harm in that. Only here one must be careful. Opera is opera, symphony symphony; and I don't think it is a good idea to insert a symphonic piece into an opera just for the pleasure of letting the orchestra cut loose once in a while.

I say this just by the way, so don't attach any importance to it; I am not even absolutely sure I have said a true thing, but I am sure I have said something that runs counter to the spirit of the times. Each age has its own stamp.

History will decide later what ages were good, what ages bad. Who knows how many people in the 17th century admired Achillini's sonnet, *Sudate, o fuochi,* more than a canto of Dante?

But whatever may be good or bad, you in the meantime must keep your good health and your good humor, and that for a long time to come!

To Franco Faccio   *Montecatini, June 20, 1884* (A)

Giulio Ricordi (Burgmein) had written a "French Serenade" for the opening of the Exposition at Turin, and Faccio had contributed a cantata.

Dear Faccio: Be so good when you pass by the Trombetta restaurant as to give the enclosed five lire to the poor devil of an omnibus driver. True, he almost made us miss our train. But now my anger is past, and I'm sorry I didn't leave anything for him. Drop me a line and tell me without any composer's modesty how Giulio's piece and your piece went. We arrived quite safely. They all send you their best. I thank you just as if I were in Turin, and press your hand.

To Franco Faccio   *St. Agata, August 19, 1887* (A)

With "creators," Verdi exploded once more against stars who "create" their roles at a première, and almost seem to think that they are the ones who have created the work itself.

[373]

Thank you for your telegram and letter and please excuse me for not answering immediately. Even if I'm not writing any operas, I am extremely busy putting my things in order and straightening out my affairs, so that I can . . . live quietly for a while, if I'm capable of it!

Well, well! So "Otello" is making its way even without its *creators?!!* I had got so used to hearing people proclaim the glory of those two that I was practically convinced that *they* had written "Otello"! You take away all my illusions when you tell me that the Moor is getting along all right without either diva or divo! Is it possible?

By the way, I was quite consoled to hear that the first night audience at Brescia was chary of applause, just as they were at first in Venice. . . . "Well done," I said to myself, "those are progressive audiences!" It was a demonstration of mistrust against the master of once upon a time, and showed a passionate and extremely praiseworthy desire for a new kind of beauty. It was absolutely logical and right. But if they should go to the theater now and simply applaud, then . . . oh dear! I should lose my courage. . . . It would be I who would lose all faith!

In closing, I can only congratulate both of us that you have made the leaky boat sail!

To Clarina Maffei   *St. Agata, September 2, 1884* (A)

Giulio Carcano (1812-1884), the poet and translator of Shakespeare, had just died.

Dear Clarina: I received the sad news quite unexpectedly. Peppina had known it for 24 hours and wanted to keep it from me. But the mail yesterday brought me your letter and the announcement from the family, with its black border.

I don't want to mouth a lot of words; you can well imagine how great is my sorrow at a loss like that of our sainted friend. When I saw him a few months ago in Milan, I found him very weak, but I hoped he would recover and I might see him again. Poor Carcano! I still remember his final words. It was Sunday, I came to see him at one o'clock, and found him bustling around as if to go out. "Don't go to a lot of bother," I said, but he answered with adorable simplicity: "My dear Verdi, I am still among those who go to Mass on Sunday." All right, all right; and I went with him to the church door. "Till we meet again!" Alas, I shall never see him again!!

You are quite right: when one gets to be our age, there is fresh emptiness about us every day, and when you are resigned to that too, you no longer have the strength that allowed our last saint (really the last) to suffer without a murmur. Don't mind what I say, dear Clarina!

And so he is no more, and he leaves his good wife and daughter in deepest affliction. He will certainly be long mourned by his fellow citizens as a graceful and admirable poet, but immeasurably more by his friends and family, who knew all his tremendous kindness, his public and private virtues.

Poor Carcano! Farewell!

And you, keep your peace and health! Take comfort in the consciousness that all your friends from far and near, heartily wish you well.

To Clarina Maffei   *Genoa, December 17, 1884* (A)

Dear Clarina: I am very happy to hear your news, and thank you for the poem by Maffei. Please give him my best.

The sonnet is fine and true; but the evil that it laments does not frighten me too much. Whatever happens had to happen. It is in the nature of things.

Dilettantism, always disastrous in every art, runs after the vague and odd in its craze for novelty, its pursuit of fashion; feigning enthusiasm, it submits to boredom from a foreign style of music, which it calls classical, "great" music. Why classical, why "great" music? . . . Who can say? And journalism (the other scourge of our times) praises this music in order to attract attention and to make people think it understands what others do not, or at least not wholly. The crowd, uncertain and wavering, says nothing and follows along. And yet I am not afraid, I repeat, being convinced that this highly artificial art, often odd by intention, is not suited to our nature. We are positivists, and for the most part sceptics. We believe little, and in the long run we cannot believe in the eccentricities of a foreign art that is lacking in naturalness and simplicity. An art without naturalness and simplicity is no art. Inspiration, in the very nature of things, produces simplicity. Sooner or a little later some young genius will surely rise to sweep all this away, and give us back the music of our better days. He will avoid the faults and profit by the discoveries of the present. I mean, of course: the good discoveries!

Oh, what chatter! And what for? Forgive me!

To Signor Frignani, Busseto   *Genoa, February 16, 1885* (A)

Dear Frignani: In the *Corriere della Sera* of yesterday I saw, along with a few lines about the hospital, this sentence: "It is reported that Verdi proposes to restore the church of St. Agata, which is in a bad state of repair."

[376]

I have never had any such intention, as you know. Nevertheless I shall not issue a disavowal of the statement, though I regard it as a form of extortion intended to commit me more or less to something I have no intention of doing.

I turn to you as the architect of the church so that you may warn those concerned not to count on me. Believe me always devotedly yours.

To Opprandino Arrivabene   *Milan, May 2, 1885* (A)

I have the number of *Ars Nova* that you sent me. I have not had time to read it carefully; but so far as I can see it is one of the usual screeds that do not discuss, but simply pronounce judgment with unbelievable intolerance. On the last page I see, among other things: "If you suppose that music is the expression of feelings of love, grief, etc., give it up. . . . It is not for you!"

And why, pray tell, must I not suppose that music is the expression of love, grief, etc.?

The fellow begins by citing as the *non plus ultra* of music Bach's Mass, Beethoven's Ninth Symphony, and the Mass of Pope Marcellus. Personally I would not be at all surprised if somebody were to tell me, for instance, that Bach's Mass is a trifle dry; that the Ninth Symphony is badly written at some points, and that among the nine symphonies he prefers certain movements that are not in the Ninth; and that there are even better things in Palestrina than in his Mass of Pope Marcellus.

Why not? Simply because someone holds that opinion, why can he not be one of the elect, and why is music necessarily not for him?

Anyway, I am not going to argue. I don't know anything,

and don't want to know anything. But I do know that if the great man of the *Ars Nova* should be born among us, he would abjure much of the past, and disdain the pretentious utopias of the present, which do no more than substitute new faults and conventions for the faults and conventions of other days, clothing intellectual emptiness in baroque garments.

And now, keep well and cheerful, which is much more important to us than *Ars Nova*.

To Signor Maurel   *Genoa, December 30, 1885* (A)

"Otello" is not quite finished, as has been stated, but it is well on toward the end. I am in no hurry to complete the task, because I have never thus far considered having it performed, nor am I considering that course now. The conditions in our theaters are such that, even with a success, the exorbitant cost of artists and staging almost always means a loss to the impresario. Therefore I do not want to have anyone's ruin on my conscience as a result of an opera of mine. Matters thus remain suspended between heaven and earth like the tomb of Mohammed, and I have not decided on any practical steps.

Before closing, I would like to clear up and explain a misunderstanding. I do not believe I ever promised to write the part of Iago for you. It is not my habit to make any promise unless I am very sure I can keep it. But I may very likely have told you the part of Iago was one that perhaps nobody could interpret better than you. If I said that, I stick to it. That, however, does not involve a promise: it would simply be a thoroughly feasible wish if unforeseen circumstances do not arise.

Well, let us not talk more of "Otello" for the present.

[378]

Allow me, my dear Maurel, to offer you my best wishes for the New Year, and sign myself your sincere admirer.

To Signor Augusto Conti   *Genoa, January 10, 1886* (A)

Professor Augusto Conti had proposed that Verdi give ten thousand lire for the new façade of the Florence cathedral. A medallion on the façade was to perpetuate Verdi's likeness.

I regard it as an honor to have received a letter from the hand of a man whom I, like everyone else, most warmly admire, and I would have been delighted to make your personal acquaintance.

Now perhaps you will allow me to explain candidly certain considerations relative to the scheme you present.

Does it not seem to you, esteemed Signor Conti, that if I spend the amount you mention for the *lunette* where my name is to be put, some people might be able to say—and not without a show of reason—that I had bought the honor? The case of Senator Rossi is different. It is quite all right for the nineteenth-century wool-weaver of Schio to join and do homage to the Florentine wool-weavers of the thirteenth century. But our art is one born yesterday, an art altogether modern and still in ferment. Of course there is the *beautiful and Christian art* of Palestrina's century, but it has nothing to do with our present art, and we, veritable outcasts, cannot enter the temple.

The other consideration is positive and insurmountable. My finances would not allow me the luxury of such expenditures. You, like many others, may perhaps suppose me richer than I am; but I, knowing what sums I have at my disposal, and knowing how large and numerous are my expenses at home and abroad, must of necessity regulate my steps so as not to lose my balance.

I am very anxious, also, that the proposal should be known only to you and me; and hoping you will approve my reasons, I beg you to consider me, with great admiration, esteemed Signor Conti, faithfully yours.

To Opprandino Arrivabene   Genoa, January 19, 1886 (c)

Amilcare Ponchielli (1834-1886) is best known for his opera, "La Gioconda."

Dear Arrivabene: How handsome you are! How handsome you are, and how lucky you are to keep yourself as fresh as a rose, if the photograph is telling the truth. I understand that at the time of the sitting you arranged your beard, mustache, hair, etc., etc., but at the same time it's a very good picture.

Nothing new to tell you. At home Peppina is tormented with a bad cough. I feel the changeable weather of this bad season very much. Hence, boredom and sadness on all sides. And a very great sorrow over Ponchielli's death.

To Francesco Tamagno   Genoa, January 31, 1886 (A)

Dear Tamagno: I am delighted to know the gratification it would give you to play the role of Otello. But at the same time I must complain of the people who have made promises in my name, which they had no power to make.

I have not yet finished the opera. And even if it were finished, I have not definitely decided to put it on. I wrote it purely for my own pleasure, without the intention of publishing it. And just now neither I nor anybody else can say what it will seem best to do! There is yet another difficulty: to find the right artists for the various parts. You know better than I that no artist, however distinguished he may be, is suited for all roles; and I don't want to sacrifice anybody, least of all you! Now then, my dear Tamagno (but this is to be a secret between us two), when you return from Madrid, let us meet in Genoa or somewhere, and we can talk it all over frankly and honestly. For the time being, however, nothing can be decided, the less so because, I repeat, I have not yet finished, and have not yet formally promised to put on the opera.

To Giulio Ricordi   (G)

Pro memoria. Assuming that I can complete what still remains to be done on "Otello," it would be well if the house of Ricordi were to fix the terms now, particularly with La Scala.

1. The house of Ricordi together with the theater management will determine the sum from which my share will be paid, etc.

2. I shall attend all the rehearsals (which I deem necessary); but I do not want to make any promises to the audience, and so I want printed on the posters only

OTELLO
TEXT BY BOITO   MUSIC BY VERDI

Nobody, not a soul, can be allowed to attend rehearsals—as usual. I alone have the full right to stop rehearsals and to forbid the performance, even after the dress rehearsal. This if

the performance

the staging

or anything else in the representation should not suit me.

[381]

The personnel taking part in "Otello" is under my immediate direction . . . as are the orchestral and choral conductor, the *régisseur*, etc.

To Opprandino Arrivabene   *Genoa, April 28, 1886* (C)

Dear Arrivabene: A few words in haste to thank you for your note—you're always original—and to wish you too twenty-five more Easters.

We leave tomorrow for St. Agata, and I'm very happy over it. A little quiet after Paris and after Milan! What a lot of bothersome things!

Farewell, farewell. Greetings from Peppina.

To Antonio Ghislanzoni   *St. Agata, July 22, 1886* (A)

Dear Ghislanzoni: Thank you for the kindly remembrance, always dear to me, and for the book you sent. It is something of yours and so I shall read it with the greatest pleasure. And this collection of humorous and satirical pieces will make a healthy book. Books of the kind are indeed rare now!

You know about poor Countess Maffei! I arrived in Milan just in time to see her die! Poor Clarina! She was so good, so considerate, so understanding! Oh, I can never forget her. Our friendship was of 44 years' standing. . . . Poor Clarina!

To Arrigo Boito   *November 1, 1886* (A)

"Otello" was finished! Verdi was 73.
Dear Boito: I have finished!
All hail to us . . . (and to *him* too!!)
                                        Farewell.

[382]

To Opprandino Arrivabene
                                    St. Agata, November 4, 1886 (c)

Verdi's friend, Arrivabene, was not destined to witness the
première of "Otello" (February 1887). He died just before
the performance. Verdi's bereavement was all the greater
"because he had set his heart on having his faithful friend
attend this première."

Dear Arrivabene: What the Devil has got into your mind,
and what the Devil are you saying? Drive away your melancholy and think of getting well. I understand about your age,
but after all, your health is fundamentally good, you're wiry
and spare by nature, and besides it's the fashion now to live
to 90, 115, or 139 years. I was reading last night of a woman
of that age who left two baby children of hers, one 85 years
old, the other 94.

So away with melancholy, and get well soon, for I hope to
embrace you next spring when, after my work is done, I shall
come to Rome. I'm a bit tired, but I'm well, I've completely
finished "Otello"! Now . . . . . *à la grace de Dieu!* Courage. I greet you in Peppina's name and I press both your
hands in mine with the old affection.

To Signor Spatz   *March 18, 1887* (A)

Spatz, the keeper of the Hôtel de Milan at Milan, had a
picture painted of his celebrated lodger, Verdi. He proposed
to put a tablet with Verdi's name on the door of the com-
poser's apartment. (Verdi died at the Hôtel de Milan 14
years later.)

Dear Signor Spatz: Do with the portrait as you think best.
I don't believe it would be a good thing to put my name on

the room. It seems to me that people who occupy it in the future would not be much pleased to find their apartment tagged with a name.

To the President of the International Art Circle, Rome
Genoa, March 7, 1887 (A)

Various newspapers have come to me, stating that the Circolo Artistico Jnternazionale is gathering signatures for a petition to invite me to Rome for the first performance of "Otello."

I do not know if this is the case; but if it is, allow me to warn you, Mr. President, that I cannot and must not go to Rome under the circumstances.

Artistically speaking, my presence would be quite useless. Then, why go to Rome? To put myself on display? To gather applause?

My feeling is not one of either modesty or pride; it is a feeling of personal dignity, which I cannot possibly give up.

If matters are as rumor reports, I would ask you, Signor President, to arrange that the petition shall not be sent, in order to spare me the extreme regret of refusing.

Forgive the intrusion of this letter, and believe me, with highest esteem, faithfully yours.

To Arrigo Boito　　　　　　*St. Agata, October 5, 1887* (A)

Boito asked for six names, one of which was to be given to a school of choral singing whose establishment was under consideration.

Dear Boito: If you will promise neither to praise nor blame me for it, I will send you a few names as they first occur to

[384]

GIUSEPPE VERDI, 1887

me. There are more than six, but there are so many good
masters during the period that it is hard to choose.

16th century:

 *) Palestrina (*in primis et ante omnia*)

 Victoria

 Luca Marenzio (who wrote with the greatest purity)

 Allegri (of the *Miserere*)

 and many other good composers of that century, except
  Monteverde, who was an awkward part-writer.

Beginning of the 17th century:

 *) Carissimi

 Cavalli

Later:

 Lotti

 *) Alessandro Scarlatti (in whose work harmonic treas-
  ures are also to be found)

 *) Marcello

 Leo

Beginning of the 18th century:

 *) Pergolesi

 Jomelli

Later period:

 *) Piccini (the first, I think, who wrote quintets and
  sextets; composer of the very first *opera-buffa,*
  "Cechina").

If you really want only six, the ones with the asterisks *
seem to me to deserve preference

Nearer to the present day there are:

 Paisiello

 Cimarosa

Guglielmi Pietro, etc.; then

Cherubini

I wish you all success; and if you succeed, you will have done a good deed, for the young people (I am not talking about schools, all of which may be good) do not learn the right things; in fact they are already off the path; and if music is what you understand by music, (and it is) one has to know a little about meter and declamation as well, and be educated enough to grasp essentials. Then if you really understand the subject you are putting to music, and you have to shape a character, to portray passions, you won't be so easily led astray by extravagant vocal or instrumental mannerisms or eccentricities of any kind.

Send me news of how you are and what you are doing and have achieved.

To Signor Rocchi   *Genoa, January 6, 1888* (A)

This letter is addressed to a Signor Rocchi of Perugia, otherwise unknown.

Sir: You allow yourself to read me a lecture which I shall not accept.

I ask you in turn:

Why do you, who do not know me, send me one of your works?

And why should I spend time on it?

Do you know how many letters, pamphlets, and compositions I receive every day from all over the world? Am I supposed to answer them all?

You may think it is my duty, but I say to you on the contrary that it would be sheer *tyranny* to demand that I waste my time answering all the letters and looking at all the

[386]

pamphlets and compositions, almost invariably foolish and futile.

P.S. I do not remember your book exactly. But if it was sent in August it must be at my estate, and I will have it sent to you from there as soon as I have returned.

To Giulio Ricordi   *St. Agata, November 9, 1888* (A)

The newspaper "Perseveranza" had proposed celebrating the fiftieth anniversary of "Oberto," Verdi's first published opera (1839). "Die two months ago and not forgotten yet," comes from "Hamlet."

Dear Giulio: I see that the papers are talking about a jubilee!! Have pity on me! Of all the useless things in the world that is the worst; and I, who have done so many useless things, hate them heartily. Besides it is impracticable, and an imitation of foreign customs that opens the door to suppositions that are untrue, cannot be true, and must not be true. In repertory theaters this jubilee would be, though useless, nevertheless possible. But here it can only result in a miserable, ridiculous business. They are even talking of artist-stars! Ugh! Patti, who is a true artist, might in a moment of madness say yes; but the others, without really refusing, would later conveniently remember "obligations," outside the known world if need be. You, who can be sensible when you want to, must write a couple of lines opposing this idea as useless and impracticable. You, who are an authority in these matters, will certainly be believed. And if you find that some kind of concession is necessary, suggest that the jubilee be set for fifty days after my death. Three days are enough to consign men and things to oblivion! "O heavens," says the poet of all poets, "die two months ago, and not forgotten yet?!"

I am counting on the three days. Farewell!

To Signor Borrani, director of the Hospital at Villanova
Genoa, January 16, 1889 (A)

I think it right to acquaint you with the fact that I have had bad reports from the hospital at Villanova, which I can only hope and wish are not true. This is what I hear:

1. That the food is stinted.
2. The wine even more so (yet the cellar is well provided!)
3. That the milk costs too much and that it is not whole milk.
4. That the commonest sort of oil is used, with a bad effect on both food and lighting.
5. That they wanted to buy half-spoiled rice and coarse, dark native spaghetti.
6. That funeral expenses are charged, even with people of absolutely no means.
7. Many more things which I do not mention for the sake of brevity.

I am far away and can say nothing to this; I can neither believe nor disbelieve it; but in any case these reports distress me extremely. Is it then impossible to achieve what I planned when I devoted part of my fortune to endowing this charitable foundation?

I think that the hospital is sufficiently provided for and that no small economies should be necessary. But to tell you the truth, rather than hear more of these complaints I would prefer that the hospital be closed and nothing more said about it. However, I hope none of this is true, and that you will be so kind as to reassure me immediately with a couple of words.

To the firm of Ricordi   *Genoa, February 4, 1889*

The following letter refers to "Otello"

I shall be told that this finale, like the chorus of the second act, is not effective. It may be true that someone else would have done it better, but I could not; and the worst of it is that I am unhappily convinced that the effect did not come off because for one reason or another the performance was never good, or at least the interpretation never corresponded to my intentions. Afterwards I regretted, and I still regret, that I was not fundamentally more inflexible and more demanding. What do you expect? There were many things that did not satisfy me, but I thought that with my seventy-four years I could not allow myself the outbreaks of temperament of the years of "Aida" much less of "La Forza del Destino." For once in my life I wanted to show myself as the inflexible man I am, but I failed. . . . I shall never try again!

Once again: rehearse according to my directions! I repeat: rehearse, and don't just say it is impossible. . . . Why should it be? Rehearse, rehearse; it can do no harm.

To Arrigo Boito   *Genoa, February 17, 1889* (A)

Dear Boito: I hate to divert you from your work even for a moment, but I feel I must talk to you about this jubilee, which seems to me senseless and quite without any possible benefit.

Putting aside my ego, my modesty, my pride, and all that, I ask: What are you going to put on for the evening of November 17? A concert of assorted operatic pieces?

Good God, how horrible!

Performances of some of the operas?

But then, if the performances are to mean anything, there ought to be at least three or four—the earliest, the latest, and another between those. The last two would not be hard to put on. But the first would be difficult and expensive; it would need four first-rate performers (who could also sing), and as elaborate staging and rehearsals as for a new opera. And what would be the outcome? I ask you: would our present audience, so different from that of fifty years back, ever have the patience to sit through the two long acts of "Oberto"? Either they would be bored to death in polite silence (always a humiliating business) or they would show their disapproval. In that case it would be a scandal, not a festival.

About the other project, establishing a perpetual endowment by national subscription, I ask again:

What amount could be collected?

A small sum would be useless except to give one of the usual competitive prizes, which do no good either to art or to the prize-winner. A sum that would really do any good (which would be hard to raise in these critical times) would have to be very substantial indeed, so that the interest on the capital would suffice to assist a young man with his first attempt in the theater. And *then* what difficulties we find!

First, to guarantee the quality of the opera to the impresario;

[390]

Second, to guarantee the quality of the performance to the composer.

For this there is no recourse except to appoint a commission, or rather two (and even that would not be sure). One to examine the verse; the other to examine the music. The first would be easy to choose, and I can name it for you at once: Boito and two others. The second would be more difficult: again Boito . . . and who else? Furthermore, the Commissions would have the thankless and difficult task of supervising the *mise-en-scène* and musical rendering, in order that the impresario should not be able to have the opera performed as a *pis-aller,* for the sole purpose of pocketing some money.

Here another question arises: Where is the opera to be performed? At Milan? But if it is done by national subscription, why might not the Romans, for instance, claim it for Rome, the Neapolitans for Naples, etc.?

What a multitude of difficulties! I am finished. Let me conclude by saying to you what I have been telling to Giulio since early last November: that the jubilee, besides being supremely distasteful to me, is neither useful nor practicable. If you agree with me, why don't you see to it at the first meeting you hold—since you, as both composer and librettist, speak with greater authority than the others—that the whole business is quietly buried? Don't leave any opening for it to be revived, and you will be doing a good deed.

Of course this letter is confidential. There is nothing in it that I could not say aloud, but there is no sense in my letting my voice be heard further. I have cost you a little time, and I am sorry for it. Forgive me. Good-bye. Peppina sends her greetings and I clasp both your hands affectionately.

To Joseph Joachim   *St. Agata, May 7, 1889* (A)

Esteemed Joseph Joachim, President of the Musical Society of the Beethoven House in Bonn. Although it is foreign to my nature to take part in any celebration that receives publicity, in this case I cannot refuse the honor that is offered me. It is for Beethoven's sake! Before that name we must all prostrate ourselves in veneration!

To Franco Faccio, Lyceum Theatre, London

Montecatini, July 14, 1889 (A)

From the telegrams and from Muzio I have had word of the London "Otello." Now you confirm the report, and it rejoices me, though at my age, and in the present state of our musical affairs, a success is of no avail. You speak of a triumph of Italian art! You are mistaken there! Our young Italian composers are not good patriots. If the Germans, proceeding from Bach, have come to Wagner, they do so as good Germans, and all is well. But when we, the descendants of Palestrina, imitate Wagner, we are committing a musical crime and are doing a useless, nay, harmful thing.

I know that Boito has been very well spoken of, and it gives me the greatest pleasure: for praise of "Otello" in Shakespeare's native land means a great deal. So one more greeting! And once more, I am glad, and I clasp your hand!

To Arrigo Boito   *Montecatini, July 17, 1889* (A)

Dear Boito: . . . . When you were sketching "Falstaff," did you ever think of my huge accumulation of years? Of course I know you will reply by exaggerating the state of my health which is good, splendid, robust.

Assuming that it were, you will still admit that I could be accused of great rashness, if I were to undertake such a task. And suppose I could not master my weariness? Suppose I could not finish the music? Then you would have your time and pains for nothing! And I would not want that to happen for all the money in the world. The thought is intolerable to me. The more so if, by writing "Falstaff," you should, I will not say abandon, but even neglect your "Nero" or delay its production. I should be blamed for the delay, and the thunderbolts of public ill-will would descend upon my head.

To Giosuè Carducci   *Milan, December 3, 1889* (A)

Until now I have not had the courage to send a line to you —to you, our greatest poet!

But now I can no longer resist the wish, the duty, to thank you for your personal letter to Ugo Pesci.

I would never have dared hope that you would remember my name in such kind, and truly marvelous terms.

I bow to you, thank you, and I am, with deepest admiration, devotedly yours.

To Ugo Pesci [*Carducci's letter*]
                    Bologna, November 14, 1889 (A)

Dear Cavaliere Pesci: With the first throbs of his early art, Giuseppe Verdi sensed and proclaimed the resurgence of the fatherland. What unforgettable and sacred songs to anyone born before 1848!

Giuseppe Verdi, with the flower of his enduring art, honors and uplifts the reborn fatherland in the sight of all nations.

[393]

Glory to him! Immortal, serene and triumphant, as the ideal of his art and his fatherland!

Dear Signor Pesci, I am a religious man: before deities I worship and am silent. Your, Giosuè Carducci.

To Giuseppe De Sanctis   *Genoa, January 2, 1890* (B)

From Giuseppina (referring to projects for operas).

I've received your kind letter of December 28, and I thank you for myself and in Verdi's name too, for your cordial good wishes. We both send our best greetings to your whole family. We are well enough considering our age, and hope you are all in good health yourselves. Be careful of the influenza, that seems to want to pay a visit everywhere as it has already done even at our house. One of our servants has had it but has recovered.

"Don Quixote," "Romeo and Juliet," and "King Lear," are sleeping the sleep of the just. Let the journals and the journalists print what they like, for from time to time they need to fill up their columns.

Affectionate greetings from Verdi and Giuseppina.

To Aldo Noseda   *Genoa, April 1, 1890* (A)

Noseda was President of the Scala Orchestral Society. The works mentioned in this letter are listed in the index of Verdi's works at the end of the volume.

I have never been so tenderly attached to my work that I kept it in my portfolio to fondle and admire. Everything I have done has been published.

But—stay: About sixty years ago before I came to Milan, I composed some choruses for Manzoni's tragedies and his "Cinque Maggio" (Fifth of May). (They shall never see the

[394]

light.) And then just recently I set a few notes to a puzzle bass that I found in the *Gazzetta Musicale*. Nothing worth mentioning.

This is Easter, and I thought I was making a general confession. I have no other sins in my portfolio!

I rejoice with you, Mr. President, in the Orchestral Society, to which I wish the best of good fortune.

To Giulio Ricordi　　　*St. Agata, November 4, 1890* (A)

The following letter was written after the death of Emanuele Muzio.

Dear Giulio: Just now my head is no good, and I can hardly gather my wits. Poor Muzio wrote these exact words to me under date of October 25: "I have put my affairs in order." I know he is an orderly man, and will certainly have thought of everything. Still, if anything should be amiss, please ask Signor Pisa to do on my behalf anything, and in the most convenient fashion, that ought to be done under these distressing circumstances.

Peppina and I are absolutely distraught. If I weren't 77 . . . and in a season as hard as this. . . . But I am 77. Good-bye.

To Monsieur Erard [*Written in French*]
　　　　　Busseto-St. Agata, November 7, 1890 (A)

Some months ago Monsieur Bossola of Genoa was entrusted on my behalf with sending one of my pianos, which was in need of repairs, to the House of Erard in Paris.

I learn that the piano has been returned to Genoa in perfect order—Maestro Bossola has just written to me—and I am aware that the House of Erard has declined compensation

[395]

for its expenses and labor. I am abashed, and at the same time deeply grateful for this great kindness. The task was long and laborious enough, and my gratitude to the House of Erard must be equally lively and steadfast.

To Gino Monaldi   *Genoa, December 3, 1890* (A)

What can I tell you? For forty years now I have been wanting to write a comic opera, and for fifty years I have known "The Merry Wives of Windsor." However—the usual *buts,* that are present everywhere, always stood in the way of a fulfillment of my wish. Now Boito has swept aside all the *buts,* and has written me a lyric comedy unlike any other.

I am amusing myself by writing the music; without any plan. And I don't even know whether I shall finish it . . . I repeat, I am amusing myself.

Falstaff is a rogue who does all sorts of bad things, but in an amusing way. He is a type. There are so many different types! The opera is completely comic! Amen. . . .

To Maria Waldmann   *Genoa, December 6, 1890* (A)

Your letters, dear Maria, are a comfort to me. But the last one was a healing balm during the sad days I have been going through. Within a fortnight I have lost my two oldest friends!

Senator Piroli, a learned, sincere, and upright man, of a rectitude without compare. A faithful, dependable friend for sixty years! Dead!!

Emanuele Muzio, whom you knew in the days when he was conducting the orchestra for "Aida" in Paris. A true friend, devoted to me for almost fifty years! Dead!!

And both of them were younger than I!! Everything is ending now! What a sad business life is!

You can imagine what anguish it was, and still is. And so I am little in the mood to work on an opera, which I have begun but not got very far with. Pay no attention to the scribblings of the newspapers! Will I finish it? Will I not? Who knows? I am writing without a plan, with no end in view; I simply want to occupy a few hours of the day.

So far as our health goes Peppina and I are doing quite well, in spite of our years.

To Giulio Ricordi *January 1, 1891* (A)

And now let's come to "Falstaff." It really seems to me that any plans for the future are folly, absolute folly. I will explain. I began "Falstaff" as a mere pastime, without any preconceived ideas, without any plans—I repeat: *to pass the time.* Nothing else! Now, the talk that's going on about it, the proposals, however vague, and the words they drag out of you, will finally turn into undertakings and obligations that I absolutely refuse to assume. I told you, and I repeat: I am writing *as a pastime.* I also told you that the music was about half done. . . . Let's make this perfectly clear. I mean: "half sketched out." And in that half, the greater part of the work remains to be done: the ensemble of the parts, revision, and adjustment, in addition to the instrumentation which will be most fatiguing. In short, the whole year 1891 will not suffice to finish it. So why make plans, enter on undertakings, however vaguely worded? Moreover, if I felt myself bound, even to the slightest degree, I should no longer feel *à mon aise,* and I couldn't do anything well. When I was a young fellow I was able, in spite of ill health, to stay at my writing table from ten to twelve hours, working steadily. Often I began work at four o'clock in the morning, and kept on until four in the afternoon with only a cup of coffee in my stomach—working continuously. I can't do that any more. In those days I was master of my body and my time. Now, alas, I no longer am.

In conclusion, the best thing to do now and in the future, is to tell everyone, everyone, that I can't and won't make the slightest promise about "Falstaff." If it is to be, it will be, and it will be as it is to be!

The *Perseveranza* said that it was publishing a New Year's supplement about "Falstaff." The supplement hasn't arrived here. Be kind enough to send it to me. So much has been said, and not very well said, about "Falstaff," who knows whether the *Perseveranza* may not have thought of something good to say.

To Ambroise Thomas [Written in French]
                              Genoa, January 23, 1891 (A)

Ambroise Thomas, composer of "Mignon" and "Hamlet," was Director of the Paris Conservatory.

My dear Maestro: Having been away from Genoa for some days, I did not hear of the death of our lamented Délibes until my return.

Knowing the interest you took in that courageous artist, I turn to you, sir, with my sincere condolences. The loss of this composer is doubly regrettable, for along with his brilliant abilities he did great honor to the musical art of France.

Please accept, my dear Maestro, my regrets for poor Délibes, with my high esteem and devotion to yourself.

To Mr. I. M. Buel, 3940 Market Street, Philadelphia
[*No date*] (A)

Commendatore is an honorary title which is bestowed by the King of Italy.

Commendatore Ricordi has given me the copy of "The Great Operas," Part One. It is a tremendous work, magnificent, worthy of the highest admiration.

I am therefore deeply sensible of the honor you bestow on me by dedicating such a work to me.

I thank you, esteemed Signor Buel, most particularly, and hope this tremendous work will receive the admiration it so richly deserves. With deepest respect, I am, faithfully yours.

To Countess Negroni-Prati   *Genoa, March 8, 1891* (A)

[. . . .] You too are having your afflictions? Listen to me: sorrows are the daily bread of our life; but once you have reached a certain age, they grow with astonishing force. People say that you should bear it, and take courage—but at the moment I am richly endowed with them and they are great and grievous. I must re-read the Book of Job to find strength to bear them. To be sure, even he cursed mightily.

So courage, and forward, as long as may be.

To Arrigo Boito   *Genoa, April 26, 1891* (A)

Dear Boito: I must leave at once for St. Agata to look after some business of mine, and I could not go to Milan at present. They are packing our valises now, tomorrow the servants leave, and day after tomorrow we shall leave at seven in the morning and be at St. Agata around three in the afternoon.

However I couldn't be of any great service to you in ap-

[399]

pointing a conductor for La Scala. Since I very rarely go to the theater, I don't know the best conductors. In any case, I shouldn't be in favor of a competition. You judge a conductor *on the podium.* Those with the best names are Mancinelli and Mascheroni.

I think I told you that Luisa Cora came to see Peppina one day, to tell her that her husband would give up the riches of Madrid and London if he could find a permanent, respectable, well-paid position here. Later we discovered that this was only a wish of Luisa's. Now then, since you can't count on Mancinelli, the best choice would be *Marino* or *Mascheroni.* Of the two, I should take the latter, for many reasons, above all because I'm told he is a hard worker (and you need a hard worker at La Scala), a conscientious man without sympathies, and better still, without antipathies.

But it's not enough to choose a conductor. He must be independent of the management, and assume the full musical responsibility before the Commission, the management, and the public.

Moreover, you need a good chorus-master, who is always subordinate to the conductor. He should not only take charge of the musical instruction but also concern himself with the stage, as if he were a *régisseur,* and at the performances either the chorus-master or his assistant should slip into a costume and sing along with the members of the chorus.

Furthermore, you need a stage manager who is always subordinate to the conductor.

Finally, a clear and precise program should be drawn up, and neither the operas, nor the singers who are to perform them, should be chosen haphazard, as has been done in recent years.

Two stable companies should be formed complete for the whole season, and they should be engaged in time to have two operas ready at the opening of the season. Thus you would avoid putting the public in a bad humor, which sometimes lasts all through the season.

All this would be smooth sailing, but . . . there is always a *but!* It all depends on finding the MAN!

I shall write you from St. Agata.

To the Mayor of Parma   *St. Agata, April 29, 1891* (A)

About a fortnight ago, just as I was leaving for Genoa, I received here at St. Agata your kind letter of the 12th of April, signed by yourself and the honorable Aldermen of the Municipality of Parma.

Rereading this letter, I find myself rather embarrassed for an answer; I do not know whether to claim for myself, at least in part, the many courtesies in which the letter abounds. —I am writing "Falstaff," it is true. But I am writing it in moments of absolute leisure, simply for my own amusement, and without any definite goal in view; and I do not know whether or when I shall finish it. Everything that has been written in the newspapers is without any basis whatsoever, and "Falstaff" today is still a thing of the future.

However, I deeply appreciate your flattering expressions of esteem and wish to convey my thanks to you and to the honorable Aldermen.

To Giulio Ricordi   *St. Agata, June 9, 1891* (A)

Ricordi had evidently written Verdi that La Scala would not miss a subvention so much if he would introduce "Falstaff" there.

You're joking, my dear Giulio! and I'm glad to know you are in a good mood! What? Six or seven months ago, not a soul was thinking either of "Falstaff" or of the "Venerable Patriarch" of St. Agata. The theater was going along as usual with fiascos and successes (very few of the latter), and now you come and tell me that the theater would not be so badly off without a subvention!! Let's leave joking aside. It's not the time now to broach the subject of "Falstaff," which is progressing slowly, but I am more and more convinced that the vast size of La Scala would vitiate its effect. In writing "Falstaff," I have had neither theater nor singers in mind. I have written for my own pleasure, just for myself, and it seems to me that instead of La Scala, it ought to be performed at St. Agata.

To Ferdinando Resasco   *St. Agata, October 21, 1891* (A)

Dear Signor Resasco: I have no unpublished material to offer you for the special number of *Genova-Iberia*. But since you speak to me of agriculture, in which I am only a dilettante, I really wish that this noble science were more widely cultivated here. What a source of riches it would be for our country!

A few less musicians, lawyers, doctors, etc., and a few more agriculturists: that is the wish I make for my country....

To Giuseppe Gallignani   *Milan, November 15, 1891* (A)

Dear Gallignani: I am sorry not to have been able to attend your concerts of sacred music. I know they were very successful and I am glad of it.—I am particularly glad for the performance of Palestrina's music: he is the real king of sacred music, and the Eternal Father of Italian Music.

Palestrina cannot compete with the bold harmonic innovations of modern music, but if he were better known and studied, we would write in a more Italian spirit, and we would be better patriots (in music, I mean).

Keep on in Parma with the work you have begun so well here, and you will be doing an artist's work.

To Edoardo Mascheroni   Genoa, the last day of 1891 (A)

[. . . .] I have heard about the scant success of "Die Walküre." Who knows whether it may not do better in the future? I should think it possible.

The remarks of the apostles were to be expected. But they were right when they said that La Scala is too big, and that a curtain ten yards away is impossible! And I myself add that the two rows of boxes on the stage are horrible. But, alas, nothing can be done about them. If there had been anything to do, it would have been done at the time of "Aida" or before. But all these people who talk theater know very little about it, and they wander about with their ideals in an atmosphere of impracticality.

To Hans von Bülow   Genoa, April 14, 1892 (A)

Hans von Bülow, the celebrated German pianist, composer, and conductor, was married for a time to Cosima Liszt, who later became Wagner's wife. As early as 1844 he had heard and enjoyed "Ernani" in Vienna. The "Requiem," however, did not please him at first; he thought it too theatrical. But then, studying it again, he grew enthusiastic. He wrote an ecstatic letter to Verdi, and this is Verdi's reply.

To the illustrious Maestro Bülow: There is not a shadow

of sin in you! And there is no reason to talk of repentance and absolution!

If your former opinions differed from your present ones, you were quite right to express them; I should never have ventured to complain.

Besides, who knows . . . you may have been right then.

However that may be, this unexpected letter of yours, written by a musician of your stature and your standing in the world of art, was a great pleasure to receive! Not because of my personal vanity, but because I see that truly superior artists judge without prejudice of school, nationality, or period.

If the artists of the North and South have different tendencies, it is well that they are different! They all should hold fast to the character of their own people, as Wagner very rightly says.

You are fortunate to be still the sons of Bach. But we? We, the sons of Palestrina, once had a great school, and it was our own. Now it is a bastard growth, and ruin threatens.

Can we begin again?

I am sorry that I cannot attend the Musical Exposition in Vienna, where I should not only have had the good fortune to meet many distinguished musicians, but have enjoyed the pleasure of shaking your hand in particular. I hope that the gentlemen who so kindly invited me will remember my advanced age and forgive my absence. I am your sincere admirer.

To Giulio Ricordi   *1892* [?] (A)

The great French baritone, Victor Maurel (born 1848, died 1923 in New York), was the first Falstaff in the Scala per-

*formances, as he had been the first Iago in "Otello." In 1881
he was Boccanegra in the revival of that work. Still Verdi
refused his request for a sort of monopoly on Falstaff. But
Maurel also sang Falstaff at the New York première in 1895,
and as early as 1873 he had sung Amonasro in the first New
York "Aida." In 1909 he settled there as a teacher. He also
designed the settings for the New York performance of
Gounod's "Mireille." He wrote four books on singing, and
an autobiography.*

Dear Giulio: We are wasting our time with letters and
telegrams. I tell you, you are all outsiders, off your own preserves. Only I am at home here and I cannot allow anyone
to evict me from my property.

There is no sense in pressing me to put on "Falstaff" to
suit others.

1. Do not pay the artists exorbitantly.

2. Do not hold paid rehearsals.

3. I will not undertake to give "Falstaff" where other people choose.

Firstly, I don't want the firm to lose money, in spite of a
success, on a new opera of mine.

Secondly, paid rehearsals would be a disastrous precedent,
set by "Falstaff."

Thirdly, let us assume for the sake of the argument that
after the performance at La Scala I decided to make a few
changes. Could I then allow an artist to come to me and
say: "But I have no time to wait because I want to play this
opera in Madrid, in London". . . . My God, that would
be too much of a humiliation! I have told you that you are
all off your own preserve and I may say that Maurel is, too.
Can't he see that if the libretto of "Falstaff" is good and the

music tolerable, and he plays the part in such a superior fashion, he will automatically become indispensable without having to make demands that are useless to him and offensive to others?

Madame Maurel, who is a very intelligent woman, but a little annoyed just now, will say I am wrong. A month from now she will say: *"Le maître avait raison."*

Let's put things in their proper places! I simply ask to remain master of what is mine, and not to ruin anyone. I may add that if I had to choose between accepting those conditions and burning the score, I would light the fire immediately and put "Falstaff" on the funeral pyre myself, together with his great belly.

P.S. These demands themselves have excited me quite enough.

To Giulio Ricordi   *St. Agata, September 18, 1892* (A)

The Scala stage designer, Hohenstein, had been sent specially to England "to absorb the atmosphere of Windsor and to copy the old houses in Holborn" (Toye).

Dear Giulio: I am returning the piano score with a few remarks, and the libretto to you. . . .

Now that it is printed the libretto seems even better. . . .

You ask some questions about the entrances and the exits of the players. Nothing is easier or simpler than this *mise-en-scène,* if the painter does a set as I saw it before me while I was composing.

Just a large practicable garden with paths, lots of plants and bushes here and there, so that the people can hide themselves, at will, as the drama and the music demand.

In this way the men will have their separate place, and

[406]

can later invade that of the women, when the latter are no longer on the stage. Then toward the end of the act the

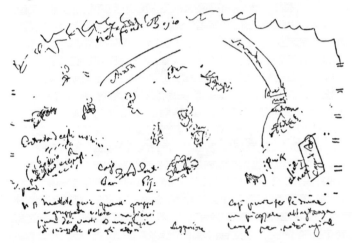

women can occupy the place where the men were. Don't tell anyone about these ink-splotches of mine, not even Boito, but be sure that Hohenstein's ideas are approximately like mine.

Tito tells me that Hohenstein suggested putting the screen close to the wings "because it is natural and logical for a screen to lean against the wall." Not at all.

This screen, so to speak, takes part in the action and must be put where the action requires; the more so because Alice says at one point: "This way, more that way, wider open still," . . . etc.

The stage for the second-act finale should be almost completely free, so that there will be room for the action, and so that the principal groups can be clearly distinguished: the group by the screen, the one by the basket, the one by the window.

FALSTAFF, FINALE SECOND ACT

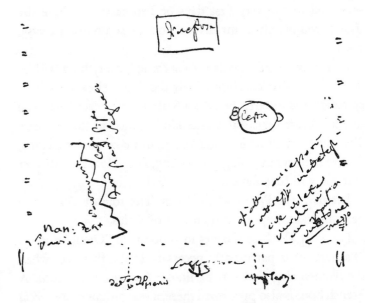

I repeat: don't say anything to anybody, for I don't want to meddle with anyone's business; I would much rather that others should think of something better. . . . But on the other hand I shan't approve anything unless it convinces me completely and in every way.

I was just going to mail this when I received your letter of the 17th. Peppina and I are both deeply grieved at your misfortune and we feel for you and your Giuditta in your affliction. We can only say to you, have patience and courage.

In the matter of "Falstaff" I do not wish to obligate myself to anyone, but I promise the publishing house of Ricordi that I will give "Falstaff" at La Scala during the Carnival season of 1892-93, if the troupe of which we spoke is completely assembled—reserving to myself the right to replace anyone found unsatisfactory at rehearsals. "Falstaff" can be produced in the very first days of February, if I have the theater completely at my disposal on the second of January, 1893.

As far as the rehearsals are concerned, everything will be done as on other occasions. Only the dress rehearsal should be conducted differently. At La Scala I have never been able to get a dress rehearsal of the kind needed in that theater. This time I shall be inexorable. I shall make no complaints, but the moment anything goes wrong, I shall leave the theater and you will then have to withdraw the score.

Let us leave Paroli where he is. The role of Bardolf is perhaps more important than that of Caius.

[. . . .] The bass clarinet in *A* occurs in "Otello" too. In "Falstaff" it is particularly necessary in the third act when the women sing that sort of litany: *Domine fallo casto*. A French horn is also prescribed there, a real old *corno da caccia* without valves, with the fundamental low *A* flat. The instrument should have a fairly full tone; it will sound more easily. Enough for today.

Has Pasqua been engaged?

And how about Cesari? As far as I know, he won't be at La Scala this year.

To the Parisian Critics [*Written in French*]

January 5, 1893 (A)

Henry Bauer of the "Echo de Paris," Charles Darcours of "Figaro," Leon Kerst of the "Petit Journal" and Alfred Bruneau of "Gil-Blas."

Esteemed Sirs: I am deeply sorry to be obliged to tell you that the custom and house rules of La Scala do not permit attendance at rehearsals.

This is a regulation that I have always approved of, and I feel I should be the last to violate it.

I am truly distressed, and I beg you, esteemed sirs, to accepts my regrets and apologies.

To Camille Bellaigue [Written in French]
February 9, 1893 (A)

The French music critic Camille Bellaigue (1858-1930) was greatly admired by Verdi. He afterwards wrote a biography of Verdi.

I was greatly pleased to receive your letter. I only regret that you are not to be here today. Perhaps that is as well for you.

"Falstaff" this evening, then!

I don't know whether I have hit the gay note, the true note, and above all the sincere note. Some very fine things are being done in music nowadays, and in certain respects, if one does not pursue the matter too far, there is real progress. But in general people are not sincere and they always do as their neighbors do!

Don't let us talk about politics. Tomorrow or very soon you will receive the score and libretto.

To Minister Ferdinando Martini
Milan, February 11, 1893 (A)

After the opening of "Falstaff" it was seriously suggested that Verdi be made Marquis of Busseto.

In the *Perseveranza* I read that the title of Marquis is being conferred on me. I call upon you as an artist to do everything to stop it. My gratitude will be much greater if I do not receive the title.

To Giuseppe De Sanctis   *Milan, February 15, 1893* (B)

From Giuseppina.

It's true, the first triumphal days of "Falstaff" have passed, but the confusion of letters, notes, telegrams, visits, etc., has not yet ended. So in spite of my determination, and the demands of my age and my physical strength, not to write any more letters, I still have to write a few. Although this is brief, I do it willingly for you, thanking you in Verdi's name for all the fine things you say about "Falstaff" and its author. Without false modesty, Verdi really deserves them. It's impossible to surpass him as to loftiness of genius and uprightness of character! I repeat with you: May God preserve him still for many years!

To Edoardo Mascheroni   *Genoa, April 23, 1893* (A)

Farfarello: nickname of the conductor Edoardo Mascheroni, who had become the chief conductor at the Scala after Faccio's death; he conducted at the première of "Falstaff." Verdi had borrowed 100 lire from him at the Rome railway station, and forgotten to repay it. Zanardelli was a young patriotic deputy. "Tutto nel mondo è burla" (All the world's a jest) is the first line in the final chorus of "Falstaff."

Dear Mascheroni: Ha! Ha! Ha! Ha! Ha! Ha! I sang, just like the merry wives, when I read your letter!

Poor Farfarello. . . . All that work and bother, and then the awful peril of losing 100 lire too!

Ha! Ha! Ha! Ha!

I wired Giulio immediately, and he immediately wired Nuti, who has perhaps already liquidated the debt. So be it!

And you tell me no news of the happenings at the Teatro

[412]

Argentina!!? I don't mean in the parterre, but on the stage.

You shall report some other time!

A really wasted evening!! Poor Piontelli will shed tears of blood!!

Only 30 thousand lire!!!

And what about us? . . . And art? . . . But who are "we," and what sort of "art"? We? Poor supers, who have to beat the big drum, until they tell us: "Be quiet . . ."

Tutto nel mondo è burla. . . .

Ha ha ha ha.

Giulio will send me the photographs, and just imagine, I shall send one immediately to Zanardelli; or rather I shall send it to you if you're still in Rome.

Give everybody on the stage that asks after me, my greetings. You may not have to greet anyone!

I'm not going to say any nice things to you (I've already done that) and I won't say thank you, because I'm going to plague you again soon!

To Edoardo Mascheroni   *Genoa, April 27, 1893* (A)

Another of the merry letters from the period of "Falstaff." The music is also from "Falstaff."

Dear Mascheroni: You aren't the only privileged one! I made a big boner too!!

Don't laugh—I'm in danger of committing suicide!

Hearken and tremble!

For once in my life I wanted to be pleasant, and I didn't succeed! . . . I sent a picture to the proprietor of the Hotel Quirinale, and I addressed it: "To Sig. Bruni, proprietor of the Hotel Quirinale, etc., etc.," As Boito was leaving for Milan yesterday, he shouted in a voice in F sharp:

[413]

"Bruni isn't the proprietor of the Quirinale at all." Ahhhh!

Who is it then? He couldn't tell me! . . . In my rage I took a *revolver* (it was made of chocolate) and fired it into my mouth! . . .

And I'm still alive!!! Oh, oh! AND I'M STILL ALIVE!!

e vi-vo an- co - - - - ra

I throw myself into your arms: *Save me, save me.* . . .
What can you do?
What should I do?

To Edoardo Mascheroni   *St. Agata, May 7, 1893* (A)

Mascheroni was to go to Vienna as conductor of "Falstaff."

Dear Mascheroni: I am back at St. Agata and breathing deep breaths of relief. [. . .]

I haven't heard much about Venice. I received only two newspapers, sent, I think, by Meg and Quickly, and the telegrams. If you think there is any point in using the instruments in the quartet (on condition that they can't be heard), do so. But take out the

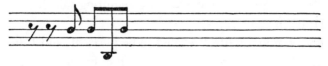

in the oboes; the low B is too awkward in the oboe.

Have a good trip to Vienna. I don't believe the trip on to Berlin will be good. Artistically speaking it was a mistake.

[414]

I could have stopped it, but knowing how far Giulio's agreements went, I didn't want to put him in too difficult a position. But Giulio was wrong to act so arbitrarily and so little from the artistic point of view. The most sensible thing is to be sceptical; it spares you further difficulties!

How are the merry wives getting along? Have no jealousies sprung up between the old ones and the new ones? What wonderful comedies there always are in the theater —and outside too!

Tutto nel mondo è burla!

And now I send you my greetings, seriously, and go to work . . . not music! . . . No, no, no, no!! Farewell.

To Edoardo Mascheroni   *St. Agata, May 15, 1893* (A)

In his letters, referring to "Falstaff," Verdi is almost intoxicated. He is parodying himself: he would never call the conductor a "creator" as he does the composer and, sometimes, the librettist. He is also parodying Wagner—in whose music the orchestra so often carries the melody, while the singer serves "as accompaniment." The part of Dame Quickly was played by Pasqua.

Congratulations, congratulations, and congratulations again to you, the third creator of "Falstaff"! Who will be the fourth one? P. perhaps . . .

And the fifth?

The merry wives.

By the by, I have had a very gracious and particularly kind letter from Pasqua.

Thank her for me and tell her that I shall answer her later because I am busy now putting the finishing touches on an opera in twelve acts plus a prologue and an overture which is as long as all nine of Beethoven's symphonies put together. Besides every act has an introduction in which all the violins, violas, 'celli and double basses play a melody in octaves, not like those in "Traviata," "Rigoletto" and so on, but a modern melody, one of those lovely ones that have no beginning and no end, and hang suspended in air like Mohammed's tomb. . . . I have no time to explain to you how all the singers will furnish the accompaniment. I hope I shall be inspired enough to imitate the crash-bang of the cymbals with the singers' voices; but I will tell you about that some other time. Adieu!

To Edoardo Mascheroni   *St. Agata, June 8, 1893* (A)

I declare that I never got your letters from Vienna. The last news from you was dated May 12th from Trieste. After that I heard almost nothing more about "Falstaff"; I am not sorry. After my worries, I can imagine yours! On top of all the exertions, the gossip, the whims, and then, as you say yourself, the insults! That is bad, very bad; but have no illusions. In the future too, you will find yourself in similar surroundings. The theater is made that way, and it has to be!

Ordinary seasons are soon over. One person turns right, one left, and good-night. But on a tour like this the artists are together too much, and know each other too well; each one thinks himself indispensable, each one thinks that when he is at it that he has the sole right to applause, they all try to be important, important, important, and end by believing themselves heaven only knows what! But there is no cure for it! Perhaps, in moments of supreme exaltation, one might try pouring a stream of cold water on their heads, which would also flood the stage and the boxes and everything else.

If you wait for a performance of "La Forza del Destino"

INSCRIBED TO ARTURO TOSCANINI   *Courtesy Arturo Toscanini*

GIUSEPPE VERDI, 1899

to come to Busseto, you will have a long wait. The finances of Busseto do not permit any theatrical performances. But if we shouldn't meet even at Montecatini, the house of St. Agata stands here immovable and it is always open to you.

To Edoardo Mascheroni   *St. Agata, June 15, 1893* (A)

Dear Mascheroni: I have received your letter of the 13th, and rejoice with you at the ovations you received in Vienna and Berlin. Real, solid ovations, which crystallized into the brilliant offers which have been made to you from Berlin and Hamburg. Splendid!

You ask me for an opinion? What opinion? And who should really give one?

It might be a serious mistake to tell you to go, and it might be just as serious to tell you to stay here.

Of course conditions in our theaters are lamentable. Nothing is more certain than that! Even our capital has no theater!! La Scala alone keeps on going, but no one can guarantee that it too may not have to close soon.

None of the projects that have been proposed recently could be easily realized. Here, with a public like ours, a steady repertory is impossible. For example, let this year's company of singers appear for two consecutive years, even with the best operas in their repertoire, including Maurel in "Rigoletto," "Hamlet," etc., and then you can tell me more about it. Every country must be allowed its own peculiarities, and so here we have to tolerate all the unseemly noise and the stupid verdicts. It's bad, but that's the way it is!

These are really deplorable conditions, and in the German theaters they are better in many respects, particularly because wages are assured and because you have the right to

[417]

a pension after ten years of service. But over and against that there is, of course, the repertory system, the language for which must absolutely be mastered. And then there is the hostility, which may not be apparent now, but will break out sooner or later, and then all the maestri and non-maestri will declare war against "the Italian."

All this is inevitable! Will you have the courage to confront such malice with a shield of equanimity? That is the only valid and reliable weapon, but it is hard to wield.

Then there is something else you spoke of yourself: the children's education! That is a dangerous snag. Either you must leave your family in Italy for nine months, which costs a lot of money, and go up there alone—or you take your family with you and give your children an education which will be neither German nor Italian. You may say that you can have your children educated as you please. No! you are deceiving yourself. Your children will breathe the air there, and that air will change both their minds and temperaments. . . .

After this picture do you still want my opinion?

God forbid!

To Edoardo Mascheroni   St. Agata, August 10, 1893 (A)

The "disgrace" concerning Catalani's funeral refers to the many people who did not attend the rites. The young musician, Ricci, was given Italian citizenship, through the intervention of Zanardelli, the deputy.

Dear Mascheroni: We are born to suffer: And do you really believe that we can be composers and conductors without eating our hearts out day by day, a bit for breakfast, a bit for dinner, with always a little saved for the morrow?

[418]

I can well imagine everything you tell me. I am too familiar with theaters, big and little, not to realize the difficulties you have had; and you are lucky indeed if you have been able to overcome them at least in part. [. . . .]

Poor Catalani! A splendid man and an excellent musician. Too bad, too bad. I must congratulate you and Giulio on the few fine words you said over the poor fellow. What a disgrace, what a reproach to the others!

Give my respect to the illustrious Zanardelli; tell him that I remember with gratitude his kindness to the poor young man who but for him might now be carrying an Austrian musket instead of playing in your orchestra.

What about you? You know that we are at Sant'Agata, and you are always welcome on any occasion, at any season, at any hour.

To Signora Zilli   *Genoa, December 15, 1893* (A)

Signora Zilli played Alice in "Falstaff."
Dear Signora Zilli: It's true, it's true!

A whole year has passed since we began working with "Falstaff," first at my house and then in the room at La Scala. A wonderful time, when we all lived and breathed nothing but art! I remember our moments of happy emotion and . . . Do you remember the third performance of "Falstaff"? I took leave of you all. You were all a little moved, particularly you and Pasqua. Just think what that farewell was to me. It meant: "Never shall we meet again as artists!!!"

To be sure, we did see each other again in Milan, in Genoa, in Rome. But memory always carried us back to that third evening, which meant:

This is the end!

Le ultime note del Falstaff

Tutto è finito!

Va, va, vecchio John . . .
Cammina per la tua via
Fin che tu puoi. . . .
Divertente tipo di briccone
Eternamente vero sotto
Maschera diversa in ogni
Tempo, in ogni lugo!!
Va. . . . va. . . .
Cammina, cammina,
Addio!!!

The last notes of Falstaff

All is done!

Go, go, ancient John,
Be off upon your ways
As far as life will take you. . . .
Laughable figure of a rogue
Forever real beneath
A thousand masks in every
Age and countryside,
Go, go!
Be off, be off!
Farewell!!!

VERDI'S ADDIO TO FALSTAFF

This note belongs to Arturo Toscanini and has graciously been
put at our disposal by him for this volume.

You are fortunate to have so much of your career before you; may it always be as brilliant as you deserve.

Thank you for your good wishes for the holidays. They are a little early, but they can be renewed, and I return them with all my heart.

To Edoardo Mascheroni   *Genoa, December, 1893* (A)

Dear Mascheroni: I have received the *Lombardia* you sent me, and in my opinion, you were wrong to write that letter.

Just let people have their say, and you do, as far as possible, what it is up to you to do. An invisible orchestra! . . . The idea is so old that everybody, or at least a great many people, have dreamed of it. I too would like to have an invisible orchestra in the theater, but not just half invisible. I want a *completely invisible* orchestra! To have the orchestra, which is a part of the poetical world of the ideal, play in the middle of an audience which is applauding or hissing, is the most ridiculous thing in the world. The tremendous advantages of an invisible orchestra would more than compensate for the inevitable loss of power and sonority, and the nasal, rather childish sound which would result from its playing, so to speak, with mutes.

But if we can't have a completely *invisible orchestra* as is proved not only by the Paris Opéra, but by many German theaters and even by Munich and Berlin (I repeat, *completely invisible*), then any other arrangement you may try will be puerile and will have nothing to do with art; and alas, I am afraid that 30 years from now people will laugh at these poor ideas of ours.

As for me, I don't think your harmonic resonance chamber

[421]

underneath the orchestra is worth anything. Whether it's there or not, the sonority will be the same.

I also think that the orchestra, such as it is, is well grouped and arranged. And I don't say this because I am guilty of the arrangement, having had it set up that way when I did "Aida," but because the instruments blend well, with the strings surrounding the wind instruments and enclosing them, particularly the brasses, in the middle. They would not blend so well if you were to put all the double-basses in a single row against the stage. The brasses wouldn't be sufficiently covered and their sound would be reflected back from the walls of the theater. If you leave the double-basses where they have been up to now, you can avoid the problem of their sticking up too high and obstructing the view. . . . But then where would you put the harps, which stand even higher?

And what about the conductor being up so high, with his stick always in motion, up and down, back and forth, and all over the place?

You would have to do away with the conductor!!!

Mother of God! What problems to waste time about!

On the contrary, on the contrary! There is only one, very simple problem. *Amen!* You devil of a Farfarello! making me waste half an hour writing all this nonsense, and useless nonsense at that!

To Monsieur Gailhard [*Written in French*]
                    Genoa, January 31, 1894 (A)

Monsieur Gailhard was Co-director of the Opéra in Paris.

Dear M. Gailhard: "Otello" at the Opéra in Italian?! I am surprised and astonished.

I am not arguing your right to perform works in Italian at the Opéra; but personally when I think of the Opéra, your great *Théâtre National,* I cannot understand having any work there that is not French. There is something stunning, shocking in the combination of the Opéra and an Italian work.

It is perfectly true that "Aida" was given in Italian before it was given in French; but that is a different matter. "Aida" was first performed in Paris at a wholly Italian theater.

Accordingly, if "Otello" is to be given at the Opéra, I think it should be done in French translation.

I am sorry, my dear Monsieur Gailhard, that I cannot agree with you, but trust it will not prevent you from accepting my assurances of esteem and friendship.

To Camille Du Locle   *Genoa, February 8, 1894* (A)

Charles Nuitter, archivist of the Paris Opéra, made French translations of many operatic libretti.

Dear Du Locle: I am exceedingly embarrassed by our Paris musical affairs. They concern not only myself but my collaborators on "Otello" and "Falstaff."

As you know, "Falstaff" is shortly to be given at the Opéra-Comique; and subsequently "Otello" at the Opéra. This is an important and possibly a serious matter, and no false steps must be made.

In Paris they are saying that Carvalho is not the Carvalho he once was; that his theater is going downhill; that his partners are distressed at the choice of operas and the slim profits, etc., etc. Some of the papers are echoing this talk, and spreading an atmosphere of gloom. Probably you think all this is nothing to you. Not for the moment, it is true; but when "Otello" comes to be put on, it is to everyone's interest, yours included, that the atmosphere should not be black.

I no longer have any dependable friend in Paris who can inform me accurately of the situation. Nuitter would be the person to turn to; but I am not sufficiently intimate with him, and have no right to question him on so delicate a matter.

What about you? You have been a true, intimate, and faithful friend for many years. Could you do it? Would you do it? If so, you would be doing me the greatest of favors, relieving me of innumerable embarrassments, and making a decision that could do no harm to our artistic reputation or our personal dignity. Nuitter may be assured of my word of honor, my silence, and my discretion.

P.S. If you do, I urge the greatest dispatch, there is no time to lose.

To Léon Carvalho [*Written in French*]
Genoa, February 11, 1894 (A)

Thank you for your gracious letter. I saw Maurel yesterday, and he told me again what you had already written.

You are very, very kind. But you have forgotten just one, tiny little detail. You have forgotten my four-score years!! At this age one needs quiet and rest, and though I feel relatively well, I no longer can stand either the work or the fatigue or the irritations which are inevitable in the theater. I know what you will answer to all this, but I have been acquainted with the theater for a long time (unfortunately) and I know what to expect.

For the rest, I can only repeat my words to Maurel: "If

my health, my strength, and my eighty years permit, I shall come to Paris."

In the meantime take good care of the role of Alice. It needs first of all, of course, a very agile, beautiful voice, but at the same time an actress with tremendous temperament. The role of Alice is not developed at such length as Falstaff, but it is just as important from a scenic point of view. Alice leads all the intrigues of the comedy.

Please accept, my dear M. Carvalho, my warmest compliments; and for both you and myself I wish the best of luck for "Falstaff."

To Camille Bellaigue [*Written in French*]
Milan, March 3, 1894 (A)

Dear Mr. Camille Bellaigue: I am greatly at fault. It is a long time since your fine book, "L'Année Musicale," reached me, and I have not said a word about it. Horrors! I might say in extenuation that recently I have had to shuttle back and forth by train between Genoa, Sant' Agata, and Milan, where I shall be until three days hence. A poor excuse! I repeat that I am greatly at fault.

Your book is very fine, showing a true mastery of the subject; your criticism is honest, sincere, and of a high tone. I was most struck by the Geneva lecture. Apart from the indulgent words devoted to myself, for which I thank you, I find there confirmation of some ideas that have been pattering about in my head for a long time.

Everywhere the cry is: "The true, the true!" and perhaps we are less close to the true (despite our orchestral and harmonic riches) than the artists of other ages. But music, you

[425]

say, will keep on changing: the pendulum will keep on swinging back and forth until—etc., etc. So be it.

I am done. Once more my apologies, compliments, and thanks. Please accept this expression of our warmest friendship from my wife and myself.

To Giuseppe De Sanctis   Genoa, March *13, 1894* (B)

Your letter, which, in spite of its enthusiasm, is clear, unprejudiced, and carries the imprint of the truth, gave me (and I think Verdi too) real pleasure. Thank you for your impatience for the happy announcement of the great success. But don't have any illusions about new operas to come. Verdi has worked enough, and certainly has the right to rest. Let others follow this example, not only of his activity, but also of his upright character in the full meaning of the word.

PEPPINA

To Giuseppe Gallignani   Genoa, June *20, 1894* (A)

Gallignani, although he was Director of the Parma Conservatory, did not have the last word in administrative matters.

Last year, as you may remember, I asked you to use your influence to have the son of my coachman accepted at the Conservatory of Parma. You replied that the date for applications was past.

Now I am returning to the subject. I repeat the recommendation I made last year, and ask you please to do your best to have my request put through.

Beg the authorities, implore them on bended knee, in my name. Amen! With a thousand excuses and thanks, I am yours.

To Giuseppe Gallignani   *Genoa, October 29, 1894* (A)

The last time I had the pleasure of seeing you at St. Agata,
I introduced my coachman, Luigi Veroni, to you, whose son
hopes to be enrolled as a pupil in your Conservatory. As the
testimonials of his teacher state, he seems to be extraordinarily gifted for music.

You took such an interest in the matter that I hoped and
still hope for results.

Now school is about to open on the third of November
and poor father Veroni is all excited, because he has heard
no more about the matter. He will bring this letter to you
and I hope to hear that his wishes and my hopes have been
fulfilled.

To Giuseppe Gallignani   *Genoa, November 4, 1894* (A)

Dear Gallignani: *Nemo propheta in patria* . . .

If I had been born in *Turkey* I might have put it through!
But I bow to the exalted wisdom of the Minister!
How lucky we are! Nursed with such severity we shall
surely yet become a nation of perfect beings. . . .
Forgive me! Farewell.

To Dr. Angelo Carrara   *Genoa, March 23, 1895* (A)

Dear Doctor Carrara: Within a few days I shall be at St.
Agata to look after all my chores.

I wrote you from Milan that "my business and other obligations make it imperative for me to know down to the last
cent how much income I can count on from my rents." I
repeat that now, word for word, particularly because I have
no more large, extra receipts from new operas, nor will I

have them in the future! Where I am concerned, nobody bothers about paying punctually—under the pretext that *I have plenty*!! That is not true! The modest possessor of 3000 lire with a well-balanced budget, is richer and more *à son aise* than I, who am always having large, new, unforeseen expenses, and never know exactly what sum I own!

This state of affairs must stop, and if you can give me a few hours of your time we shall discuss the matter when I get back, and try to find some good, practicable solution, before a radical decision becomes necessary!

Meanwhile in order to save time, will you please prepare the contracts of the tenant farmers for me with a guarantee that the rents will be paid when they are due. In one of your letters you wrote me concerning this: "I hope they will be prompt." *Hope* is an alarming word in this case. Then why did I make the sacrifice of reducing the land rentals so generously?

To Enrico Bossi   *Busseto-St. Agata, June 11, 1895* (A)

Dear Maestro Bossi: I have just received your esteemed letter, which I hasten to answer before your compositions arrive.

I am quite capable, in private, of giving an informal opinion of a musical work—but no more than that.

Judgments are of no value, even when they are sincere. Every one judges according to his own feelings, and the public interprets other people's judgments in the same way.

But what need have you of my verdict? And why should the Conservatory of Pesaro need it . . . for you who are so well known?

I shall admire your works as before. But you will permit

me to confine myself to the admiration, which I have and
have always had for you.

St. Agata, June 21, 1895 (A)

To the Director of the "Deutsche Verlags-Anstalt," Stuttgart
    [Written in French]
Never, never shall I write my memoirs!

It is quite enough that the musical world has tolerated my
music so long! Never shall I condemn it to read my prose.

To G. Tebaldini   *February, 1896* (K)

[. . . .] I know some old settings of the Te Deum and
I have heard quite a lot of modern ones. But to me no performance of this hymn has ever been convincing, quite aside
from the quality of the music.

Such performances generally take place as part of the
pompous ceremonies in celebration of some victory or coro-
nation, etc. At the beginning, Heaven and earth exult: *Sanctus, sanctus Deus Sabaoth.* But about half way through, the
work takes on a different color, so to speak: *Tu ad liberan-
dum.* . . . The Saviour is born of the Virgin and proclaims
the *regnum coelorum* to mankind. . . . Mankind believes in
the *judex venturus,* and calls upon him: *salvum fac;* ending
with the prayer, *Dignare Deo, die isto* . . . in pathos, darkness, mourning and even in terror. [. . . .]

To Camille Bellaigue   *Genoa, April 17, 1896* (A)

Dear Bellaigue: I am very grateful to you, my dear B., for
your kindness in sending me your book, *"Portraits de Musiciens."*

I already knew the portraits of Palestrina, Marcello, and

Pergolese. Of the new ones I like "Rossini" and "Wagner" best . . . aside, that is, from the expression, "Punchinello." Rossini's humor was biting, caustic, sometimes malicious, but he was never a Punchinello.

You quote the phrase as somebody else's expression. Then this somebody else was wrong.

You speak of "the great man of tomorrow." Oh, he will certainly come; but there is no hurry! A great deal must be done yet along present-day lines and with the present tendencies before we get tired of this kind of music which (some people believe) is so coarse and inflated that it explodes without producing anything.

To Edoardo Mascheroni   *Milan, January 28, 1898* (A)

Dear Farfarello: [. . . .] My health is just the same. I'm not sick, but I am too old!! Think of spending your life without being able to do anything!

It is very hard.

To Camille Bellaigue   *Milan, May 2, 1898* (A)

The titles of Bellaigue's books were "Portraits et Silhouettes de Musiciens" and "Etudes Musicales et Nouvelles Silhouettes de Musiciens."

Dear Bellaigue: I am answering belatedly because I wanted to read your book, "Les Musiciens," with the greatest attention. It is very beautiful, profoundly thought out and masterfully written. I shall talk to you only about music, about music alone, and I join you in your praise of the three giants: Palestrina, Bach, and Beethoven. When I think of the petty, poverty-stricken melody and harmony of our times, Palestrina seems a miracle.

[430]

Everybody thinks as you do about Gluck, but I can't help feeling that in spite of his powerful dramatic temperament, he was not far superior to the greatest of his day, and as a musician he was inferior to Handel.

The silhouettes of Chopin, Schubert, Saint-Saëns and so on, are splendid, and the magnificent portrait of St. Cecilia is on an exalted plane.

You say a lot about Rossini and Bellini which may be true, but I confess I can't help thinking that, for abundance of real musical ideas, for comical verve, and truthful declamation, the "Barber of Seville" is the finest *opera buffa* in existence. Like you, I admire "William Tell," but how many other magnificent, sublime things there are in various of Rossini's other operas.

Bellini is weak instrumentally and harmonically, it's true; but he is rich in feeling and in a certain personal melancholy, which is completely his own! Even in his less well-known operas like "La Straniera" and "Il Pirata," there are long, long, long spun out melodies, like nothing that had been written before. How powerful and true the declamation is, for example, in the duet between Pollione and Norma! And what a lofty flight of thought there is in the first phrase of the introduction to "Norma," which is followed after a few measures by another theme:

badly orchestrated, certainly! But no one has ever written anything of more heavenly beauty.

Please notice, my dear Bellaigue, that I do not pretend to

be pronouncing judgments. Heaven preserve me from that! I am only relating my impressions . . .

You speak very indulgently about "Otello" and "Falstaff"! . . . The composer does not complain, and Giuseppe Verdi presses your hand in gratitude and thanks you.

To the Countess Negroni Prati
                        Montecatini, July 23, 1898 (A)

For several days I have been intending to answer your dear, sad, beautiful letter, but I shouldn't have had anything very cheerful to say either! . . .

Life is suffering! When we are young our ignorance of life, the bustle and distractions and intoxication of it all, dazzle and fascinate us so that we take our bit of happiness and misfortune in our stride without even being conscious of living. Now we know what life is, we feel it, and the suffering oppresses and tortures us. What can we do? Nothing. Only live on, sick, tired and disillusioned until. . . .

To Pilade Polazzi   *St. Agata, October 18, 1898* (A)

Thank you very much indeed for the number of *La Scena* which you have so kindly dedicated to me.

Now, to answer the question of the deputy, Professor Bovio, I must say that I have nothing to report regarding my nervous system, which has grown stronger with the years so that I now need not envy the most robust worker in the fields.

The opinion which you ask me to give of your publication, *La Scena,* is comprised in the following sentence: I beg you to renew my subscription for which I enclose the fee for one year.

INSCRIBED TO THE SINGER, TERESA STOLZ   *Courtesy Arturo Toscanini*

GIUSEPPE VERDI, 1900

To Arrigo Boito   *Genoa, December 15, 1898* (A)

Three of the four "Pezzi Sacri" (Stabat Mater, Laudi alla Vergine, and Te Deum) were to be performed at La Scala in April, 1898. The performance took place in spite of Verdi's objections.

Dear Boito: At the meeting you are going to have at La Scala today, Giulio is going to request that the performance of my "Pezzi Sacri" be stopped. Please defend my cause and leave these poor little works in peace. You ask: why? First because I don't believe they would be effective in La Scala in view of the setting and present-day circumstances; second, because my name is too old and boresome. It even makes me bored, myself, to say it. And add to this the newspaper comments! . . . though it's true that I don't have to read them.

To Giuseppe De Sanctis   *Milan, January 3, 1899* (B)

I am most grateful for your greetings, and I send the same to you and to your family.

You will excuse me if I do not write at length; my hand is not steady and I write with difficulty.

To Giuseppe De Sanctis   *Busseto, October 21, 1899* (B)

Signora Verdi's last letter to her godson. Not quite one month later she died, on November 14, at the age of eighty.

Dear Don Peppino: Please excuse my too long delay in answering to thank you in Verdi's name for the affectionate and gracious wishes for his eighty-fourth birthday. He is well and carries his blessed old age with marvelous vigor! Thanks from both of us, to you and your family, for your kind words, and I shall pray God to bless and prosper your talent and the

[433]

efforts of all of you, so that they may win your family at least a position of modest ease.

I have had a long and weary illness, and I ask you to forgive me if I write little. I echo the good wishes of health and happiness to you and to your family, also in Verdi's name, and with the most cordial greetings, I sign myself affectionately,

PEPPINA.

To the Countess Negroni Prati
St. Agata, August 16, 1900 (A)

The following letter was written after the murder of King Umberto.

Dear Signora: I was so distracted by the horrible tragedy of these last few days, that I could not answer your letter immediately.

I had already wanted to do what you suggest, but I am almost an invalid and can undertake nothing.

In its lofty simplicity, the Queen's prayer seems as if it had been written by one of the early Church Fathers. Inspired by a profound religious emotion, she has found words of such truth and simplicity that it would be impossible to match them in swollen and artificial music. We should have to go back three centuries, to Palestrina.

To Gerardo Laurini
St. Agata, August 18, 1900 (A)

Professor Gerardo Laurini had put the Queen's prayer into verse.

My years, my health, and my doctors all forbid me even the slightest exertion. Moreover I should never have composed the prayer in a versified arrangement. The original

[434]

words of the Queen have more sincerity, more feeling and a *simplicity,* which is naturally lacking in verse.

[Addressee unknown]   *November 13, 1900* (J)

Very true . . . it is comforting to think that there is some friendly person, even though he be far away, who is concerned for us, especially on days which recall the saddest events of our lives. Tomorrow, the fourteenth of November, is a day of misfortune for me, as the day was for you that robbed you of your beloved wife. But you had sons who loved you dearly. . . . I am alone. It is sad, sad, sad!

To Maria Waldmann   *Milan, December 22, 1900* (B)

Dearest Duchess: Thank you a thousand times for your affectionate letter. I take the greatest pleasure in your joys and in those of your family. May you always be happy!

As for myself, I hardly know what to say. I am not ill, but my life and my strength diminish from day to day. Everything tires me! It's only natural! . . .

Please excuse the brevity of this letter. I write with difficulty.

Keep your affection for me, as I shall always keep mine for you. Best wishes to your family.

It is a joy for me every time you write. I press both your hands in old friendship.

To Giuseppe de Amicis
                    The beginning of January, 1901 (J)

Even though the doctors tell me I am not sick, I still feel that everything tires me. I can no longer read, nor write; my eyes are giving out; my feeling dims; and even my legs don't want to carry me around any more. Why am I still in this world?

To Victor Sauchon   *Milan, January 17, 1901* (A)

This letter, written in French to Victor Sauchon, agent général of the Society of Authors in Paris, and dated ten days before Verdi's death, is the last of the "Copialettere" and probably the very last that Verdi wrote.

My dear M. Sauchon: I have received the cheque for 2691.80 lire for my composer's royalties up to the end of 1900. Please accept my thanks and my compliments.

VERDI'S LAST WILL

Verdi's will, written in his own hand, is dated May 14, 1900, and was registered in Busseto on February 1, 1901.

This is my will.

I revoke all previous depositions and declare them invalid. I nominate and appoint Maria Verdi, the wife of Signor Alberto Carrara of Busseto, as my universal heir. She is to be required to give no bond and shall be free of any obligation to make an inventory.

1. I bequeath to the central Almshouses of the City of Genoa the sum of twenty thousand lire.

2. I bequeath to the Institute for Rachitics of the City of Genoa the sum of ten thousand lire.

3. I bequeath to the Institute for the Deaf and Dumb of the City of Genoa the sum of ten thousand lire.

4. I bequeath to the Institute for the Blind of the City of Genoa the sum of ten thousand lire.

5. I bequeath to Guerino Balestieri, who has been many years in my service, the sum of ten thousand lire.

6. I bequeath to the domestic servants who shall have been ten years in my service, the sum of four thousand lire each; to the other domestic servants, one thousand lire apiece.

7. I bequeath to Dr. Angelo Carrara of Busseto my gold repeater-watch with the gold chain, and further bequeath to his son, Alberto, all my firearms together with the chest in which they are contained, and also my gold shirt-studs.

All these bequests shall be paid and executed by my heiress within six months from the day of my death.

[8 to 13]

14. I bequeath to the House of Repose for Aged Musicians, which has been constituted a legal person by decree of the 31st of December, 1889, aside from the building which I have had constructed on the Piazzale Michelangelo, Milan:

1. Fifty thousand lire in five per-cent consolidated Italian Bonds, presently registered for me with certificate N four.

2. Twenty-five thousand lire in Italian bonds payable to the bearer.

3. All my composer's royalties from Italy as well as foreign countries on all my operas, including the amounts which accrue to me from contracts ceding the rights to such works. Of this income, the Board of Directors shall be empowered to use only five thousand lire each year during the first ten years, in order that the remaining monies shall constitute a capital sum to be added to the endowment of the foundation.

[4-5]

6. I bequeath to the above-mentioned House of Repose for Aged Musicians, the Erard grand piano, which is in my apartment in Genoa, my spinet at St. Agata, my decorations, my artistic mementos, the pictures which I have specified in a letter to my heiress, and other objects which

my heiress may find appropriate, to be preserved in a room of the above-mentioned institute.

15. I bequeath to the farmer, Basilio Pizzola, who has worked for many years in my garden at St. Agata, the sum of three thousand lire to be paid immediately after my death.

16. I bequeath to my valet, Gaiani Giuseppe, and to Teresa Nepoti, for their faithful services, the sum of four thousand lire each, though they have not been ten years in my service.

[17-20]

I prescribe that my heiress shall pay these bequests as indicated within six months after my death, and that she shall consign the securities bequeathed to the House of Repose for Aged Musicians immediately after my death.

It is my urgent desire to be buried with my wife in Milan in the chapel which is to be built in the House of Repose for Aged Musicians which I founded.

If this expressed desire should not be fulfilled, then I direct that a monument shall be placed for me in the burial plot of the Cimitero Monumentale of Milan, which has been acquired for me by my attorney, Umberto Campanari. If no further arrangements shall have been made in this matter, the necessary sum shall be paid by my heiress, but it is not to exceed twenty thousand lire.

As executors of my will, I appoint Dr. Angelo Carrara of Busseto and his son, Alberto Carrara, and I bequeath to each of them the sum of five thousand lire.

In all matters regarding the execution of this my will, I request the executors to be guided by my attorney, Umberto Campanari of Milan.

I enjoin upon my heiress to retain my house and garden in St. Agata in their present condition and request her to leave all the fields surrounding the garden as they now are.

The same obligation holds for her heirs or their representatives.

I direct that my funeral shall be very modest, at dawn or at the time of the Ave Maria in the evening, without singing or music.

I do not wish my death to be announced with the usual formalities.

To the poor of the village of St. Agata, six thousand lire shall be distributed on the day after my death.

GIUSEPPE VERDI

COMPLETE LIST OF VERDI'S WORKS

Compiled by Franz Werfel

DRAMATIC WORKS

1 *Rochester* (Text by PIAZZA), circa 1836-1837, unpublished

2 *Oberto, Conte di San Bonifacio* (Text by PIAZZA and SOLERA). First performed at La Scala, Milan; November 17, 1839

3 *Il Finto Stanislao* or *Un Giorno di Regno* (ROMANI), La Scala, Milan; September 5, 1840

4 *Nabucodonosor* ["*Nabucco*"] (SOLERA), La Scala, Milan; March 9, 1842

5 *I Lombardi alla Prima Crociata* (SOLERA), La Scala, Milan; February 11, 1843

6 *Ernani* (PIAVE), Teatro la Fenice, Venice; March 9, 1844

7 *I Due Foscari* (PIAVE), Teatro Argentina, Rome; November 3, 1844

8 *Giovanno d'Arco* (SOLERA), La Scala, Milan; February 15, 1845

9 *Alzira* (CAMMARANO), San Carlo, Naples; August 12, 1845

10 *Attila* (SOLERA), Teatro la Fenice, Venice; March 17, 1846

11 *Macbeth* (PIAVE), Teatro Pergola, Florence; March 14, 1847

[441]

12 *I Masnadieri* (MAFFEI), Her Majesty's Theatre, London; July 22, 1847

13 *Jérusalem* (ROYER and VAËZ), Académie Royale de Musique, Paris; November 26, 1847 (Completely revised version of *I Lombardi*)

14 *Il Corsaro* (PIAVE), Teatro Grande, Triest; October 25, 1848

15 *La Battaglia di Legnano* (CAMMARANO), Teatro Argentina, Rome; January 27, 1849.

16 *Luisa Miller* (CAMMARANO), San Carlo, Naples; December 8, 1849

17 *Stiffelio* (PIAVE), Teatro Grande, Trieste; November 16, 1850

18 *Rigoletto* (PIAVE), Teatro La Fenice, Venice; March 11, 1851.

19 *Il Trovatore* (CAMMARANO and BARDARE), Teatro Apollo, Rome; January 13, 1853

20 *La Traviata* (PIAVE), Teatro La Fenice, Venice; March 6, 1853

21 *Les Vêpres Siciliennes* (SCRIBE and DUVEYRIER), Opéra, Paris; June 13, 1855 (This opera was revised for Italy under the title of *Giovanna da Guzman*)

22 *Simone Boccanegra* (PIAVE), Teatro la Fenice, Venice; March 12, 1857

23 *Aroldo* (PIAVE), Teatro Nuovo, Rimini; August 16, 1857 (Revised version of *Stiffelio*)

24 *Un Ballo in Maschera* (SOMMA), Teatro Apollo, Rome; February 17, 1859

25 *La Forza del Destino* (PIAVE), Imperial Opera, St. Petersburg; November 10, 1862

26 *Macbeth* (NUITTER and BEAUMONT), Théâtre-Lyrique, Paris; April 21, 1865 (Completely revised version,

with cuts, additions, and reinstrumentation of the
original score)

27 *Don Carlos* (MÉRY and DU LOCLE), Opéra, Paris; March
11, 1867 (Five-act version)

28 *La Forza del Destino* (Completely revised version), La
Scala, Milan; February 20, 1869

29 *Aida* (GHISLANZONI), Cairo; December 24, 1871, for the
opening of the Suez Canal

30 *Simone Boccanegra* (Completely revised version, with
additions, and textual improvements by BOITO), La
Scala, Milan; March 24, 1881

31 *Don Carlos* (Largely revised version cut down to four
acts), La Scala, Milan; January 10, 1884

32 *Otello* (BOITO), La Scala, Milan; February 5, 1887

33 *Falstaff* (BOITO), La Scala, Milan; February 9, 1893

*The revised versions of Verdi's operas must definitely be considered new
works, since the greater part of the music was composed anew, and few
pages remained unchanged.*

OPERAS VERDI WISHED TO COMPOSE

Autograph sketches of plot and dialogue for these projected
are preserved at St. Agata.

Shakespeare's *King Lear, Hamlet* and *The Tempest;* Byron's
Cain; Grillparzer's *Die Ahnfrau;* Dumas' *Kean;* Euripides'
Phaedra; Calderón's *A Secreto Agravio, Secreta Venganza;*
Chateaubriand's *Atala;* Victor Hugo's *Marion Delorme* and
Ruy Blas; Giacoma di Valenza (after Chapter XXX of Sis-
mondi's "History"); *Arria* (after Book XII of the "Annals"
of Tacitus); Molière's *Tartuffe;* Pushkin's *Boris Godunov.*

CANTATAS AND HYMNS

(for chorus, orchestra, and soli)

1 *Festival Cantata* for a wedding in the family of Count Borromeo, Milan, 1835
2 *Three choruses* from Manzoni's tragedies, about 1840
3 *Il Cinque Maggio,* hymn by Manzoni, about 1840
4 *Suona la Tromba,* hymn by Mameli, 1848
5 *Guarda che bianco luna,* Notturno for soprano, tenor, bass, and wood-winds
6 *Inno delle Nazioni,* dramatic cantata for baritone, chorus, and orchestra, written for the London Exhibition, to a text by Boito. Performed at Her Majesty's Theatre, 1862

RELIGIOUS MUSIC

Youthful works written when Verdi was organist in Busseto (around 1830)

1 A big *Mass,* three *Tantum Ergo,* a *Stabat Mater* (Some of these works are preserved in the Museum of Busseto)
2 *Messa da Requiem* in memory of Alessandro Manzoni, Church of San Marco, Milan; May 22, 1874
3 *Pater Noster* by Dante, for five-part chorus; Milan, April 18, 1880
4 *Ave Maria* by Dante, for soprano and string quartet, Milan, April 18, 1880
5 *Ave Maria, scala enigmatica armonizzata a 4 voci* (soprano, alto, tenor, and bass), composed about 1889
6 *Stabat Mater,* chorus and orchestra; Paris, April 7, 1898
7 *Le Laudi alla Vergine* by Dante, for four-part women's chorus, unaccompanied; Paris, April 7, 1898
8 *Te Deum* for double chorus and orchestra; Paris, April 7, 1898

INSTRUMENTAL MUSIC

1 Youthful works (1825-1840): *Overtures* and one hundred *Marches* for the orchestra of Busseto. *Short symphonic pieces, Concert pieces for piano* (Capriccios). Autograph manuscripts of these works are preserved in the Museum at Busseto.
2 An unpublished *Overture* to *La Forza del Destino*
3 An unpublished *Overture* to *Aida*
4 *String Quartet in E minor,* Naples; April 1, 1873

BALLET MUSIC COMPOSED FOR PARIS

1 *Grand Ballet* for *Jérusalem*
2 *Grand Ballet* for *Il Trovatore*
3 *Grand Ballet* for *Les Vêpres Siciliennes*
4 *Grand Ballet* for *Macbeth*
5 *Grand Ballet* for *Don Carlos*
6 *Grand Ballet* for *Otello* (This ballet is a complete symphonic composition in itself, the single movements of which are entitled: "Arabian Song," "Greek Song," "Hymn to Mohamet," and "Dance of the Warriors"

SHORT VOCAL PIECES

1 Youthful works (around 1830): *Arias, Serenades, Duets, Trios,* and other vocal pieces for church and concert performance (preserved at Busseto)
2 *Sei Romanze* (1838):
   Non t'accostar all'urna
   Muore, Elisa, lo stanco poeta
   In solitaria stanza
   Nell' orror di nott' oscura
   Perduto ho la pace
   Deh! pietoso

3 *L'Esule* (poem by Solera), ballade for bass, 1839
4 *La Seduzione* (poem by Balestra), ballade for bass, 1839
5 *Album di Sei Romanze* (1845):
    Il Tramonto (poem by Maffei)
    La Zingara (poem by Maggioni)
    Ad una Stella (poem by Maffei)
    Lo Spazzocamino (poem by Maggioni)
    Il Mistero (poem by Romani)
    Brindisi (poem by Maffei)
6 *Il Poveretto,* romanza, 1847
7 *Stornello:* "Tu dici che non m'ami," 1869, for the album
    published in honor of Piave
8 *Arias* and *Romanzas* composed for the use of certain sing-
    ers, to be inserted into the scores of the earlier operas

EPILOGUE

W E TRUST that the reader has gained increased understanding of Verdi's letters from Franz Werfel's Foreword and from my Notes. The source of every letter is apparent from the symbols employed, which are explained after this Epilogue. The List of Recipients and the Index should also be useful for study and enjoyment of the text.

This book has a history. In Vienna, in 1926, Franz Werfel and I brought out an anthology of Verdi's letters, based almost exclusively on "Copialettere," the Italian collection of 1913. Having made that translation myself, I know how difficult it is to reproduce the monumental simplicity of Verdi's style in another language, and can appreciate Edward Downes's success with this task in the present volume. Since 1926, however, several collections of Verdi's letters have appeared in the original Italian—the last, "Carteggi Verdiani," published by the Italian Academy—and we have now drawn upon them to round out our Viennese selection. It is the first attempt of the sort. This and the Vienna edition are the only translations extant.

As in our earlier selection, we have placed a letter at the beginning in which Verdi—the least vain of operatic composers—protested against the publication of musicians' letters. For himself, he was doubtless right; but posterity, seeking to learn about an artist's life from every source, has its rights as well. His works do not tell enough. Biographical data are bound to be insufficient. Verdi's letters alone reveal his world.

In this book we encounter not merely a century of Italian history and a century of the theater—Italian, French, and German. We also see Verdi's great antagonist, Richard Wagner, at work. Verdi emerges as an artist, a genius, an iron-willed, passionate, yet always kindly man. He is a humanist, a free spirit, a cosmopolite, although a great patriot. His grasp of political matters is astounding; his outbursts against future barbarism are prophetic. Let no one scoff at Verdi as a composer of hurdy-gurdy arias. His operas, today, have been vindicated.

In our selection, we hope that we have portrayed his genius. We think a true picture of the composer can emerge only from a chronological arrangement of the letters, which none of the Italian editions offers. Likewise, almost all of them are over-loaded with explanations, while we have sought to give only the essential ones.

Inevitably, there are gaps in our work. This volume, otherwise, would have had to be much longer. In spite of this and the shortcomings inherent in any new effort, we hope that the book will be received with the sympathy which its predecessor found.

PAUL STEFAN

The source of each Verdi letter is indicated by a symbol in the date line, according to the following key:

(A) I. Copialettere di Giuseppe Verdi, ed. G. Cesari and A. Luzio. Milan, 1913
(B) Carteggi Verdiani, ed. A. Luzio. Rome, Reale Accademia d'Italia, 1935 (2 vols.).
(C) Verdi Intimo—Carteggio di Giuseppe Verdi con il Conte Opprandino Arrivabene. Milan, 1931
(D) Re Lear e Ballo in Maschera—Lettere de Giuseppe Verdi ad Antonio Somma, ed. A. Pascolato, Citta di Castello, 1902
(E) Giuseppe Verdi nelle lettere di Emmanuele Muzio ad Antonio Barezzi, ed. A. L. Garibaldi. Milan, 1931
(F) Verdi's Letters to Du Locle, Musical Quarterly, 1921; and Letters to Léon Escudier, Music and Letters, 1923
(G) General: other sources
(H) Lettere inedite di Giuseppe Verdi, etc., ed. Morazzoni. Milan, 1929
(I) Arthur Pougin, Verdi. Paris, 1886
(J) Bragagnolo-Bertazzi, La vita di Giuseppe Verdi narrata al popolo. Milan, 1904
(K) Gino Marchese Monaldi, Verdi. Turin, 1921 (2nd ed.)

LIST OF RECIPIENTS

INDEX

This index does not refer to the recipients of the letters, to the list of Verdi's works or to the list of symbols:

INDEX

Busch, Hans, 237
Busseto, 16-23, 26, 60, 64, 65, 75, 82,
    83, 85, 86, 97, 98, 104, 113, 148,
    150, 152, 156, 158, 159, 161, 163,
    164, 168 sq., 171-174, 178-180, 190,
    191, 203, 205, 206, 208, 210, 211,
    216-225, 227, 228, 232, 242-246,
    252, 253, 265, 298, 316, 331, 335,
    376 sq., 395, 411, 417, 433, 437
    sq., 439

Cabaletta, 10, 49, 278, 279, 284, 360
    sq.
Cagnoni, composer, 262
Cairo, 70, 71, 219, 273-274, 293,
    294, 295, 305, 308, 333
Cammarano, Salvatore, librettist, 102,
    103, 110, 112, 113, 149, 151
    sq., 158, 172, 173, 176, 192;
    "Alzira," 109; "La Battaglia di
    Legnano," 139, 140, 144; "Re
    Lear," 152 sq.; "Trovatore" out-
    lined, 164 sq.; death (1852), 171
Campanini, Umberto, lawyer, 439
Caponi-Folchetto, music critic, 97,
    354
Capua, 235
Carcano, G., 137; suggests "Ham-
    let," 158; death, 374
Carducci, Giosuè, 393
Carissimi, 385
Carrara, Angelo, lawyer, 65, 298,
    427 sq., 437 sq.; Alberto, son of
    Angelo, 437 sq.
Caruso, 36
Carvalho, Léon, director of Paris
    Opéra Comique, 239, 423, 424
Casa di Riposo, 65, 66, 78, 438 sq.
Castel San Giovanni, 219
"Catherine Howard," opera project,
    110
Catalani, composer, 418
Cavaignac, general, 136, 142
Cavagnari, mayor of Parma, 342, 343
Cavaliere, Giuseppe, 101
Cavalli, composer, 28, 385
Cavour, 10, 11, 22, 216 sq., 240, 334
    sq.

Cencetti, Giuseppe, 324
Censorship, 141, 150, "Rigoletto,"
    158; "Stiffelio," 163; "Ballo,"
    147, 207 sq., 212
Chamber music, 51, 349
Charivari, Paris newspaper, 132
Chiarpa, Giuseppe, 225
Cherubini, 272, 297, 386
Cimarosa, 34, 385
Chopin, 431
Civitavecchia, 214
Classical, 346, 376
Clausetti, 325
Coblenz, 125 sq.
"Cola di Rienzo," opera project, 100
Coletti, singer, 36, 103, 110, 201, 211
Cologne, 125 sq., 129; festival, 337
    sq.
Comic opera, 31, 32, 85, 87, 351,
    385, 396
Commander of the Italian crown, V.
    refuses decoration as, 256
Commission to reform musical in-
    struction, 291, 296, 299, 301, 302,
    394, sq.
Como, lake of, 124, 228
Consecutive fifths and octaves, V.
    forbids, 104
Conservatory, Milan, 21, 22, 50, 297;
    Parma, 426; Naples, 95, V. de-
    clines directorship of, 290 sq., 296;
    Paris, 297, 302, 303; Italian Con-
    servatories, 291, 301, 334, 343,
    394
Conti, Augusto, 379
Contracts, 109, 110, 119, 139, 156,
    194; "I Lombardi," 99; "Mac-
    beth," 120; with Lucca released,
    123, 131; "Jérusalem," 132, 134;
    "Luisa Miller," 149 sq.; "Rigo-
    letto," 161; "Vêpres" in Paris,
    197; "Traviata," 201; "Ballo" in
    Naples, 211, 214; "Forza," 259;
    "Aida," 273, 277; "Otello," 294,
    320, 327, 353; "Falstaff," 409
Contra-bassoon, "Macbeth," 147,
    235, 242; marches for, 21, 242
Copialettere, 436

[455]